D1246417

GENERAL
ANTHROPOLOGY

About the Authors

MELVILLE JACOBS is Professor of Anthropology at the University of Washington, where he has instructed since 1928. Prior to his appointment to the University faculty, he taught English in the public school system of New York City. Dr. Jacobs has conducted numerous field researches in linguistics, folklore, and ethnography among the Oregon and Washington Indians, and has published a number of articles and books on these subjects. For five years Associate Editor of *American Anthropologist*, Jacobs is a member of many professional organizations, including the American Ethnological Society, the American Anthropological Society, the Linguist Society of America, and Sigma Xi. Dr. Jacobs holds the B.A. degree from the City College of New York, and the M.A. and Ph.D. degrees from Columbia University.

BERNHARD J. STERN was awarded a B.A. and M.A. from the University of Cincinatti and a Ph.D. from Columbia University; he also studied at the Universities of Chicago and Michigan and the London School of Economics. Before his death in 1956 he was Lecturer in Sociology at Columbia University and Lecturer in Anthropology at the New School for Social Research; he had also taught at Yale University and the University of Washington. In addition, he had completed extensive research in human relations and medical progress and had published numerous books and articles in many phases of social research. He held memberships in many professional organizations; he was Assistant Editor of *Encyclopedia of the Social Sciences* (Vol. IIIf.) and was Chairman of the Board of Editors of *Science and Society*. He edited, with A. Locke, *When Peoples Meet*.

GENERAL ANTHROPOLOGY

By Melville Jacobs

Bernhard J. Stern

BARNES & NOBLE BOOKS

A DIVISION OF HARPER & ROW, PUBLISHERS

New York, Evanston, San Francisco, London

©

Second Edition, 1952, 1955

Copyright, 1947, 1952, 1955

BY BARNES & NOBLE, INC.

L. C. Catalogue Card Number: 55–12151

SBN 389 00013 2

Manufactured in the United States of America

PREFACE

Anthropology has always delighted the intellectually curious. For a long time its appeal was primarily to lovers of the exotic. Accounts of strange customs, divergent sex practices, bizarre magical and religious behavior, and new kinds of arts have fascinated young and old alike. Often, descriptions of the modes of life of non-European peoples have functioned as escapist literature, and cults of primitivism have been based on the behavior and on the arts of natives of other lands. Great spurts in intellectual and artistic progress have occurred during periods of exploration and culture contact, when discovery of the ways of other peoples has helped to dispel smugness and provincialism and has served as yeast to social change.

As anthropology has matured as a science, as its methods of research have become more thorough and its techniques of analysis more exacting, it has lost none of its intrinsic humanistic appeal. Scientific findings in relation to prehuman or fossil types and to the technologies and manufactures of prehistoric eras have vastly extended the time span of human history, have put other modern peoples as well as ourselves in more correct perspectives, and have given fascinating evidence of human inventiveness among all peoples during hundreds of thousands of years. Comparative studies of the physical and psychological characteristics of living populations have countered the traditional beliefs and rationalizations of those who would justify unequal treatment of their fellow men on grounds of racial differences. Studies of the varieties of behavior, beliefs, languages, and arts among populations of diverse culture have given insights into the potential range of development of personality, cultures, and institutions, and have negated earlier static or limited concepts of human nature. Analyses of the functional interrelationships of different aspects of culture in the processes of culture change have laid bases for the eventual formulation of laws of cultural change and of the dynamics of personality formation.

Because scientists, teachers, and laymen are becoming cognizant of the many contributions that anthropology can make to other sciences, to programs of social and educational policy, and to an enrichment of human understanding and a quickening of human sensitivities, the demand for courses in anthropology is rapidly increasing in colleges and universities, and the subject is also being introduced in classes below the college level. This book has been prepared as an introductory text to facilitate the studies of beginning students and other interested persons who wish a broad and contemporary view of the science. It is, by design, an outline whose purpose is to chart *all* the main highways in present-day anthropology, with the hope that readers will later follow many interesting avenues and side roads the ramifications of which must needs be bypassed in this initial guide.

Grateful acknowledgment is made for the valuable suggestions of Professor Willard W. Hill of the University of New Mexico, Professor Elmer R. Smith of the University of Utah, Dr. William W. Elmendorf of the University of Washington, and Bess D. Langdon (Mrs. Melville Jacobs), who read preliminary drafts of the entire manuscript, and also of Professor Ruth Benedict of Columbia University, Professor Viola E. Garfield and Dr. Arden R. King of the University of Washington, and Dr. Amelia Susman, who read sections of the manuscript. The assistance rendered by Miss Anita Huovar, of the Issaquah, Washington, high school, and by Mrs. Adele Gottlieb is deeply appreciated. The authors wish to express their indebtedness also to countless persons here unnamed who have contributed to the scientific tradition which this book seeks to further.

In the preparation of this revised edition, the authors have had the benefit of valuable suggestions by many anthropologists and especially of those by Carroll A. Burroughs, H. Douglas Osborne, Professor William W. Elmendorf, and Professor Frederick S. Hulse, of the Department of Anthropology, University of Washington, and Professor George Herzog of Indiana University.

M. J.
B. J. S.

CONTENTS

CHARTS

GENERAL
ANTHROPOLOGY

CHAPTER ONE

INTRODUCTION

The Fields of Anthropology. Anthropology is the scientific study of the physical, social, and cultural development and behavior of human beings since their appearance on earth. It includes several distinct and at the same time interconnected scientific fields. These are human evolution, or the study of fossil man; physical anthropology, which is concerned with the classification of modern geographical populations and with their processes of physical change; archeology, or prehistory; cultural anthropology; and scientific linguistics.

Human Evolution, or the Study of Fossil Man. The basic task in the study of human evolution has been to recover and interpret fossil remains which reveal why, how, when, and where the populations from apes to modern human beings have changed in their skeletal make-up and in the structure of their central nervous system. Fossils of apelike antecedents of humans are rare and hard to find. On the basis of the few skeletons and the parts of many others which have thus far been discovered, however, and of the finds of skeletons of more recent near-humans and true humans, preliminary generalizations can be made regarding the ascent of human beings from remote and apelike ancestors.

Physical Anthropology. The biological changes in, and interrelationships between, modern geographical populations of humans have been studied on a basis of anatomical comparisons of living peoples and of the human remains found in recent cemeteries. Modern geographical populations and their ethnic subdivisions cannot be set apart sharply from one another because there is a continuous series of variations in all anatomical features. Nevertheless, race classification and comparison based upon physical observations and measurements, or upon differences in genetic inheritance, or both, is a legitimate scientific pursuit. The difficulties and limitations of interpretation of the data obtained must, however, be pointed up with special care. This is required because unfortunately the labels used in the classification of distinguishable major populations and ethnic subdivisions of these populations have been widely misinterpreted. They have been improperly employed by large numbers of prejudiced and unscientific people, who have ascribed hereditary superiorities and inferiorities to specific populations and to ethnic subdivisions of the latter. An analysis of the nature and error of such forms of racism has become an important contribution of physical anthropology.

Observations and measurements are also made on differences in physiological growth and behavior of living populations. Inferences drawn from such studies must likewise be made with utmost caution. At all times the physical and physiological processes found in humans are considered in the context of their geographical and cultural environments.

Archeology, or Prehistory.   History studies peoples who have left written records. Prehistory studies all other ancient peoples. Since written records give perspectives of human history for only a few regions during the past several thousands of years, the million or more years of prehistoric technology and culture can be examined directly solely by recourse to the study of objects discovered by archeological excavations. The objects obtained by these methods have been very revealing. They show that there must have been progressive advances in the technology of cutting tools made of stone. They also provide a vast quantity of other material objects used by humans during the several thousands of years just preceding the recent invention of writing. When the prehistoric tools, implements, and other objects dug from the ground are interpreted in the framework of a scientific theory of the processes of human history, social life, and culture, they indicate general features of ancient social life. Archeological science, now about a century old, has vastly extended knowledge of prehistoric times and has revolutionized our perspectives of the past.

Cultural Anthropology.   Humans, as distinct from other animals, have a culture—that is, a social heritage—transmitted not biologically through the germ cells but independently of genetic inheritance.

Cultural anthropologists—who are also often called social anthropologists, ethnologists, and ethnographers—describe, analyze, and attempt to account for the wide variety of customs and forms of social life of humans, particularly of peoples with primitive technologies. They therefore study technology or material culture, economic life, community organization, family life, clans, secret societies, government and law, magic and religion, the arts, and all other forms of cultural behavior. Their studies have revealed the extraordinary range of human behavior in society, and hence the diverse potentialities and plasticity of human nature.

Scientific Linguistics. Scientific linguists record and analyze the sounds, vocabulary, and grammatical structure of one or another of the approximately 2700 languages of the world. They compare the characteristics of some of these languages, in order to arrive at formulations regarding the interrelationships between languages and the manner of past linguistic changes. Attempts are also made to determine the social and cultural factors which have brought about such changes.

Scientific linguistics does not limit its researches to well-known languages or to those of peoples who have a written literature. It is equally interested in hitherto unwritten languages—that is, in the languages of the peoples of primitive technological levels. Important discoveries regarding the nature of language have been derived from recent research in this field.

The preceding fields constitute the major subdivisions or component sciences of anthropology. Their methods vary because of the different kinds of subject matter. Two of the fields—that of the study of fossil man, or human evolution, and that of physical anthropology, or the study of living geographical populations—are associated with biology and genetics in an especially intimate way. They are, however, also social sciences because the biological developments which they reveal have been affected by social and geographical environments. On the other hand, cultural anthropology and linguistics, and the subsidiary scientific studies of the economics, religion, and art of nonliterate peoples, have little relation to the biological sciences or to their methods of research.

The anthropological fields serve as a means for ever fuller comprehension of man's past and of the nature of physical, cultural, and mental characteristics of the peoples of the world. These studies have helped to counteract cultural provincialism and have suggested broad vistas and humanistic insights for more enlightened understanding of man's behavior. Although individual anthropologists may conduct researches without concern for the consequences to mankind of their contributions to knowledge, the expanding reservoirs of anthropological knowledge constitute resources for the building of a better world, where the potentialities of all human beings will be fulfilled.

The Terminology of a Scientific Anthropologist. In order to facilitate scientific research in anthropology, the popular comprehension of anthropological formulations, and the greatest possible use of anthropological knowledge for the benefit of mankind, the terminology must be rigidly scientific. Terms such as *race* and *primitive* are therefore employed only with specific, well-defined meanings. By a human "race" is meant a geographical population which differs from other populations in one or more inherited anatomical features, or in the genetic characteristics responsible for such features. The term does not refer to tribe, nation, culture, or language. The term "primitive" is used only to designate peoples who are technologically or economically primitive.

Such terms as *the backward races, aborigines, savagery* or *savages, uncivilized, barbarism* or *barbarians, the simpler peoples, primitive men,* and *primitive folk* are pointedly omitted in this book either because with advances in knowledge they now lack scientific utility, or because they have come to have derogatory connotations. Scientifically precise terms have been substituted to facilitate more effective understanding and use of anthropological materials. Anthropologists still put to scientific service lay terms such as *magic, secret society, horde, clan, tribe, the state, chief, property, civilization, culture, progress, totem, spirits, art, nomad,* and *crime.* The problem is to divest these terms of whatever unscientific implications they may have in daily parlance and to be so precise in definition that they can serve as efficient descriptive and analytic tools.

Anthropology as a Science. The science of anthropology has a well-defined set of objectives. It seeks (1) to describe phenomena of human life and culture accurately; (2) to classify the variable phenomena studied in order to achieve revealing general formulations; (3) to locate the origins of the changes and processes that are characteristic of such classified data and to describe those changes and processes accurately; and (4) to predict or indicate the general directions of change likely to be taken by the phenomena under examination. The proper sphere of anthropology as a science is therefore to strive to secure historical, sociological, and psychological laws that describe over-all trends or processes among the peoples of all prehistoric and historic periods. To do this it must first be descriptive, factual, and chronological in order to acquire data from which generalizations or laws can be formulated.

Anthropologists have usually limited their scientific search for data, as well as for laws, trends, or processes, to the peoples who have or had a technology simpler than that of the civilizations of the eastern Mediterranean such as Egypt, Babylon, and Persia in pre-Christian centuries, and to peoples who have had no technique of writing. However, their findings and methods have been relevant to and have assisted in a better understanding of the behavior of all peoples. Recently anthropologists have become increasingly interested in contacts between peoples of different levels of technology and have also ventured into the field of cultural change in modernized societies, and into the relations of culture to personality in contemporary cultures.

Anthropology has as yet accurately described or formulated but few laws and it has rarely been possible to present these laws in mathematical form. There has, however, been valuable scientific work directed towards the discovery and statement of laws. The search for scientific laws is relatively simple when the phenomena observed are numerous and similar, so that the observer may ignore variable individual behavior, minor exceptions, or other details in order to express the average behavior of a great mass of similar items. That is what the chemist, physicist, or bacteriologist is able to do. He describes the average behavior of multitudes of units, and the laws he formulates are kinds of statistical approximations.

The pursuit of scientific laws is, on the other hand, relatively difficult when the phenomena observed are few in number, are restricted to special circumstances of time and place, and are marked by detailed exceptions in which the observers are interested. It is made all the more difficult when the observers are unable to achieve the degree of emotional detachment, impartiality, and objectivity which physicists possess as they study billions of ions. It is one thing to formulate laws concerning multitudes of entities about which no one is emotional or biased, and another to be objective regarding very small communities with markedly different concepts and practices from those of the investigator. History, psychology, sociology, linguistics, mathematical statistics, and the amalgam of these disciplines which constitutes anthropology usually deal with small numbers of very human entities functioning in special situations. That is why generalizations in terms of dynamic processes of origin, change, and interrelations have been difficult, although by no means impossible, in the social sciences.

Anthropology as a Vocation. The majority of American anthropologists are associated with colleges or universities where they give lecture courses in general anthropology and in specialized subjects such as race and physical anthropology, archeology, religion, linguistics, and art, and on the cultures of American Indians, Africans, or other peoples. The numbers of institutions of higher education where anthropology is taught are increasing rapidly and most larger institutions now have anthropologists on their staffs. A smaller number of anthropologists are employed by museums supported by federal, state, or city governments or private organizations. A few anthropologists are connected with federal bureaus. All anthropologists conduct their researches either in campus halls or museums, or on field expeditions.

The funds for anthropological research are derived largely from college or university budgets. Considerable sums for research are also granted by museums and government bureaus, and by a number of privately endowed foundations. The printing of results of research is financed by a number of universities, museums, and government agencies, as well as by professional organizations supported by the anthropologists themselves, by a few private foundations, and by a few other persons interested in such research.

In recent years a number of new opportunities for teaching an·l research in anthropology have developed. Interracial organizations on a national and local level are utilizing the services of anthropologically trained personnel. Government departments are requiring the services of anthropologists as investments in foreign lands create interests in native peoples. The United Nations and its agencies such as the United Nations Educational, Scientific and Cultural Organization (UNESCO) have utilized anthropologists in the field of race and cultural relations. The development of teaching of anthropological, interracial, and intercultural courses in teachers' training colleges, junior colleges, and high schools appears to be in the offing and if this occurs, many more persons trained in anthropology will be required. Whereas at present there are less than a thousand Americans, and only a few hundred Europeans outside of Holland and the Soviet Union, employed in all types of anthropological work, this number will probably be multiplied many times within a generation.

SELECTED READINGS

Boas, F. "Anthropology," in *Encyclopedia of the Social Sciences,* II (1930), 73–110.
——. *Anthropology and Modern Life.* New York: Norton, 1928.
Gillin, J. *The Ways of Men.* New York: Appleton-Century, 1948. Pp. ⊁-?0.
Goldenweiser, A. A. *Anthropology.* New York: Crofts, 1937.
Herskovits, M. J. *Man and His Works.* New York: Knopf, 1948. Pp. 3–14.
Hoebel, E. A. *Man in the Primitive World.* New York: McGraw-Hill, 1949. Pp. 1–7.
Kluckhohn, C. *Mirror for Man.* New York: Whittlesey, 1949. Pp. 1–16, 168–195, 290–300.
Kroeber, A. L. *Anthropology.* New York: Harcourt, Brace, 1948. Pp. 1–13.
Linton, R., ed. *The Science of Man in the World Crisis.* New York: Columbia Univ. Press, 1945. *Passim.*
Lowie, R. H. *Are We Civilized?* New York: Harcourt, Brace, 1929.
Piddington, R. *An Introduction to Social Anthropology.* Vol. 1. Edinburgh: Oliver and Boyd, 1950. Pp. 1–3. Vol. II. 1957. *Passim.*
Thomas, W. I. *Primitive Behavior.* New York: McGraw-Hill, 1937. Pp. 1–7, *et passim.*
Turney-High, H. H. *General Anthropology.* New York: Crowell, 1940. Pp. 3–12.

CHAPTER TWO

HUMAN EVOLUTION

Introduction. For centuries, but especially since the 1830's and the development of an evolutionary point of view which culminated in Charles Darwin's classic *Origin of Species* (1859) and his *Descent of Man* (1871), scientists have been interested in man's relations to other animals, from the simple one-celled amoeba to the highly developed primate.

Contemporary knowledge of man's evolutionary development is largely derived from the findings of paleontology, which is the study of fossils of ancient animals, and from the comparative study of man with other living animals, particularly with the subhuman primates, in respect to structure, embryology and growth, physiology, susceptibility to disease, and behavior. In these fields available knowledge is incomplete. The science of the laws of arrangement or classification of members of a species, which is called *taxonomy,* has unfortunately often been narrowed to mean classification on the basis of only a few arbitrarily selected structural characters. Sufficient evidence is available, however, from these and other sources to establish the hypothesis of man's evolutionary relationship to the primate ancestor of the anthropoid group, the surviving members of which are man, gorilla, chimpanzee, orang, and gibbon. This genetic relationship to other primates, however remote the relationship may be, cannot now be seriously questioned. It is clear, however, that the inference often conveyed in popular discussion of the evolution of man, that man is descended from apes as they exist today, is erroneous. Apes of kinds now living and human beings (*Homo sapiens*) are only cousins of a great degree of remoteness and their lines of descent diverged at least seven million years ago.

No scientist challenges the fact of the evolution of human beings from apelike ancestors or other essential aspects of the theory of biological evolution. The controversies that agitate scientific circles are over the details of the progressive changes, and the dynamic causes underlying evolution. This chapter will present the important established facts about the successive steps in human evolution and the scientific interpretations as to the meaning of these facts.

Early Geologic Epochs. Following the Archeozoic and Proterozoic eras, the main geological epochs conventionally designated by geologists are the Proterozoic, Paleozoic, Mesozoic, and Cenozoic (or Tertiary and Quaternary). In early geological epochs primitive forms of animals evolved from one-celled organisms. Eventually reptiles appeared and, still later, bird and mammal orders. The primates, the most complex of the mammal orders, evolved during the Tertiary epoch, which is often termed the Age of Mammals. During successive divisions of the Tertiary epoch, designated the Paleocene, Eocene, Oligocene, Miocene, and Pliocene, each of which lasted 6,000,000 or more years, the primate line related to modern human

Epoch	Division		Years ago at start of epoch
Cenozoic	Quaternary	Recent	20,000
		Pleistocene	1,000,000
	Tertiary: The Age of Mammals	Pliocene	13,000,000
		Miocene	25,000,000
		Oligocene	36,000,000
		Eocene	58,000,000
		Paleocene	63,000,000
Mesozoic			230,000,000
Paleozoic			550,000,000
Proterozoic			925,000,000
Archeozoic			1,500,000,000
Azoic			

Fɪɢ. ɪ. The perspective of geological epochs. Numbers are within wide margins of probable error. Many writers equate Quaternary with Pleistocene.

beings advanced through successive biological levels by means of mutation, normal variation, and natural selection. The present fragmentary knowledge of the anatomy of this ancestral line on each of these levels is summarized in the following sections.

Paleocene Primates. Fossilized remaining parts of the lowest existing primate suborder, sometimes considered a pre-primate and termed the lemurs, are found in Paleocene deposits of over fifty million years ago. The more than eighty species of living lemurs known today in Madagascar, Africa, and Indonesia suggest that these Paleocene predecessors were largely arboreal and nocturnal, quadrupedal, furry, and of mouse to cat size, with a central nervous system inferior to that of the tarsiers and monkeys. All lemurs differ from other primates in lacking the bony wall separating eyes from jaw muscles. They appear to lack stereoscopic vision and depend largely on sense of smell. It is unlikely that they were on the direct line of evolution to modern humans.

Another Paleocene suborder of the primates, the rat-sized arboreal tarsiers, together with the lemurs, probably evolved from a common insectivore ancestor. Once dwellers on every continent, only one species (in Indonesia) has survived into the modern period. Since they are capable of erect sitting posture, their forepaws are frequently freed for dextrous manipulations. They appear to surpass lemurs in intelligence. They are nocturnal and leap rather than scamper through the trees. Vision is bifocal not stereoscopic. Reduced dependence upon the sense of smell has permitted a reduced snout, so that the eyes are close together. Brain area for vision is enlarged; for smell, reduced. Their opposable thumbs and big toes allowed manual behavior that was unprecedented in efficiency. Early fossils of tarsiers show these features. Their diet was probably largely made up of insects. Because the stimuli which came to them from the environment were progressively less by way of smell and more by way of touch, handling, and vision, the tarsiers learned more than lemurs. Natural selection during the Paleocene period favored those primate lineages and populations that came to possess opposable thumbs, stereoscopic vision, and reduced brain area for smell. In the Eocene period which followed the Paleocene, from 30,000,000 to 4⁻.000,000 years ago, it is probable that one of the tarsier types had become the ancestor of all types of monkeys. Most tarsier populations eventually died out, leaving modern survivors only in Indonesia.

Eocene Predecessors and Oligocene Monkeys. The most complex central nervous system which evolved during the Eocene and Oligocene periods was in that line evolving towards a monkey. Diversely structured populations evolved during these epochs because of the living conditions in different tropical forest environments. Monkey populations in America appear to have evolved separately from Old World monkeys.

There have been found in a Lower Oligocene stratum in Egypt fossil jaws of primates that were equal to large squirrels in size. One primate, called *Propliopithecus,* is thought to have been midway between an Eocene tarsier and a later anthropoid level. The same stratum yielded another lower jaw of a primate called *Parapithecus,* which is the earliest monkey so far recorded.

The brain of the monkeys notably surpassed that of the Paleocene tarsiers in its superior auditory and visual acuity and its diminished olfactory sensitivity. Monkeys also developed beyond bifocal to true stereoscopic vision. Such vision had especial survival value for arboreal creatures, since it permitted better judgments of distances. All Old World monkeys today remain largely arboreal except for one specialized group, the baboons.

Miocene Apes. Students of evolution have often found that some types of animals which have made successful adjustments to their surroundings have attained a much larger size. Giantism often has certain advantages. No American monkeys ever evolved far in this direction; the ecological factors that may have failed to support such a trend are unclear. In the Old World Lower Miocene or even earlier, some primates were already very large. During all of the Miocene these bigger primates lived in many parts of Europe, Asia, and Africa. Fossil remains of their teeth and jaws and of a few other bones have been found in many places. Most scientists now believe that some of these creatures could have been ancestral to modern humans and modern apes.

Among most large primates the typical way of moving about in the trees is by brachiation, which involves swinging by the arms from branches rather than running along on branches. This form of locomotion appears to be associated with great weight. Creatures that brachiate are also often of an erect instead of a horizontal posture. Up to the present only a few fossils of bones which indicate the posture of Miocene apes have been found. Nevertheless, scientists infer that increased size led to new forms of natural selection. The large creatures frequently visited and moved about on the ground and may have had better chances of survival due to a wider range of more nutritious foods, tumbled less frequently, and obtained nourishment and protected themselves in treeless areas. Another inference is that the greater hazards and the stimuli of ground life tended to select the more intelligent and posturally upright creatures.

Dryopithecus and Proconsul. The general name of *Dryopithecus* is given to many Miocene and Pliocene apes. Others, very similar in many ways, are *Sivapithecus,* with teeth of human like pattern, and *Proconsul,* of whom a number of fossils have recently been found in East Africa. Arm, leg, and foot bones of *Proconsul* strongly suggest that it walked on hind legs without need for support from the arms as in the living apes. Its teeth and jaws also were more nearly human in shape than are those of other apes living or extinct. No fossil brain cases of *Proconsul* have been found, nor of any other ape of this period; consequently, no estimations of brain size or contours are available. The geographical extension of Miocene ape populations is, however, such as to suggest that they were rather successful animals in their time. Later events warrant the conclusion that in the long run those among them that were best adapted to ground life by erect posture, bipedal locomotion and perhaps other traits, were the most successful. The largely arboreal apes of today are of course few and confined to relatively small regions. Anatomists assert that the *Dryopithecus* line had already gone beyond the restricted and largely vegetarian diet of monkeys and of arboreal apes and had become omnivorous. Because it was able to make use of bipedal locomotion, the arms of the Dryopithecus type were relieved of locomotive operations, and the forearms of this population were entirely freed for the manipulation of objects. Some scientists have suggested, on the basis of meager evidence, that the Dryopithecus population was at least as intelligent as modern gorillas. The geographical populations of a type as widely diffused as was the *Dryopithecus* became diversified rapidly in the varied regions they inhabited. As millions of years went by, the descendants of the Late Miocene *Dryopitheci* were selected, because of the hazards of living on the ground, in a direction of progressive change towards the development of types with increasingly complex brain structures. Five million or more years later, in the Middle Pliocene to Late Pliocene periods, the brains of the descendants of *Dryopithecus* had developed to a different and immeasurably superior level. An omnivorous, erect, ground-dwelling ape had changed at length into a much more intelligent but still prehuman creature.

Comparison of Man with Other Primates. The order of the primates embraces tarsiers and lemurs, monkeys, the extinct *Dryopitheci* and all later apes, and man, most of whom possess the following characteristics: relatively large and complicated brains; hands or feet capable of seizing or derived from types that are; the presence of a certain kind of clavicle or collarbone; free mobility of the digits, and opposability of either the thumb or big toe or both; some or all of the fingers and toes with flattened nails instead of claws; and the presence, as a rule, of only two mammae. Several characteristics of the apes indicate their close relationship to human beings. For example, they may breed at any time; they are capable of a variety of facial movements expressing emotions; they have diurnal, color, and stereoscopic vision; they are superior to tarsiers in discrimination of form, size, and distance. Apes possess the blood groups and blood sera found among men and suffer from the same diseases.

It was specifically through the evolution of the brain that man achieved his pre-eminence over other animals. The reduction of the snout in the tarsiers had allowed the visual fields of the two eyes to overlap and thus made stereoscopic vision possible. As this vision in depth improved with the true monkeys, more effective visualization of objects and events and better co-ordinated use of the limbs were made possible.

Erect posture had great influence on the further growth of the brain. Arboreal anthropoid apes are distinguished from monkeys by the fact that they carry their bodies at right angles to their plane of movement in the branches of trees rather than horizontally, although

among the apes the arms continue to play an important part in movement of the kind termed brachiation. After their descent from the
trees the adaptation of the earliest hominids, or prehumans, to the life
on the ground, associated with the progressive growth of the brain
and the possession of stereoscopic vision, led finally to the specialization of the limbs. The position of the head, caused by the movement forward of the opening at the base of the skull, through which
the spinal cord passes to the brain, rendered superfluous much of the
muscle at the back of the neck formerly required to maintain the
head. Both of these developments favored the expansion of the brain.
Moreover, when the hands were relieved from a direct share in
movement, growth in manual dexterity in the handling of tools
was made possible. Further, the employment of the hands for feeding
lessened the demands on the jaws and teeth and thus relieved the
skull from muscular pressure, while at the same time it altered the
balance of the head.

Thomas Huxley once declared, "The structural differences which
separate Man from the Gorilla and the Chimpanzee are not so great
as those which separate the Gorilla from the lower apes." At the
same time he emphasized that "every bone of the Gorilla bears marks
by which it might be distinguished from the corresponding bone in
Man." Similarly G. Elliot Smith declared that "no structure is found
in the brain of the ape that is lacking in the human brain, and on
the other hand the human brain reveals no formation of any sort
that is not present in the brain of the gorilla or chimpanzee. As far
as we can judge, the only distinctive feature of the human brain is
a quantitative one, namely a marked increase in the extent of the
three areas in the cerebral cortex . . . which are relatively smaller in
the brain of the anthropoid apes." The average brain capacity of
modern Europeans is about 1500 c.c., which is more than double
that of the largest ape brain ever recorded (650 c.c.) and more than
three times that of the average gorilla (450 c.c.). This increase
is due to the development of the parietal and frontal regions of the
brain and the lower part of the temporal area.

Although the mental superiority of man is evident, the limits of
animal intelligence are not yet defined. Man is not the only tool-
using or tool-making animal nor is he alone capable of methodical

planned behavior as was once believed. Recent experiments and observations of the psychology of the apes have shown that apes are capable of some purposeful activity, and of a limited use of objects to obtain food. They are reported to be capable of solving certain problems by methodical exploration of situations, and of a small measure of thinking. They have limited memory and respond to symbolic rewards on occasion. Their behavior anticipates that of humans but differs from it because of the absence of articulate speech which enables man to communicate, transmit, and accumulate knowledge. The apes lack true language and possess only a large inventory of interjections, ejaculations, and other simple signals or emotional cries, whereas man's possession of language has given him the power to devise a culture and thus has enabled him to utilize his environment more effectively for his own ends.

Evolution during the Late Pliocene Period. No specific fossils of the later Pliocene descendants of *Dryopithecus* of directly prehuman lineage have as yet been located. Nevertheless, generalized observations regarding the kind and degree of progress of the ancestors of humans during the later Pliocene period can be offered as speculations, through the application of present knowledge of the processes of natural selection and of the nature of primitive ways of living. These observations are as follows:

1. If biological evolution from the Late Miocene *Dryopitheci* to modern humans is conceived as a continuum subdivided into successive levels, the types of the Late Pliocene period must already have been much closer to the human species than to the *Dryopithecus*. Such levels are (1) *Dryopithecus* of Late Miocene, (2) *Dryopithecus* of Early Pliocene, (3) *Dryopithecus* of Middle Pliocene, (4) prehumans of Late Pliocene, (5) near-humans of Early Pleistocene, (6) modern humans of Late Pleistocene. One may therefore postulate the existence of Late Pliocene prehumans, who had evolved beyond *Dryopithecus* levels.

2. Progressive developments in the complexity of structure of the Late Pliocene prehuman brain were such as to make entirely new forms of behavior possible. This was an era of strategic advance from an ape brain to one with some of the potentialities of the human brain.

Geological level	Probably ancestral to humans	Possibly ancestral to humans	Of interest but not ancestral to humans
QUATERNARY			
Recent	Homo sapiens		
Late Pleistocene	Homo sapiens		
Middle Pleistocene	Near-humans: Pithecanthropus, Sinanthropus	Neandertal	
Early Pleistocene	Near-humans	Gigantopithecus Meganthropus	Australopithecenes
TERTIARY			
Late Pliocene	Prehumans		
Middle Pliocene	Dryopithecus		
Early Pliocene	Dryopithecus		
Late Miocene	Dryopithecus		
Middle Miocene	Dryopithecus (Ramapithecus)	Some Dryopithecenes	
Early Miocene	Proconsul	Proconsul Maximus	
Late Oligocene			
Middle Oligocene	Propliopithecus gibbonoid		
Early Oligocene		Parapithecus monkey Tarsiers	
Eocene			Lemurs
Paleocene			
SECONDARY	Pre-primates (insectivora)		

Fig. 2. Developmental levels in the primates leading to *Homo sapiens*.

3. The successive levels of *Dryopithecus* from Late Miocene to Middle Pliocene comprised creatures completely undomesticated, whose behavior was determined, in all probability, largely by learning based upon trial and error, as among other higher mammals. Almost all living primates live in groups in which the young learn by observation and imitation; doubtless this was true in Pliocene times. Such learned behavior appears to be a necessary precondition for behavior that constitutes responses that are intentionally taught by the more experienced members of the group. Probably by the Late Pliocene, the prehumans had already created and were therefore transmitting a primitive cultural heritage. Wild creatures were thus changing into self-domesticated creatures of an unprecedented kind. They were progressively more plastic, adaptable, and free to hit upon, invent, and recall new and more efficient stimulus-response reactions.

4. Teeth, toes, and fingers were progressively supplemented by crude tools, weapons, utensils, and containers. Most of these were made of wood and bamboo, of creepers, grasses, and fibers, and of other tractable, soft, pliable, decayable substances. Stones must have been difficult to fashion and they are inefficient in their natural forms. The Late Pliocene period was thus an era of early, if not initial, manufacture and use of artifacts. Because these crude artifacts were perishable, they cannot be uncovered by archeological excavations today. Those who possessed and made them survived because they were better able to cope with environmental conditions than were the forest denizens who possessed only instincts, teeth, and digits. Artifacts thus became increasingly a means for effectuating survival.

5. The inventory of specific instinctive cries, shrieks, calls, and other sound signals of the *Dryopithecus* ape was being supplemented and replaced by an ever-expanding inventory of noninstinctive learned call signals. The more apt, precise, and specific the sound signals became the more they contributed to the survival of their possessors. These primitive beginnings of true language constituted tools of a new kind for more successful survival, and they progressively replaced instinctive cries.

6. Learned signals and taught behavior constituted bases for new

patterns of social relationships which, because of their flexibility, had greater survival value under diverse circumstances than instinct-determined relationships. Scientific researches may never reveal the manner and forms of such learned relationships, but it can be supposed that they may have taken the form of hunting parties of males; sprout-, root-, fruit-, and berry-collecting parties of females; husband-wife family patterns for the sake of tending babies and sharing domestic chores; clusterings of families in bands or encampments for the sake of more efficient production and defense; and several others.

Some idea of the anatomical level of the Middle Pliocene to Late Pliocene ancestors of humans may be derived from the fossil remains of a number of African near-humans termed the *Australopithecenes*. They lived as late as the Middle Pleistocene and probably in earlier periods as well. The teeth are remarkably human, and recent discoveries of leg and hip bones show that they must have walked erect. Apparently they made use of tools and included smaller animals in their diet. Yet their brains remained small and apelike and the general conformation of their skulls was not human. This population, which was limited to one continent as far as is now known, was composed of humanlike higher primates which lived too recently to be ancestral to humans. However, the earlier Australopithecenes of the Middle Pliocene may be judged possible steps on the direct line of human evolution; proof in the form of additional Pliocene fossils is needed. The Australopithecene fossils contribute to the present comprehension of human evolution by their display of progressive development which was parallel, in many aspects, to the evolution of human anatomical structure.

Pleistocene Developmental Levels. Geological knowledge of Europe is especially detailed for the Pleistocene, which is the last 500,000 to 1,000,000 years. The known and successive geological levels of Pleistocene Europe are therefore arbitrarily employed as calendrical markers for human developments. These calendrical steps of the Pleistocene are listed in Fig. 3, which follows the convenient although not proved assumption that the Pleistocene lasted about a million years.

Early Pleistocene Fossils. Part of a large and thick fossil jaw found in 1941 in Java, termed *Meganthropus paleojavanicus,* and the

Period	Age in years	Time-levels
RECENT		last 20,000 years
PLEISTOCENE	50,000	4th glacial (Würm) or pluvial
		3rd interglacial
	250,000	3rd glacial (Riss) or pluvial
	500,000	2nd interglacial
	750,000	2nd glacial (Mindel) or pluvial
		1st interglacial
	900,000	1st glacial (Gunz) or pluvial
	1,000,000	preglacial

FIG. 3. Quaternary time-levels, with years ago indicated within wide margins of probable error.

three fossilized molar teeth of enormous size found in Hong Kong apothecary shops between 1934 and 1939, termed *Gigantopithecus,* are obviously those of huge-jawed giant primates. They may be ancestral to Pleistocene humans, or possibly to the orangutan. Until fuller data are obtained, speculations regarding their significance for human evolution will be premature.

Earliest Known Hominids: The *Pithecanthropus* Group. Between 1891 and 1940, scientists found in Java fragmentary fossils of a near-human population termed *Pithecanthropus erectus* (erect ape man) which lived between 500,000 and 800,000 years ago. Parts of five different skulls were found, a half-dozen thigh bones (femurs), and a number of teeth. The teeth were large but near-human, the jaws were massive, the supraorbital ridges were heavy and protruding, and the forehead was sloping or flat. The brain size varied from 700 c.c. to 1000 c.c. or more. The latter figure is within the modern human range. The topography of the inside of the skullcap showed a near-human developmental level of the brain, especially in relation to its speech area. Muscle attachments on the femurs indicated erect posture.

Variability in the size of the features of these fossils was considerable, although the absence of a sufficiently large series of complete skeletons precludes a mathematical phrasing of the average and variability of any of the features of this ancestral population. A three-year-old child's skull found at Modiokerto in Java in 1936 appears to be a member of the *Pithecanthropus* population and is probably geologically earlier than the adult specimens.

Between 1929 and 1937 scientists recovered fossilized parts of almost forty members of a near-human population in northeastern China termed *Sinanthropus,* the developmental level of which was probably slightly more advanced than *Pithecanthropus.* Nine or ten complete skulls were found, with a range in brain capacity from 900 c.c. to 1250 c.c.; a portion of this range overlaps that of modern humans. The bones of *Sinanthropus* are much more numerous and are better reported upon than *Pithecanthropus,* but they are nevertheless too few for mathematical determination of the average and variability of any one feature. As in the instance of *Pithecanthropus* the variability in features is impressive. It may indicate hybridization of genetically divergent groups.

In the strata in which the *Sinanthropus* bones were found there is evidence that this population had knowledge of the control and use of fire, a discovery of capital importance, and that it possessed cutting tools of stone of by no means a primitive level. There are also some evidences of cannibalism, which fact however may be of no special significance since moderns have also on occasion eaten human flesh.

The developmental level of the structure of the brain and the teeth was more advanced in the direction of modern humans than was that of the large lower jaw. Anatomists term such differences in the degree of advance of the features of a species *asymmetrical evolution.* The progressive reduction in size of teeth, which appears to have proceeded at a more rapid rate than did the humanization of the jaw, has been further exemplified by the massive lower jaw discovered near Heidelberg, Germany, in 1907, the geological age of which is the same or earlier. Reasons that used to be given for classifying it in the human genus, while *Sinanthropus* and *Pithecanthropus* are excluded, now seem inadequate. The best taxonomic opinion at present includes all three within a single genus.

The extensive areas inhabited by near-human populations of the

Middle Pleistocene or earlier are suggested by the fact that Europe, North China, and Java have all contributed fossil remains. Even more widespread are the finds of stone artifacts of this period. The near-humans lived in temperate as well as tropical climates. At least in the case of *Sinanthropus* they were demonstrably in control of fire. However, the use of fire may have been widespread or even universal during this time; lately some evidence, as mentioned above, indicates that the South African *Australopithecenes* possessed this feature of culture. There is every reason to suppose that the inventory of perishable and now unknown artifacts made with cutting tools of stone was much larger than was the variety of stone artifacts. The style traditions exhibited in the stone artifacts, as well as the information derived from endocranial casts and details of jaw anatomy, point to a likelihood that various forms of language were also employed.

However, populations were very likely quite sparse because of the prevailingly low technological level. Bands of the near-humans may have been widely separated and have had minimal intercommunication. Although the meager evidences point to a generally similar standard of technology in cutting tools, the conditions of living probably varied from region to region because of the general poverty of the means of manipulation of various types of environment.

During the course of some thousands of generations, selection of genetic mutations in the direction of truly human types must have taken place, and in all probability these were of sufficient survival value to have spread widely. Intermixtures between communities in contact have always occurred among humans. Therefore there seems to be little if any reason for doubting that this occurred among near-humans. But the opportunities for their intermixture may have been few, and the survival of the African *Australopithecenes* for so long a time suggests this.

The final extinction of the *Australopithecenes,* whenever it took place, may also be interpreted as a demonstration of the survival value of the mutations that had been selected and that had led the human ancestral line in the direction of human types. This applies especially to changes that involved the central nervous system. *Australopithecene* brains were far smaller and much less adequate, in all probability, than those of the near-humans, and a humanlike brain appears to have been necessary for the full exploitation of the way of life that had developed by the end of the Pleistocene second interglacial period. Populations which survived this period undoubtedly had attained a necessary degree of complexity and adaptability of psychic organization. They may also be presumed to have been little dissimilar in their inherited determinants of ability, as appears to have been the case among human populations ever since. At the same time they may have been as diverse in exterior appearance or in relatively nonadaptive traits of external anatomy as are the modern human populations. In fact, there have been claims that *Sinanthropus* possessed incipient Mongoloid, *Pithecanthropus* incipient Australoid, and Heidelberg incipient Neandertaloid characteristics. Further skeletal finds, and especially ones which interconnect with more recent populations in those areas, are required before such claims can be accepted.

Study and interpretation of the groups of near-human remains of the first half of the Pleistocene period indicate that humanlike domestication had clearly begun. Primitive cultures were in existence. In spite of the paucity of specific information regarding culture, it may be said that the near-humans had entered new evolutionary paths: they were subject to unique forms of selection for survival. These forms were determined by culture as well as by nature because the environment in which they lived was, to a degree, changed and shaped by their cultural habits. The major course of human biological development, from at least the second interglacial on, has been distinctive, and it may have been distinctive in much earlier Pleistocene eras, too. It has differentiated and set apart the human line from other animal species throughout the epochs when cultural factors contributed to the environmental setting.

An assortment of skull fragments were uncovered in East Africa in 1935. These remains offer inconclusive suggestions of the presence of a near-human population in this area during the second interglacial period. However, it is very uncertain whether the dating of the finds is second interglacial, and their state of preservation is too poor to permit the drawing of any conclusions about the anatomy and relationships of the population, termed *Africanthropus*.

Quaternary epoch	Name and dating of type	Name of type less certainly placed
	Living populations	
Shortly following 4th Ice Age	Tepexpan Boskop Brünn, Předmost	Wadjak, Talgai, Keilor, Aitape
4th Ice Age	*Homo sapiens* (Cromagnon) Later Neandertaloids	
3rd interglacial	Ehringsdorf, Krapina, Carmel Earlier Neandertaloids Fontéchavade	Steinheim Solo Rhodesian
2nd interglacial	Swanscombe	
Early 2nd interglacial	*Pithecanthropus, Sinanthropus* Heidelberg	*Africanthropus*
Early Pleistocene		*Gigantopithecus Meganthropus*

Fig. 4. Principal types of the Quaternary arranged in developmental levels.

Early Varieties of the Genus *Homo*. The course of anatomical change between Middle Pleistocene near-humans and much later types is not clearly known, although the quantities of stone implements are great enough to suggest an increase in population density. The dating of many of the Middle Pleistocene near-human and human fossil remains is doubtful and their anatomical characteristics sometimes permit more than one interpretation. Additional discoveries will improve the interpretation of the data. The fossils which might fit into a sequence from near-human to human types are too fragmentary to warrant more than tentative sketching. In 1921 a skull of excessively puzzling type was found in Rhodesia in South Africa together with a thigh bone and fragments of a second skeleton. The brain case, estimated at about 1300 c.c., is no larger than are some of those of *Sinanthropus,* but the supraorbital ridges are larger. The upper jaw projects considerably. On the other hand, the teeth and the general conformation of the skull are far more human. Unfortunately the strata from which these specimens were obtained have not been ascertained, and examination of additional relics *in situ* is necessary to determine the period of the Pleistocene in which they lived. However, they show a combination of advanced ape and human features rather than a transition between them. The Rhodesian finds definitely indicate asymmetrical evolution.

A comparable combination of apish and human traits also appears in the famous Piltdown fragments reported in southern England between 1909 and 1915. Recently (1953) these specimens were exposed as a modern skull and an orang jaw. However, for almost forty years these fragments generated intense interest because of their curious assemblage of traits. Some scientists correctly claimed that the parts were of two different creatures. Accompanying the revelation that the specimens had been dishonestly handled, fluorine technique showed that the bones were modern. If the remains had come from one race, they would have illustrated asymmetrical evolution. Rates of evolutionary change seem to have been variable among different populations, and the changes in different body parts in the same race certainly did not always occur at an even tempo.

Eleven partial skulls that lacked facial bones were found in a Middle Pleistocene deposit at Solo in Java in 1931. In some ways they resemble the Rhodesian finds; in others they do not. The average size of brain appears to be considerably greater than in *Pithecanthropus,* an earlier inhabitant of Java, but it is still below that of more recent humans. Some students have classified the Solo group as a species, *Homo soloensis.* Others have thought it a distant ancestor of the modern Australoids.

In 1935–36 two thick bones (occipital and parietal) of a skullcap were discovered at Swanscombe in Kent, England. The inference from recent fluorine testing agrees with inferences from geological study of the site, that the Swanscombe skullcap bones must be presumed to be of second interglacial age. Aside from their thickness, they are quite modern and indicate a modern-like brain. It would be reasonable to classify them as *Homo sapiens.* Neither face nor jaw is known from Solo or Swanscombe, but the skullcaps indicate extremely different types of *Homo.* Through more discoveries, the progress of human evolution in different regions during the Middle Pleistocene eras will be less obscure. Evidence obtained by archeologists shows improvement in the technical skill of Middle Pleistocene populations, indicating that the populations may have been increasing.

Third Interglacial Populations. With the exception of the Swanscombe specimen, the fossils listed directly above may have all been of third rather than second interglacial eras. There are numerous human fossils that are rather definitely third interglacial, but so far they come only from Europe and the contiguous Near East. In spite of their origin in a comparatively small sector of the Old World, they are characterized by great diversities of physical type.

The skullcap of a female, discovered in 1947 in a cave at Fontéchavade in France, resembles modern *Homo sapiens* more closely than the Swanscombe fragments.

A skull from Steinheim in Germany, reported about 1934, has numerous characteristics of the later Neandertal people.

Since Fontéchavade and Steinheim are very likely early third interglacial, they provide evidence that is helpful in interpreting human evolution. One of the problems which they may help to solve is whether the Neandertal type represents a developmental stage of all, of only some, or of none, of the ancestors of *Homo sapiens*. Until recently there had been good anatomical and theoretical evidence to support the first two of these three possible views. Few scientists were inclined to favor the hypothesis that Neandertal was not ancestral to *Homo sapiens*. The Steinheim, Fontéchavade, Swanscombe finds and perhaps also the spectacular improvements that may now be anticipated in the dating of Pleistocene specimens, tend to support the viewpoint that was least tenable a short time ago. Scientists are increasingly inclined to accept the plausible theory that as early as the appearance of the Neandertal type, humans existed who lacked the anatomical traits peculiar to Neandertals. It is also noteworthy that the earliest fossils that have any Neandertal characteristics have fewer such traits than are displayed in the Neandertal fossils of later dating. The series of fossils at Ehringsdorf and Krapina in Central Europe, and at caves on Mt. Carmel in Israel are of the third interglacial period. The specimens from Central Europe are not fully Neandertal. The Mt. Carmel series shows some individuals who were distinctly of *Homo sapiens* type, while others were far more Neandertaloid. Decisive discoveries are needed to establish the now plausible hypothesis that the Neandertals are a largely European specialization in the evolution of *Homo sapiens* during a relatively late Pleistocene period. Whether or not such a specialized population intermingled with *Homo sapiens* populations must also be determined.

The Neandertals. From late in the third interglacial until after the middle of the final glaciation, Neandertals seem to have been the principal if not the sole inhabitants of Europe. In its extreme form this population is characterized by large deep-sunk eyes, large supraorbital ridges, low forehead, retreating chin, considerable facial prognathism, broad nose, long flat-cheeked face, and a long low skull with protuberant occiput. Forearms and shins were short. The long bones have been interpreted as indications of a slouching bent-kneed posture and gait. However, in many features the Neandertals are less apelike than are modern humans. The average brain size is larger than that of humans. Since complexity rather than size of brain is indicative of intelligence it would be rash to conclude that the Neandertals had greater intelligence. Despite the restricted geographical range and time span of the Neandertals about a hundred complete or partial skeletons have been found, more than all earlier Pleistocene specimens together. The Neandertal remains include all ages and both sexes. Scientists have also found great numbers of associated artifacts, of a specific tradition or technical style termed Mousterian (see p. 93).

Although scientists have accumulated and have inferred far more specific information about this population than about any earlier group, there are many things which cannot be inferred warrantably from the bones and the artifacts. Many artists have attempted portraitures or sculpturings which purport to represent the external appearance of these near-moderns as well as of earlier Pleistocene populations. Even the texture and the combing of head hair, the nose shape, ear patterning, lip thickness, and amount of body hair have been portrayed. All such ventures, however, lack scientific merit in spite of whatever aesthetic or novelistic interest they may have. The soft parts of these peoples left no trace in geological deposits and so it is impossible to ascertain their color or appearance.

The Neandertals have often been represented as cave dwellers. The belief among many anthropologists, especially the archeologists and specialists in Pleistocene human evolution, that residence in caves was a central or widespread feature of Neandertal life must be challenged. Few archeologists or human paleontologists who have reported Neandertal discoveries have been familiar with the manner of life of hunting peoples of the modern period. European caves have long been valued as sites for research and study and, under favorable research conditions, have yielded pertinent data. Although the finds in caves from France to Palestine have been remarkable, the authors believe that they do not support the claim that cave residence was typical for Neandertal times. Modern hunting peoples have almost everywhere constructed various types of habitation near their hunting, fishing, and plant-gathering locales. As ancient hunting peoples, the Neandertals are believed to have followed similar procedures. Therefore, the high frequency of Neandertal finds in caves does not establish them as seasonal or all-year-round cave dwellers. A more cautious interpretation would suggest that the Neandertals often visited caves, sometimes dwelt in or near them, occasionally worked in or near them, and in general lived in types of habitations which cannot be ascertained because they have not been preserved.

Early Varieties of *Homo Sapiens*. The existing evidence indicates that the Neandertal race became extinct but does not negate the possibility that traces of Neandertal ancestry have survived in *Homo sapiens* populations. No convincing proof has been given that any living race is notably closer to the Neandertal than any other. From the third interglacial to the present the number of fossils increases and are more widely distributed. Except for the Neandertal type, all can be classified as members of *Homo sapiens*. They are not closely similar in anatomical features. Racial variety as great as that existing today appears to have characterized *Homo sapiens* at all times. In some anatomical traits the early members of *Homo sapiens* vary from living members consistently. The early ones had bigger than average modern cranial capacity. In general their skeletons are more robust. Most of them had far better teeth. Their faces tend to be rather short and broad. Possibly living through hunting tended to develop such characteristics.

Since more investigations have been made in Europe than else-where, knowledge of early *Homo sapiens* types is derived too, pre-dominantly from this small area. Hence, some current tentative con-clusions, regarding recent evolution, may be skewed.

By the end of the glacial period at the latest, *Homo sapiens* was living on all the continents and in all island regions except the most remote.

Fossils from Australia and the East Indies are few but in some instances they are significant. A skull from Keilor in Australia and another from Aitape in New Guinea appear to be Pleistocene rather than Recent. Both show many of the skeletal traits common among living natives of Australia. Two skulls from Wadjak in Java and one from Talgai in Australia may be of post-glacial age; they have also been interpreted as Australoid to a degree. All of these five skulls are clearly *Homo sapiens*. Although the browridges and the palates of Keilor and Wadjak are large, and the faces are prognathous, the general conformation is neither simian nor Neandertaloid.

South African finds are becoming more frequent. The Florisbad skull is perhaps oldest. It has broad, thick browridges and is very prognathous. Some scientists think that it is related to the proto-Australoid skulls mentioned above. A number of Late Pleistocene skulls are usually included in a so-called Boskop type. It is character-ized by a vertical rather than a retreating forehead, small jaw and teeth, broad nose, narrow orbits, and a long head. Its traits are for the most part non-apelike and, indeed, it has rather childlike char-acteristics. The modern Bushmen have similar features.

East Africa has produced numerous fossils of *Homo sapiens* type, but of uncertain dating. Most parts of Asia have offered only cultural remains. Although these reveal the presence of people from early times, they tell nothing about anatomical types and changes.

In North Africa and Europe, fossils of *Homo sapiens* succeed Neandertals climaxing the fourth glaciation, perhaps sixty thou-sand years ago. Thick skulls and big browridges are found in many individuals, but in general there are few traits which can be accepted as conclusive evidence of descent from or hybridization with earlier Neandertal inhabitants. Some scientists claim that the advanced tech-nology of the *Homo sapiens* groups enabled them to support greater numbers, and that the Neandertals were gradually absoibed rather than destroyed. However, the question arises as to whether two racial groups of similar mental potential are likely to have different levels of technology in Pleistocene times. Most scientists do not assume that the Neandertal was on the average mentally inferior to *Homo sapiens*. The assumption that *Homo sapiens* gained advantage because it possessed a technology superior to that of the Neandertal begs the question as to how long one racial type could possess a culture superior to that transmitted by another racial type, and whether this was for a time sufficient to have resulted in unequal competition for racial survival. In modern times the rapid advance of the technologically more developed Caucasoids has worked out in such a fashion, but it remains rather rash to assume the same process in eras, the cultural dynamics of which are not sufficiently known.

Many scientists hold that some degree of Neandertal ancestry, how much is uncertain, may at length be ascertained especially for Northwest Europeans. When human remains from late glacial times become more numerous scientists plan to seek evidences of Neandertal ancestry in the *Homo sapiens* populations of such epochs.

Considerable variability in anatomical details, such as in length of leg and height of nasal bridge, is found in the populations of sixty thousand years ago. But the variability is no greater than in modern inhabitants of the same regions. Some writers have improperly selected certain individual late glacial specimens as ancestral to one or another modern race. However, these European skeletons do resemble Caucasoids rather than Mongoloids or Negroids. They comprise various groups of skeletons long familiar to anthropologists as the Cromagnons, who include the female and young male from Grimaldi, claimed as partially Negroid but not proven so; and the more than forty individuals discovered at Brünn and Předmost in Czechoslovakia.

Other very late Pleistocene areas offer only a few skeletal remains. A small group of skulls and skeletal fragments found in 1933 in northeastern Asia includes individuals some of whom have distinctly Mongoloid traits. In no case are these traits as developed as in recent Chinese. In many features the resemblance is rather to other modern types such as the Ainu. In America also, probable or possible remains of the very late glacial period have been found. Perhaps the best authenticated is the Tepexpan fossil from Mexico. The skull is recognizable as that of an Indian although not typical of most present or recent Indians. It adds to the still limited evidences that modern people entered America, by way of Siberia and Alaska, during the very late glacial period.

By the end of the Pleistocene, all populations possessed a technology sufficiently advanced to permit their survival in any area which they could reach. Moreover, most areas had been entered. Among the consequences, therefore, of advance in technology, were: an increase in the amount of land surface occupied the world over, an increase in total numbers as well as in the numbers dwelling in certain naturally favored districts, some increases perhaps in numbers dwelling in areas that earlier could have permitted the survival only of extremely sparse populations, and a greater variety of racial types since so many regions were now inhabited. Anthropologists no longer believe it likely that such racial variability and numbers of racial types paralleled variability in biologically determined efficiency, either mental or muscular. All later Pleistocene fossils are of relatively robust, large-brained individuals. It seems safe to presume that the human ancestors of the Late Pleistocene required a minimum of intelligence and strength to survive.

Summary. Geneticists are no longer inclined to urge that most of the changes in the evolution from apes to modern man constituted sudden spurts ahead or mutations. Contemporary opinion leans rather in favor of gradual changes resulting from operation of the familiar processes of normal variability and selection according to environmental conditions. From the Early Pleistocene period the influence of culturally fashioned conditions of living grew constantly in all environments, and mankind became less and less dependent upon the natural ecology. Furthermore, such vast areas had been entered that the spread of genes throughout entire populations became difficult. Consequently random gene variations of little or no survival value could become fixed in the remoter populations. Thus, isolation, size of population, and cultural environments were the decisive factors involved in the process of selection of anatomical features during the Pleistocene epoch.

The evolution of man was probably also so gradual in the Pleistocene epoch, if not in earlier eras, as to constitute an unbroken continuum for every anatomical feature that has changed. Furthermore, the evidence for asymmetrical evolution or uneven speed of change of various features underscores the arbitrariness of the methodologically necessary practice of partitioning the evolutionary process during the Pleistocene epoch into a series of sharply distinguishable levels. Eventually when many thousands of skeletons are found it may be possible to illumine the entire course of human evolution, the stages for tooth evolution, for the evolution of the lower jaw, for the supraorbital ridge, and for other skeletal traits. Each trait could then be traced as if it exhibited a long series of links in a chain from the ape to modern man. At present there are too few fossils to show many of the links of the changes during the Pleistocene epoch for a single feature.

The most decisive changes, away from a *Dryopithecus* level, occurred not in the later periods for which fossils have been found, but in the Middle Pliocene to Late Pliocene periods for which not an iota of evidence is available. None of the features of the specimens of *Pithecanthropus-Sinanthropus* level are truly intermediate in the sense of being close to the center of the series of links from *Dryopithecus* to *Homo sapiens*. The Early Pleistocene to Middle Pleistocene fossils are much closer to modern humans than to Miocene *Dryopithecus* apes, and all the populations of that time already had fire and fairly well-developed cutting tools of stone.

The best that can now be done, therefore, is to describe the remains as they exist, and make tentative inferences respecting their relationship to one another, and to earlier and later forms. The samples of Pleistocene geographical populations before the Neandertals are insufficient to provide the average and the normal variability of any trait. Some inferences regarding relationships will prove to have been incorrect, when more data are at hand. However, a general tendency throughout Pleistocene times, for evolution in the direction of the modern populations, is fairly clearly displayed despite the fragmentary nature of the discoveries.

The scientific study of fossil man has barely begun. It needs to discover many more links in the chain of development of each skeletal feature, as well as many more complete skeletons, in order to describe the anatomy of each geographical population at each time-level. Only a few later links, levels, or arbitrarily denoted high points in the continuum of gradual changes have been found. The evolution of teeth will probably become best known because they are most resistant to corrosion, and considerable knowledge of the evolution of the jaw and skullcap bones will also be possible. The long bones which corrode most readily are found rarely in ancient deposits and their development will therefore be difficult to ascertain. The evolution of the soft parts will either not be known at all or will occasionally be inferred. Available knowledge supports the conclusion that during the Pleistocene epoch following the appearance of fire and of cutting tools of stone, the mental potentialities of the geographical populations were equal and have continued to be equal ever since.

SELECTED READINGS

Ashley Montagu, M. F. *An Introduction to Physical Anthropology.* Springfield: C. C Thomas, 1951 (rev. ed.). Pp. 5–228.

Boule, M. and H. V. Vallois. *Fossil Men.* New York: Dryden, 1957.

Brace, C. L. and M. F. Ashley Montagu. *Man's Evolution.* New York: Macmillan, 1965.

Clark, W. E. LeGros. *The Antecedents of Man.* Chicago: Quadrangle Books, 1959.

———. *The Fossil Evidence for Human Evolution: An Introduction to the Study of Paleoanthropology.* Chicago: Univ. of Chicago Press, 1955.

Comas, J. *Manual of Physical Anthropology.* Springfield: C. C Thomas, 1960.

Coon, C. S. *The Origin of Races.* New York: Knopf, 1962.

———. *The Story of Man.* New York: Knopf, 1962.

Dobzhansky, T. *Mankind Evolving.* New Haven: Yale Univ. Press, 1962.

Harrison, G. A., J. S. Wiener, J. M. Tanner, and N. A. Barnicot. *Human Biology.* New York: Oxford, 1964.

Howell, F. C. *Human Evolution.* New York: Random House, 1962.

Howells, W. *Back of History: The Story of Our Own Origins.* Garden City: Doubleday and Co., 1954.

———. *Mankind in the Making.* Garden City: Doubleday, 1959.

Hulse, F. S. *The Human Species.* New York: Random House, 1963.

Kraus, B. *The Basis of Human Evolution.* New York: Harper and Row, 1964.

Lasker, G. W. *The Evolution of Man.* New York: Holt, Rinehart and Winston, 1961.

Simpson, G. G. *The Meaning of Evolution.* New Haven: Yale Univ. Press, 1949.

CHAPTER THREE

THE LIVING RACES

Introduction. Problems concerning the physical characteristics of the living races and their relationships to one another have fascinated scientists and laymen alike for centuries. Anthropology offers major contributions towards the understanding of these problems. It makes no attempt to play down their complexity, yet it offers basic scientific information for the interpretation of the significance of the differences and similarities of the physical form and the behavior of the peoples of the world. It takes into consideration the contributions of the modern science of genetics, the long history of the minglings and migrations of people and resulting intermixtures, the different physical features, the instability of the human type as it adapts itself to varied physical and changing cultural environments, and other scientific data. A large portion of this field is termed physical anthropology, which is the study of features of human anatomy and the processes which change those features. However, recent scientific developments such as human genetics, physiology, and mental testing tie in so closely with physical anthropology that, for purposes of study of the living races, data from these fields have been included.

The Mechanisms of Heredity. The mechanisms of heredity in humans operate like those of other organisms but their study is complicated by circumstances unique to humans. Favorable conditions for research in heredity include controlled laboratory observations of standardized strains of organisms, such as fruit flies, over a series of generations under similar environmental conditions. Among humans such conditions for research are not present because the physical and cultural environments which affect human heredity vary widely, the special ways in which they operate on human heredity are all but unknown, and laboratory controls of relatively pure strains are beyond reach. Knowledge of many successive generations of humans is difficult because the duration of a generation is alike for the observer and the observed. Moreover, generalizations about heredity often depend upon statistical findings based on the study of many offspring, while human lineages may not be large enough for statistical deductions. Information on human heredity therefore remains fragmentary.

In hereditary transmission, the nuclei of the germ cells are central factors. When human germ cells combine, the resultant nucleus contains two sets of twenty-four chromosomes, one set from the mother, the other from the father. There is a linear arrangement of varying chemical substances, called genes, along the length of the chromosomes. Each chromosome includes a considerable number of these genes which are minimal units or entities regarded by geneticists as decisive for inheritance. The genes occupy places called *loci* on specific chromosomes. The two chromosomes of a pair are alike in the arrangement and presumably the chemical composition of their genes, and it is assumed that an individual possesses at least a pair of gene representatives for each gene-determined trait. These two partner genes are called alleles. The number of genic *loci* in human chromosomes is unknown; estimates range from 5000 to over 100,000. The prodigious number of gene combinations of different kinds possible in human mating may be seen from the fact that if the number of genes on forty-eight human chromosomes is estimated at 24,000 pairs, the possible combinations would be 16,777,-216 with twenty-four zeros. In addition to the astronomical range of possibilities that are hereditarily determined, the scientist also takes into account the environment in which the individual manifests itself. The biologist Jennings has pointed out that anatomical traits "do not fall into two classes, one exclusively hereditary (or dependent on genes), the other exclusively environmental; that every characteristic is affected both by the materials of which the organism is composed, and by the effects of the environmental conditions on these materials, and that some are more readily altered by these conditions than others." Furthermore, among humans the individual's relation to the environment, which is for the most part a peculiarly culture-fashioned environment or one made possible by features of culture, goes beyond adaptation that is primarily biological, characteristic of other animals except for the most domesticated forms. It is essentially one of learned adjustment through the cumulative knowledge, skills, habits, and psychological adaptations that can be defined as culture. Humans are distinct from other animals because they are largely or wholly uncommitted by their biological constitutions to any specific forms of cultural or psychological behavior.

Present knowledge of human genetics is still so meagre that geneticists cannot show how to breed in a direction of raising the human race to a new and higher developmental level. The best therefore that a eugenical program can now do is to lessen the frequency of a very few kinds of physical malformation or abnormality that appear in lineages where such defects are patently determined by genes. Too little is known regarding the hereditary or gene factors in mental deficiency to warrant practical programs or legislation for sterilization. Moreover, since no race has been shown to be superior or inferior to any other in mental potentialities (see p. 42), the agitation of eugenicists for racial purity has no present justification in scientific biology. Leading geneticists have therefore stressed the fact that practical and legislative proposals of the kind now advocated by eugenicists have no scientific merit. Eugenic legislation is often not merely based on unscientific premises. It has been used, as in Nazi Germany, as a weapon against political opposition, and in some states appears to have functioned as a device to lower the tax burden by sterilizing persons on the relief rolls.

Race Mixture. Contiguous communities have always intermingled. In recent millennia peoples have also migrated from area to area and associated with others whom they met. The intermingling of genes, which may have been slower in earlier than in later times, has served as a dynamic process throughout human biological history. In recent centuries the contacts of representatives of physically divergent and previously distant populations, such as the commingling of Caucasoid with Negroid in America, or of Mongoloid with Melanesian and Negrito in Oceania, have led to the formation of new physical types. There is no evidence that any mixture, due to migration, has produced especially favorable or unfavorable biological results, any more than did the earlier and possibly the slower interminglings of ancestral lines due to contiguity. Races are not static entities. New races are constantly being formed through out-breeding and inbreeding, as well as through adaptation to changes in physical and cultural environments.

There is no evidence in any hybrid populations of the undesirable "disharmony" of anatomical features asserted by some writers to have occurred in interracial crosses. There is no valid evidence in cases of human race mixture of "hybrid vigor," in physique or mentality. Nor is there proof that hybridization produces physical or psychological weakness or inferiority. There is no evidence of any special psychological or personality manifestations which can be traced directly to the biological process of mixture itself. The only known ill effects of race crossing occur where there is social dis-approval of such intermixture and where the participants and off-spring of such crossing suffer social ostracism and discrimination.

The American Negro people is a population of modern hybrids resulting from the fusing of Caucasoid, Negroid, and American Indian into a new racial type. It shows no evidence that a mechanism of Mendelian inheritance operated measurably or observably for its mixed features. In human inheritance almost every measurable or observable feature such as color or nasal profile is determined by a number or complex of genes. When a gene complex from one group such as Negroid combines with a gene complex from another group such as Caucasoid, the characteristics of resultant offspring cannot be predicted for there is a wide range of possible variants. Initially the hybrid offspring display variability for any feature within the range exhibited by the combined parental groups. If the hybrid group is segregated, and intermingling with other groups is dis-couraged by legal and extra-legal pressures, as has been true of the American Negro since slavery, its range of variability may lessen somewhat after several generations and it may become more homo-geneous.

The belief that in a hybrid human group there may be a "reversion to type"—that, for example, the dark skin color of a single Negro ancestor will reappear in an otherwise expected white descendant—is unfounded. Not one gene but a complex of genes is involved.

Human skin color has not been observed to operate according to simple Mendelian rules under which one color would be dominant and the other recessive, but rather a wide variability is manifested. Again, offspring are very rarely lighter or darker than the lightest and darkest of their four grandparents, and tend to be intermediate in skin color. The manner of operation of the laws of heredity in skin color remains obscure because of the complexity of the mechanism by which a number of genes for skin color operate together. The same observation holds for hair texture, nasal profile, lip thickness, and almost all the other measurable or observable human features.

Physical Anthropology. The gradations among populations in measurable or observable anatomical features that are directly determined by genes are so imperceptible that any race classification is merely an application of labels for convenient abstractions, termed geographical populations, races, or subraces. The scientific and pedagogic convenience of these abstractions nevertheless justifies making them. Since present knowledge of mathematically phrased differences in genes or gene frequencies is too meagre for employment as the basis of a classification, anthropology has to employ a less satisfactory procedure. It has to use measurable or observable features that differ. Eventually, it is hoped, it can classify on a sounder basis, by employing features such as blood types where the processes of inheritance are precisely determinable.

Before we present a classification of geographical populations or races which may be helpful in facilitating the description of anatomical features of the peoples of the world (see p. 46), the methods of measurement and of observation of the human body which constitute the means of providing the factual basis for such classification will be discussed. They are (a) measurements of bodily features, (b) indices which are mathematical expressions of the percentage of one measurement to another, and (c) observations which cannot be phrased mathematically.

The principal instruments used for measurements, and also therefore for indices, are a steel measuring tape, an anthropometer for reading heights and transverse diameters, a spreading caliper for head diameters and the like, a sliding compass for shorter diameters, and a head spanner for head height. Relative accuracy in measuring requires training in the employment of these instruments, together with a knowledge of anatomy and of the body landmarks that are generally accepted for purposes of measurement. The number of possible measurements is legion, but physical anthropologists agree more or less that in their field work a limited list is sufficient. Among the items which are frequently measured are the standing height or stature, maximum head length and breadth, head height, maximum nasal breadth, nasal length, and lip width. The familiar observations made are of eye color, skin color, head hair texture, the fold of upper eyelid called the epicanthic fold, and body hair.

Plasticity of Racial Type. Within the absolute boundaries determined by the genes, all physical characteristics in a population have as yet undetermined limits of plasticity depending on climate and other environmental conditions and especially on diet. The fact that racial types are subject to change does not imply that a group of modern African Negroes will necessarily become genetically lighter over a period of centuries spent in the far north, or that a group of Caucasoids will darken over a comparable period in equatorial districts. Natural selection will no longer operate to produce such results if the groups mentioned live henceforth in new ways, as modern and industrialized people. Technological levels and conditions of living have lately become so improved as to counter the manner in which natural selection always operated in the past. Therefore if natural selection no longer can effect skin color changes under modernized conditions, the genes for skin color will be changed largely by differential social selection due to varying customs.

It was formerly believed that features other than height, such as head shape, nasal width, and hair texture, were immutable no matter where an established geographical population moved. Researches by Boas about 1909, and later by other scientists who worked with various racial groups, have proved that almost all features change from environment to environment, but within as yet undefined gene-determined limits. These changes have occurred among groups whose gene frequencies remain the same—that is, populations whose hereditary characteristics have not been modified by intermixture with others. The changes have been never great enough, however, to transform the features of an Asiatic Mongoloid into those of a

Caucasoid, or of a Pygmy into a Nilotic Negroid. Stature is one of the most plastic of the features capable of being measured. An optimal diet can raise the height of a poorly fed population some inches and change to a poorer diet will lower the stature of a population. Prenatal as well as postnatal environments play a role in effecting the adult bodily dimensions.

When a physical anthropologist measures a group he measures not its genetic type or genotype but rather the present physiological form of that type, its phenotype. The plasticity of stature and head shape may be such that a description of a population as averaging five feet two in height, and .79 for the relation between head width and head length, is unrevealing since the population's potential maxima and minima for those traits have not been established. That is why the assertion that a population is short in stature and medium in head shape tells next to nothing regarding its genetic inheritance for those traits. The phenotype that is measured does not reveal the genotype.

Phenotypical plasticity in inherited color, quantity of body hair, head hair texture, and lip thickness appears to be relatively less than the plasticity of stature and head shape, which are probably determined by a much larger number of genes. That is why features such as skin color, iris color, head hair texture, epicanthic fold, quantity of body hair, nasal profile, and nasal breadth have been the best diagnostic criteria for race classification until the recent researches on blood types, and why stature, except for Pygmy populations, and head shape are less satisfactory. Present knowledge regarding the degree of possible plasticity of anatomical features does not serve to controvert the classifications given below. The races indicated here are each distinguished by a cluster of distinctive features probably determined in most instances by a relatively small number of genes.

Stature. Because stature is the most unstable of all anatomical traits it serves mainly to assist in classification of non-Pygmy as compared to Pygmy peoples. The potential height of Mediterranean Caucasoids, for example, who at present and on the average are shorter than northern European Caucasoids, cannot be determined until many more Mediterraneans have acquired a superior standard of living and diet. In the same way, there is no evidence regarding the maximum stature which will be attained by the short, poorer classes of Japan when their socio-economic system gives them an optimal intake of calories, vitamins, and minerals. The greater stature of persons of Japanese origin brought up in Hawaii or the United States suggests a potential increase in stature in the Japanese homeland of that population. Only the Pygmy populations seem held down to maxima some inches below any of the other populations. But they too can assuredly gain many inches if and when they acquire an optimal standard of living and diet.

Evidence of the stature of Pygmies in premodern eras is not available. In fact it appears that this feature is of recent evolution, which does not, however, weight a case in favor of a theory that the Pygmy populations are in general more highly evolved than the non-Pygmy populations.

Head Shape or Cephalic Index. For a century physical anthropologists have noted a mathematical expression or index called the cephalic index, which is the maximum width divided by the maximum length of the head, multiplied by 100. If the average cephalic index of a population is less than 75 it is, on the average, dolichocephalic or long headed; if from 75 to 79.9 it is mesocephalic or medium headed; and if 80 or more it is brachycephalic or wide headed. Most series of premodern skulls, that is to say, of individuals who died before the last ten thousand years, are on the average dolichocephalic. Most Negroid populations of today are dolichocephalic; so too are most northern and southern European populations and the American Indians of coastal districts. An east-west belt of peoples across Europe ranges from mesocephalic to extremely brachycephalic; as do also some Indians of the interior districts of the United States. European Caucasoids and Mongoloid groups run the gamut from extreme dolichocephaly to extreme brachycephaly. For this reason the largest geographical populations, the Mongoloids and Caucasoids, cannot be characterized as possessing essentially one or the other type of head shape. Subdivisions of these largest populations, and any other populations, may be long headed or wide headed on the average, but it is not certain whether this is mainly a consequence of genetic inheritance since proof of inheritance of a special head shape has not been given. The utility of the cephalic index as a means of characterizing a population, even if conjoined with a cluster of certainly inherited features of other kinds, is in doubt. Moreover it cannot be said that brachycephaly constitutes a higher developmental level, although the evidence of premodern skulls seems to point to a historical trend from dolichocephaly to brachycephaly. The drastic change in diet of most populations in recent thousands of years may be the only determining factor in the observed trend, rather than a consistent change of a genetic kind.

That the cephalic index of a population is unstable has recently been proved (see p. 40).

The Size and Structure of the Brain. There is notable variability in brain size within each population. The size of the brain is normally correlated with the size of the bodily frame, and prenatal and postnatal diets affect the growth of all features. Healthy and able individuals may be found anywhere within a range of as low as 1000 or 1050 c.c. to more than 1800. Within these limits any degree of intelligence may be found irrespective of brain size. Beyond such limits are diseased individuals who occur in small numbers in all populations. Apart from Pygmy populations and one or two populations that are especially poverty-stricken, averages everywhere vary between about 1300 c.c. and 1500 c.c. for the male sex, and approximately 150 to 170 c.c. less for the female sex.

The claim of a smaller average size of brain for any normally tall population has never been substantiated by evidence derived from measurements of a large series of well-fed individuals. Where the claim has been made for a Pygmy population or for one that is especially ill fed, it must be viewed in the light of the smaller physique or nutritional handicap of such a group. A wide skull tends to enclose a somewhat larger brain and therefore since some Negroid groups tend notably towards long-headedness, they have a slightly smaller average brain size. The fact that females are on the average smaller than males, both in over-all weight and in brain size, implies nothing regarding psychological potential. The same applies to smaller brain size in any population. That the largest or nearly largest average in brain size has been found among Eskimos offers no evidence that the Eskimos are racially superior to Caucasoids or to any other group.

The complexity of brain structure and the number of brain fibers appear to be the same in all populations, where comparisons are made on individuals who during their years of growth had adequate nourishment. Even where nutritional factors varied widely, racial differences in brain structure have never been demonstrated by neuro-anatomy. Wide variations in brain convolutions and foldings, however, occur within every population. Whereas differences in brain structure from individual to individual within any population are great, between the variable populations no noteworthy differences have been ascertained. That all populations today have the same complexity of structure of brain and central nervous system is decisive evidence in favor of the judgment that all races are potentially equal and that there are no genetically superior or inferior races.

Eye Color. For purposes of race classification only the Caucasoids and their ethnic subdivisions can be set apart by distinctive eye color, or rather, by iris color. All non-Caucasoid populations have a dark brown or black iris, owing to a heavy concentration of dark pigment in the front of the iris. Blue, green, or gray irises in Caucasoids are due to differing distributions and lighter concentrations of pigment. Pink iris color is found in albinos, where almost no eye pigment is present. Iris color seems helpful for classificatory purposes within the Caucasoid population, but its applicability is limited because most of humanity is much the same in respect to this trait. The inability to employ eye color observations on cemetery specimens also limits the value of this trait for classification.

Skin Color. Skin color has been observed by comparing the least sunburned portion of the body, as for example the inner surface of the upper arm, with the mixed colors of a spinning color top.

Each population displays much variability in skin color. Some persons who because of other features are most fittingly included among the Caucasoids are as dark as some African Negroids. In other words there is overlapping in skin color from population to population.

The major factor in skin pigment is the degree of concentration of microscopic dark brown or melanin granules in the deeper cell layers of the skin. An absence of such granules is termed albinism, a development which occurs rarely in every population. Melanin granules protect against the ultraviolet rays of sunlight. The heavy concentration of these granules in most equatorial populations, and the lighter concentration in peoples of temperate and more northerly belts, are patently consequences of natural selection, for light pigmentation has poorer survival value and dark pigmentation better survival value under a tropical sun. Very light and very dark pigmentation appear to be recently developed extremes comparable in kind to those found in highly specialized domesticated animals. The African Negroid is as advanced in an evolutionary sense in his dark coloring as is the North European in his meagre array of melanin granules.

No evidence has ever been adduced to show a causal interconnection between degree of concentration of melanin granules and the developmental level or quality of the central nervous system. There is thus no relationship between skin color and mental potentiality of individuals or races.

The populations with the least pigment are the Caucasoids and the Ainus. Populations of intermediate colorings are the Mongoloids, African Congo Pygmies, South African Bushmen-Hottentots, and Micronesians-Polynesians. The darkest populations are some of the African Negroids, Veddoids, Far Eastern Pygmies, Melanesians, and Australoids. (For their other characteristics see pp. 46 f.)

The Texture of Hair. Although the texture of hair of the older cemetery sources cannot be classified because head hair soon disintegrates, this trait is excellent for human taxonomy because it is less influenced by environment than other traits. It is difficult to subject it to mathematical measurement with present techniques. Straight hair tends toward round cross sections, wavy toward slightly oval, curly to oval, kinky or woolly to even more notably oval. It is also claimed that the number of bends in the hair fibers correlates with the degree of waviness, curliness, or woolliness.

Straight-haired peoples include some Caucasoids, most Mongoloids, and a very few Australoids. Wavy- to curly-haired peoples number most Caucasoids, Ainus, Australoids, Veddoids, and Micronesians-Polynesians. Kinky, woolly, or frizzly hair is found among the Pygmy, Negroid, and Melanesian groups, and a few others as among some southern Australoids. Peppercorn hair, which is the most spiraled known, is peculiar to Bushmen-Hottentots but has diffused among some southern African Negroids. The woolly and peppercorn types are specialized rather than primitive.

Body Hair. The feature of body hair is of less use in race classification than are skeletal features, since cemetery populations exhibit only remains of bones. This feature is, however, of especial value for classifications of living peoples because, as far as is known, diet change in a population has only a very slight effect upon the display of body hair.

Caucasoids, Ainus, some Veddoids, Australoids, and Congo Pygmies have heavy body hair on the average whereas other populations tend to lack much body hair. Although heavy body hair is apelike, the populations possessing this feature have one or two other features that are further removed from the ape than are the equivalent features in those populations which have little body hair.

The Epicanthic Fold. Only the continental Asiatic Mongoloids and to a much lesser degree the Bushmen-Hottentots include a large percentage of persons with inner upper eyelid or inner epicanthic folding. Inner, medial, and outer foldings occur in a number of the people of all other populations, the outer folding especially among older persons in Europe and some other countries.

The trait is not subject to measurement and can be little more than surmised from cemetery materials, but it is an excellent one for purposes of race classification because as far as is known it seems to be relatively unaffected by factors other than genes. Its principal service in race classification is, when used in conjunction with other traits, to distinguish various Mongoloid subdivisions, and the Bushmen-Hottentots. Among northerly Mongoloids the heavily fat-padded upper eyelid with its characteristic fold appears to be a recent product of selection, serving well in long cold winters. The extreme degree of inner folding so notable in northerly Asiatic Mongoloids is probably a recent evolutionary development in that part of the world.

Constitutional Types or Body Structures. Numerous attempts have been made to classify Caucasoids into contrasted body types, such as tall-slender, short-stocky, athletic, and the like. Such types are patently abstractions or ideals set up by an investigator, whereas populations witness only a continuum from one to the other extreme. Proof has not been given that hereditary differences are the major factor in the determination of differences in build. On the contrary prenatal and postnatal diet and environment are now well known to contain decisive factors in the determination of adult body structure. The human body is plastic within wide and as yet undetermined limits. The tall, slender build of Nilotic Negroids may be largely determined by genes, but until proof is given that the native diet in this area is indecisive in the shaping of such a build, one must withhold judgment regarding a genetic or racial factor. Every type of body build claimed for subdivisions of a single population can be found in other populations. For this reason, observed differences in body structural types may offer little more than clues that should be used with utmost caution in race classification.

Body Odor. Few notions regarding race differences are more widely believed than the idea that each race has its distinctive odor. The fact that very few American Negro people are of pure African ancestry does not affect the belief in racial odor because it is supposed, without any proof, that any small degree of African ancestry will produce the odor that is assumed to be present.

In many parts of Asia, where the people have mainly vegetarian diets, the body odors of carnivorous Europeans are regarded as repellent. Among the most potent odors known to chemists are valeric acid, butyric acid, and related organic compounds, which are given off as vapors through the skin by all persons who in the previous hours have digested milk, butter, cheese, or fats of various kinds. The decisive components in the body odor of Europeans may be these substances, not because they are Caucasians but because most of them eat and drink as they do. A population which eats much garlic has another characteristic odor; onions engender still other consequences; smoked salmon and venison, pickled herrings, and yams, still others.

In spite of the evidence that body odor is due to foods primarily, and to hygiene, laundry habits, and health secondarily and not to hereditary differences, many uninformed people still believe they smell distinctive group or racial odors. This erroneous belief is by no means of slight importance in the general ideology and practice of racism. It reinforces innumerable forms of segregation and discrimination.

Blood Groups. Attempts to effect or to sharpen up a race classification by employing differences in blood types have failed. The percentages of people who have one or another type of blood are about the same in some Mongoloids as in some Caucasoids, although hair texture, body hair, pigmentation, and inner epicanthic fold differ. Differences in percentages of the blood types appear to be as great within one national subdivision of a geographical population, such as the Chinese Mongoloids, as are found between Mongoloids and any other geographical populations. Furthermore the various types of blood are present in most of the geographical populations, as in apes. For example, on the basis of a large body of statistics compiled in different countries by different investigators, the ratios for 500 Swedes do not differ from those of 183 Lapps, 1391 Italians, or 502 Germans from Baden. Similarly 1000 Russians do not differ significantly from 500 American Negroes, or 500 Spanish Jews from 1000 Chinese.

Race classifications ventured by cautious scientists, which are based on clusters of distinctive features as well as on probable differences in gene frequencies, have never seemed to agree with a classification based on differences in percentages of blood types.

In spite of current unscientific policies of segregating blood or plasma according to racial type, lives can be saved by use of blood or plasma taken from any other geographical population, providing that the type taken from the donor is correct for that had by the recipient.

The long-standing notion that blood is a determinant of human quality is insupportable. There is also no such thing as German blood, Negro blood, Jewish blood, Swiss blood, or Lutheran blood. To speak of a blood relationship between populations is to speak in a literary but not scientific manner.

Race Classification. As noted in the preceding pages, race formation is dependent upon the degree of inbreeding or outbreeding of peoples, upon the adaptation of the unstable human organism to the demands of the physical and cultural environments, and upon social selection. The presence of inbreeding and outbreeding is determined by such factors as geographic isolation, the levels of technological development permitting or deterring migration or permanent settlement, and by cultural rules sanctioning or prohibiting intermixture. The human organism has shown itself to be capable of an extremely wide range of adaptive physical changes to varied climatic conditions, diets, and requirements of cultural adjustment. Social selection is practiced usually within the limits of the cultural definitions of desirable or undesirable matings, including the existing concepts of beauty or ugliness.

The history of human society since its inception has been marked by numerous migrations and the mingling of peoples, and by periods of relative stability. Were the history of past migrations and settlements known, the processes of genetic inheritance and the effects of diet and culture adequately understood, the task of classification might not be so difficult, and the judgments of the classifiers not so arbitrary. But in the absence of such knowledge there is little agreement among anthropologists on race classification.

Yet there is agreement among anthropologists that there have been in earlier periods of history, and still are, areas in the world where anatomical specializations have occurred and are occurring. These specializations make it possible to distinguish specific types from others by a cluster of observable inherited traits. Race classification is a matter of establishing genetic relationships, not merely of noting morphological similarities. When peoples are classified together under the same racial category, it is postulated that they belong to closely related family lines.

It has been customary for many anthropologists to classify the human race into three basic specialized groups, variously designated geographic populations, races, stocks, or divisions, that is the Mongoloid, Caucasoid or White, and Negroid, and then to subsume subdivisions or subraces under these heads. A tentative classification of eleven major races is offered here because of the improbability of ancient migrations adequate to explain the distributions of five Negro-like populations (African Negro, Melanesian, Congo Pygmy, Far Eastern Pygmy, and Bushman-Hottentot) which have been regarded as genetically related on the basis of anatomical similarities that can also be explained in terms of independent development. The presentation of this alternate classification rises also from the difficulty of establishing the genetic relationship of the Ainu of Japan, the Veddoids of Ceylon and the original inhabitants of Australia to the Mongoloid, Caucasoid, or Negroid populations. In the order of their numerical strength the eleven major races are (1) Caucasoid, (2) Mongoloid, (3) African Negroid, (4) Melanesian, (5) Micronesian-Polynesian, (6) Congo or Central African Pygmy, (7) Far Eastern Pygmy, (8) Australoid, (9) Bushman-Hottentot, (10) Ainu, (11) Veddoid.

These eleven populations are believed to represent the major races which existed before the sixteenth century migrations and subsequent hybridization further complicated the problem of race classification. They provide an historical and conceptual framework for other type specializations. For from the beginning there developed, and continued to develop on all continents, local and regional subtypes or subraces which also differentiated from one another through inbreeding, the effect of physical and cultural environments, and selection. These local and regional subtypes are designated subraces or racial subdivisions. In the classification of these subtypes there is no general agreement among anthropologists. Efforts at such classification will be discussed in the course of an evaluation of an alternative race classification recently offered by Coon, Garn, and Birdsell (see p. 51).

The characteristics of the eleven major races are as follows:

(1) CAUCASOIDS, who comprise approximately a billion people, display extremely variable skin color, from the lightest color to a dark brown. They cannot therefore accurately be called the white race, although this term is employed due to popular usage. Head hair is also variable, from straight to extremely curly, and body hair is often thick. Nose shapes are extremely variable but tend to be narrow and projecting. Lips on the average tend to be thin. The cephalic index runs from one extreme to the other, and stature from tall to short. There is no agreement among anthropologists on classification of Caucasoids into subraces (see p. 55).

(2) MONGOLOIDS, who number somewhat less than a billion, display variable color of skin, but their average is a yellowish light brown. Their head hair varies from straight to wavy but is more

often straight, and usually black. Except for Bushmen and Hottentots, Mongoloids have fewer head hairs and body hairs than other populations. There is great variability in nasal width and profile. Lips are variable but are on the average of medium thickness. Cheek bones project forward and laterally. More northerly Asian groups are characterized by an especially marked protection of the eyeball, caused by fatty layers which pad the lids and bring their borders close together. This type of epicanthic fold is found also in a less extreme form in some other races. Among Mongoloids, however, heavy fat padding appears to be a consequence of selection for survival in very cold winters. The highly diversified Mongoloid subraces have been variously designated (see pp. 52–53).

(3) THE AFRICAN NEGROIDS. This population numbers a hundred million and, with the exception of the Pygmies, inhabits the south Sahara extending as far south as the Cape of Good Hope in Africa. The skin of African Negroids varies from yellowish brown or dark brown to almost black. Head hair varies from very curly to woolly or frizzly and they have little body hair. Noses are variable in shape but often of great width. Ears are usually small. Some people of this race are notably prognathous—that is, have a projecting upper jaw —but others are not. Lips are variable but in some instances are thicker and more everted than those of other people. As in the case of the subraces of the Mongoloid and Caucasoid populations, the members of the African Negroid subraces vary greatly anatomically and, however they may be demarked, overlap one another (see pp. 58–59).

(4) MELANESIANS. Something under two million Negroid-like people live in the many South Pacific islands, termed Melanesia, that stretch across three thousand miles of ocean from New Guinea to Fiji. There is wide variability but generally they are characterized by deeply pigmented skin and eyes, tightly curled hair, and heavy browridges. The reasons for conceiving them to be a specialized type, independent of the African Negroids, are discussed later (see pp. 58–59).

(5) MICRONESIANS-POLYNESIANS. There are about 100,000 Micronesians in the islands north of Melanesia, and perhaps 300,000 Polynesians in the triangle of islands east of Melanesia, from Hawaii to

New Zealand to Easter Island. The body hair of these Oceanian peoples is slight. Their skin color is sometimes light, and head hair varies from straight to frizzly but is typically wavy. The hybrid nature of this group is discussed later (see pp. 60–61).

(6) THE CONGO OR CENTRAL AFRICAN PYGMIES. Numbering about 100,000 people, the Congo or Central African Pygmies have been regarded by most writers as genetically Negroid, but they appear to differ from African Negroids too greatly to warrant inclusion with that group. Their present average stature is less than five feet, although a superior diet and improved conditions of living might increase their stature considerably. They are not as dark as the African Negroids and Melanesians, and they have more body hair than these two races (see p. 59).

(7) THE FAR EASTERN PYGMIES include approximately 2000 Andaman Islanders; less than 25,000 people of Luzon, Mindanao, and other Philippine Islands; some hundreds of Semang and the partially Pygmy Sakai of the upper portions of the Malay Peninsula bulge; undetermined numbers in various Indonesian islands, New Guinea, and other portions of Melanesia. It is a moot question whether it is appropriate to include them with the Congo or Central African Pygmies in a Negrito race (see p. 59). The lips of these people are fairly thick; the head hair is woolly; their skin color is very dark; their body hair is slight; and their average height is five feet.

(8) AUSTRALOIDS. Perhaps less than 40,000 quite dark natives of Australia have survived British colonization. Their head hair varies from nearly straight to frizzly but is typically wavy. Like Caucasoids, they have much body hair but the supraorbital ridges are less pronounced in Caucasoids. With the exception of skin color their anatomical features resemble those of the Caucasoids (see p. 60).

(9) THE BUSHMEN-HOTTENTOTS are the 20,000 or more survivors of a Pygmy population in a few places in the Kalahari desert and nearby districts. Before the advance of Bantu-speaking Negroids during the Christian era, and before the recent colonization by Dutch and British, Pygmies of this type very likely occupied all of South Africa. They may have once included the full-sized *Boskop,* who are now extinct but whose characteristics may survive as components in

various South African peoples. The Bushmen average about five feet in height. Hottentots, today, are on the average much taller than Bushmen and their head hair is more often frizzly than peppercorn—which is the term used for the Bushmen's extraordinarily coiled or spiraled head hair. Their eyelids often have epicanthic folds as in the case of northern Mongoloids. Body hair is sparse, unlike the Congo Pygmies. Skin color is not dark but intermediate as among the latter. Their excessive deposition of fat on thighs and buttocks, termed *steatopygy*, may perhaps be attributed not so much to distinctive genes as to diet and postural habits with a resultant pronounced lumbar curve. The Mongoloid-like epicanthic fold has led some writers to suggest that this population acquired more Mongoloid genes than did Africans to the north, but such a hypothesis is undoubtedly less warranted than a theory of independent and parallel evolution of this feature (see pp. 58–59).

(10) AINUS. About 10,000 persons resident in Hokkaido and other smaller and outlying Japanese islands are thought to represent the ancient population of Japan. Traces of Ainu ancestry may appear to be visible in large numbers of other people in the archipelago (see pp. 52–53). The Ainu resemble the natives of southeast Australia except that their light skin color is comparable to that of brunet European Caucasoids. Ainu hair is wavy, lips are thin, and body hair is as heavy as or heavier than that of any other population.

(11) VEDDOIDS. A remnant group of at most a few hundred non-agricultural people termed the Veddas lived during the early decades of the twentieth century in the interior of Ceylon. They displayed wavy to curly hair, some body hair, chocolate-brown skin color, and rather delicate features. They seem to be anatomically intermediate between Caucasoid and Australoid (see pp. 56, 60).

Some of the problems of race classification can be understood by comparing the above tentative classification with the recent attempt at a taxonomy of the human race, also offered tentatively by Coon, Garn, and Birdsell. Their classification includes six major stocks and thirty races. Their six stocks are (1) Mongoloid, (2) White, (3) Negroid, (4) Australoid, (5) American Indian, (6) Polynesian. They note that these stocks are not races, but assemblages of groups or races which seem similar. Under Mongoloid they include all populations that have special adaptations to extremely severe winters. Negroid covers all populations which have special adaptations to extreme light and heat. White includes the Old World peoples who lack such adaptations. Their Australoid stock includes the Veddoids which are regarded separately above. The American Indian, generally treated as a subdivision of the Mongoloid, is regarded as an independent stock, as is the Polynesian.

The Mongoloid stock is subdivided by these authors into races termed Classic Mongoloid, North Chinese, Southeast Asiatic, Tibeto-Indonesian Mongoloid, and several partially Mongoloid hybrid races. *Classic Mongoloid* is used to designate northern Asian peoples with extreme epicanthic fold, flat face, and cold-selected fat padding. *North Chinese Mongoloids* are similar but with less adaptation to extreme cold.

Other anthropologists have designated the latter peoples, *Neo-asiatics*. Hundreds of millions of the people of Japan, Korea, and China represent this type, although other racial components also appear in the populations of these countries. The Japanese are largely the descendants of migrants from adjacent mainland communities of pre-Christian centuries. These immigrants commingled with the Ainus to a degree not notably different from the way Classic Mongoloids, partial Caucasoids, and others commingled for thousands of years with North Chinese Mongoloids living on the Korean-Chinese mainland. In spite of local variations in each group, there is an anatomical similarity between the populations of Japan, Korea, and China.

Southeast Asiatic Mongoloids designates, in Coon, Garn, and Birdsell's classification, hundreds of millions of people from southern China to the larger islands of Malaysia. These people are similar to North Chinese Mongoloids but have still less epicanthic folding of the Mongoloid variety. They intergrade with *Tibeto-Indonesian Mongoloids,* who include various Tibetan, Chinese, Burman, and marginal Indonesian island peoples, who are somewhat darker than other Mongoloids and display the Mongoloid epicanthic fold even less frequently.

The last two populations mentioned have had a confusing variety of appellations in anthropological literature. The former have also been termed *Malay* or *deutero-Malay,* the latter *Indonesian* or *proto-Malay,* on the assumption that two successive migrations of early Mongoloid peoples account for the present diversities of physique in the populations of southeastern Asia and Indonesia or Malaysia, apart from any other racial components also present in those regions. However, there is good reason to presume that when agriculture diffused into the southeastern Asiatic areas, the resulting increase in wealth and numbers led to Mongoloid migrations to the food-gathering districts inhabited by Pygmy and perhaps also Australoid populations. Hybridization followed, and only a few groups remained predominantly Pygmy. Difference in the percentage of Pygmy or Australoid ancestry may be suggested by the fact that in the Malaysian islands, peoples of interior districts tend to be darker-skinned and have slightly wavier hair while peoples of coastal districts often have lighter skins and straighter hair. Coon, Garn, and Birdsell use the term *Turkic* for some millions of anatomically distinctive central western Asian peoples who are hybrids of Mongoloids and Caucasoids.

Differentiations in the American Indian, as presented by Coon, Garn, and Birdsell, may have developed by the selection of certain features through diversified ways of living. They use the term *Marginal American Indians* to include largely non-agricultural natives of North and South America who are predominantly dolichocephalic and somewhat Mongoloid, while the designation *Central American Indians* is applied to all agricultural peoples of North and South America. The latter are broader-headed and less Mongoloid than the former. Not until the period following 40,000 B.C. was technology adequate to permit the survival of Asians migrating by way of the inhospitable Chukchee Peninsula, the only Old World region adjacent to America. Probably as a consequence of Upper Paleolithic technological advances (see p. 94), the Chukchee area may have been entered along several radii, especially by way of the Okhotsk Sea coast. Caucasoid and Ainu as well as Mongoloid components may have been present in these earliest pioneers in the Chukchee Peninsula. The earliest arrivals in America penetrated into the Seward Peninsula and beyond in western and central Alaska, which was then unglaciated while eastern Alaska and Canada remained glaciated. About eighteen to twenty thousand years ago, when the glaciation lessened and an ice-free channel opened along the Yukon and south along the Mackenzie, communities of food-gatherers slowly spread beyond Alaska into central western Canada and eventually filtered into all of America. Those intergrading peoples termed Marginal and Central American Indians are there-fore the numerous and slightly specialized descendants of a few original immigrants who crossed from Siberia into western Alaska by way of the Bering Strait probably about twenty thousand years ago and migrated throughout the remainder of the New World continents after about 18,000 B.C. No other people migrated to America by transoceanic canoes or other means of entry, in sufficient numbers to affect the racial composition of the American Indians, until the recent coming of the Europeans.

Anthropologists have presumed that successive waves of migrants penetrated Alaska from Siberia, although archeology has not found definite evidence to substantiate such a theory. On the other hand there is no definite evidence that food-gathering peoples succeeded in penetrating any distance through already inhabited countries in any region of the world. However, the seeming diversity of linguistic stocks among the American natives (see p. 284) suggests a series of entries into the Chukchee Peninsula and later again into Alaska from the Chukchee Peninsula. This diversity does not involve the corollary that the members of each immigrant linguistic stock were numerous, or the additional corollary that the members of each such stock ad-vanced far through an already populated district. Much further study and research is needed to explain the earliest entries of linguistic stocks, and the entries of anatomically distinctive groups of food-gatherers, if they were at all distinctive in this way. The anatomical features of many Eskimos may be ascribed to the effects of techno-logical advances associated with seal hunting, which resulted in a few thousand years of relative isolation from other natives of North America, leading to inbreeding and selection. However, Eskimos resemble Classic Mongoloids more than they do other races, and they share this resemblance with most of the Siberian aborigines. The possibility arises, then, that Eskimos may be the most recent arrivals from Siberia into North America.

Coon, Garn, and Birdsell subdivide their White or Caucasoid, into races termed Ainu, Alpine, Northwest European, Northeast European, Lapp, Hindu, Mediterranean, Nordic, and a number of partially White (Caucasoid) hybrid populations.

Difficulties in the taxonomic placing of the *Ainu,* have been discussed above (see p. 48). The captions from Alpine to Nordic constitute only the latest in a long series of attempts by anthropologists to give some genetically and historically meaningful arrangement to anatomical measurements and observations on a large number of peoples. A three-fold subdivision of European peoples was made by W. Z. Ripley in 1899 into Nordic, Alpine, and Mediterranean. In 1945 W. L. Krogman suggested a five-fold subdivision of European Caucasoids called Nordic, Alpine, Mediterranean, Armenoid, and Dinaric. Also in 1945, M. F. Ashley Montagu subdivided Caucasoids into eight races termed East Indian, Mediterranean, Alpine, Armenoid, Nordic, Dinaric, East Baltic, and Polynesian. This variety of classifications demonstrates lack of agreement among anthropologists as to the anatomical criteria that should be employed and the geographic distribution of the races they designate. Even the concepts of White or Caucasoid races are clearly subjective choices indicating arbitrary divisions in what is actually an unbroken continuum of inherited specialized physical features. Only the rather specialized *Lapps* of northern Scandinavia, and the *Gypsies* who are partial East Indians and who have resided in Europe since the Middle Ages, are relatively distinctive European races or subraces. Each of these two also includes many persons whose features are comparable to those of large numbers of non-Lapp and non-Gypsy Europeans. The other terms from Alpine to Nordic designate races only in the tentative sense that they are hypothetical arrangements of anatomical features the genetic history of which is unknown. In anthropological circles such hypotheses are employed with full recognition of their tentative nature. For most purposes of popular discussion, where racial designations are likely to be assigned a validity they do not possess, it is preferable to use such terms as Caucasians or European Caucasians or North Europeans because they do not represent classifications of technical observations and measurements. Terms such as Nordic, Alpine, and Dinaric should therefore be reserved for use in the course of specialized discussions based upon statistical data. The popular use of the concept of a Nordic race, for example, has little justification, but Nordic may serve anthropologists as a tool of analysis. Since the physical anthropologists' shifting concepts of Caucasoid or White races, or subraces, have been given wide publicity among laymen, as well as considerable attention during many decades of anthropological scholarship, the features associated with them are here presented. *Alpine* peoples live in a central east-west mountainous belt from France to central western Asia. Their average cephalic index is brachycephalic. They are mostly brunet with a somewhat higher percentage of blondness than Mediterraneans (see p. 57). Faces tend to be broad, hair straight to wavy. Stature is shorter than Nordics, taller than Mediterraneans. The factors of race hybridization and selection that may account for their features are unclear. *Northwest European* covers the peoples whose lands border the North Sea. They include individuals with heavy browridges, mixed eye colors, straight to wavy hair which is most often brown, and a wide variety of facial features. Again, the genetic components and the kinds of selection that may have been involved in this population during ancient times are uncertain, although there is no doubt that so-called Mediterraneans, Nordics, Alpines, and perhaps others are included. *Northeast European* is a catch-all term for populations from the lands that border the Baltic Sea eastwards to Siberia and south to the Carpathians or beyond. Head hair is straight to wavy and brown to blond, with many ash-blonds. Faces are broad and concave nasal profiles are frequent. Eyes are gray or mixed in color. Like Alpines and Northwest Europeans, the genetic history is obscure but certainly a mixed one. Earlier concepts termed Ladogan and East Baltic fit in the broader present concept of Northeast European. *Lapp* has already been discussed (see p. 55).

Coon, Garn, and Birdsell apply the designation *Hindu* to many of the peoples inhabiting southern Asia and especially to the people of northern India who are largely Mediterranean but darker. Perhaps they are partially descended from an ancient Veddoid population that preceded Mediterranean-like immigrants who entered India through its northwest passes before the Christian era. A theory of

Veddoid-Mediterranean hybridization, with additions of other peoples, and various specializations may account for the present diversity and range of features in northern India and elsewhere in much of southern Asia. There is insufficient evidence at present to give much support to claims that at one time Pygmy or Negroid races dwelt in India. *Mediterranean* is the term long employed for most of the populations bordering on the Mediterranean and for populations directly east of the Mediterranean into northern India. Skin color ranges from dark brown to very light. Blondness may characterize about four percent of the people in districts around the Mediterranean, but the percent of blondness diminishes east of the Mediterranean. The cephalic index is on the average dolichocephalic. Height is usually shorter than in other Caucasoids. Various subraces or types of Mediterraneans have been described: in 1939 Coon referred to *Atlanto-Mediterraneans* who are somewhat taller and whose nasal profile is straight to convex; *Irano-Afghan Mediterraneans,* who are also relatively taller but often convex in nasal profile; *Mediterraneans* proper, who are somewhat shorter and have straight and narrow noses. Other types have also been noted. Many northwestern Europeans appear to be predominantly of Atlanto-Mediterranean ancestry as a consequence of movements to the north during the Neolithic period and later. *Nordic* is currently thought of as that northerly population which is essentially Mediterranean but depigmented. The greatest concentration of Nordics is in Sweden, and relatively few Nordics appear in the countries contiguous to Sweden. People in adjacent countries who have long thought of themselves as Nordics often may be more fittingly termed Northwest or Northeast European. The genetic relationship, the factors of hybridization and selection, the reasons for depigmentation, and other aspects of Nordic origins are as obscure as are the answers to these questions for any other Caucasoids. While few anthropologists question the appropriateness of a Nordic race for classificatory purposes, no anthropologist accepts the term Aryan as synonymous with Nordic.

North American Colored is an apt designation used by Coon, Garn, and Birdsell for the so-called Negro people of North America. Genetically they are a most variable blend of Northwest European, Forest Negro (see p. 58) and Central American Indian. In other words, current popular usage which refers to the Negro people of the United States as members of the "Negro race," fails to take into account the fact that millions of people in this group have as much, or more, Northwest European ancestry as they have African (see p. 60). A similar mixture of European with Bantu and Bushman-Hottentot components may be termed *South African Colored*.

The Negroid is subdivided, by Coon, Garn, and Birdsell, into races termed Forest Negro, Melanesian, Negrito, Bushman, Bantu, Sudanese, and perhaps Hamite. In the previous classification (see pp. 49, 50) the Melanesian, Negrito, and Bushman are treated independently of the Negroid stock because of their probable genetic remoteness, and also because the Negrito is divided into two independently developed races that are separated by great distances.

Forest Negro is used by Coon, Garn, and Birdsell to include peoples from Senegal and the lands around the Gulf of Guinea Coast into much of the Congo. Skins and irises are very dark; jaws prognathous; head hair varies from very curly to woolly or frizzly but is not as extremely spiraled as in the Bushman group of South Africa. Noses are often very wide. Lips are in some instances thicker and more everted than those of any other race.

Some thousands of years ago, when agricultural and pastoral techniques diffused from northern Africa into districts south of the Sahara, Forest Negro groups seem to have advanced in numbers and wealth and expanded to the south into districts of the Congo once inhabited largely or wholly by Pygmies. The view that the Forest Negro, among all the Negroid races, may be the Negro prototype has appeared in recent writings under the caption the *True Negro*. However, the evidence for such a deduction is unsatisfactory.

The *Melanesian* race discussed earlier (see p. 49) is an anatomical counterpart of the Forest Negro, with a greater development of the browridge. This similarity led earlier anthropologists to formulate the theory that Negroids originated in southern Asia in ancient times, and subsequently migrated, during preagricultural eras, to Africa and Oceania. On the basis of the evidence now available, such a theory is untenable. Food-gatherers were never sufficient in number or adequately advanced in technology to make long-sustained migrations. Nor did they have sufficient motivation or opportunity for effective mass movement from their homeland through inhabited countries, to inhabited countries located at a considerable distance. Present knowledge of the living conditions and the situations that favor emigration of preagricultural peoples leads to the provisional conclusion that the distinctive features of the Melanesians came about through selection in the Melanesian or neighboring Indonesian islands. The Melanesians may include some significant components from contiguous races such as the Australoids and Far Eastern Pygmies.

Negrito is unfortunately employed with various meanings. It has been reserved by some writers as a designation for the Central African Pygmies; other writers have termed this African group *Negrillos*. Various authors have used the term Negrito for the Far Eastern Pygmies. Coon, Garn, and Birdsell apply it to both Congo and Far Eastern races, and also presume that the extinct Tasmanians were Negritos with an added element of Murrayian Australoid. Anatomically similar populations are thus placed under a single caption when their genetic relationship has not been demonstrated. Just as it is reasonable to deduce that the Melanesians are not Forest Negro in any genetic sense, so it seems that the Far East Pygmies are not genetically related to Congo Pygmies. Each group appeared in modern times with features that were the consequence of selection in similar equatorial environments and at a time when they were food-gatherers. Where there are similarities of features in groups as far apart as these, only a fortuitous parallelism can provisionally be inferred. The appropriateness of including *Bushman* (see p. 50) in a Negroid stock also hinges on evidence yet to be discovered concerning the ancient racial history and genetic affiliations of the group. The term *Bantu* is applied to a mixed group—of Forest Negro, Sudanese, and Bushman-Boskop—which is intermediate in color and not as tall as the Negroid groups north of it. *Sudanese* are similar to Forest Negro groups but they are often very tall and the extent of their pigmentation is extreme. They are called Nilotic Negroes or Nilotes by some anthropologists. Coon, Garn, and Birdsell employ *Hamite* for a tall group in East Africa and the Sudan, which is skeletally Mediterranean, dark in color, and possesses some external Negroid features. Presumably it is a hybrid of Caucasoid and Negroid. Other hybrid populations, with considerable **Negroid** ancestry, have been noted as North American Colored and South African Colored (see p. 58).

The Australoid stock, in the Coon, Garn, Birdsell classification, bears striking resemblance to Ainu, Veddoid-Dravidian, and Caucasoid races, but its genetic relations to these is obscure and will continue to be until more Pleistocene skeletons are unearthed. Birdsell sets up two main types within Australia, Murrayian and Carpentarian. He uses the term *Murrayian* to designate natives of southeastern Australia who possess important components of the vanished Tasmanians. Their skin is brown, hair wavy to frizzly, they have much body hair, their browridges are heavy, and their faces are similar to broader-faced Europeans. *Carpentarian* is his term for the natives of northern and central Australia. Their skin is darker than Murrayian, their hair straight to wavy, their jaws prognathous, and they have rather heavy browridges.

Dravidian appears to Coon, Garn, and Birdsell to be part of, or close to, their concept of an Australoid stock. It is used to include millions of people of southern India and Ceylon and to include the Veddoid described separately above (see p. 51). The features of the Dravidian racial type might be accounted for on the assumption that the Carpentarian Australoids had mixed with Hindu Caucasoids. However, there is now little evidence that a Carpentarian race resided in southern Asia. The genetic affiliation of people who resemble Veddoid or Dravidian types is further complicated by evidence that other peoples in Somaliland, Arabia, Baluchistan, and Celebes exhibit similar features to some degree. The problem will be clarified if future discoveries support the presence of food-gathering people of Veddoid or Dravidian features populating a continuous district bordering on the Indian Ocean, and of invasions of other races during Neolithic and later periods that led to hybridizations obscuring the earlier picture.

In the Coon, Garn, Birdsell classification, *Polynesian* stands as a race without further subdivision. The status of the Micronesians is not indicated by Coon and his colleagues, who point out the Polynesians as a hybrid group formed about two thousand years ago. The components of this hybrid are uncertain. All stocks with the exception of the American Indian, have been named as contributors. Geographical contiguity as well as anatomical characteristics weight the probabilities in favor of significant contributions from Mongoloid and Melanesian racial sources. Moreover, the Polynesian race appears to have developed after advances in the economic life, and increases in populations, of the Malaysian and Melanesian islands. The resemblance of Polynesians to Caucasoids does not warrant by itself the inference by recent authors that there are genetic components from the latter existent in the former.

Coon, Garn, and Birdsell note two additional hybrid populations, formed in modern times, which might be accorded the status of races: *Ladino,* which is used to designate the millions of people of Latin American countries who are hybrids of Central American Indian and Mediterranean, and occasionally include some of the components of Forest Negro; and *Neo-Hawaiian,* which is the term used for residents of the Hawaiian Islands who are hybrids of European, Polynesian, and other components.

As noted above (see p. 47) the term race as used by professional anthropologists refers exclusively to physical characteristics of peoples and thus classifications of races are made in terms of differences in inherited anatomical features. This important fact is obscured by the use in the classification by Coon, Garn, and Birdsell of the terms Turkic, Hindu, Bantu, Hamite, and Dravidian to designate races. These terms have been traditionally used to characterize linguistic, cultural, and religious groups and so have other than biological connotations.

The tentative nature of the classification by Coon, Garn, and Birdsell which has been analyzed in the foregoing pages is stressed in the concluding paragraph of their book: "The foregoing list of thirty 'races' might have been ten or fifty; the line of discrimination in many cases is arbitrary. In some cases we have nearly adequate data on which to base descriptions, in others almost none at all. In some we know the history of the processes of mixture, interbreeding, isolation, and selection involved; in others we have nothing but the living on which to base our deductions. . . . If this does nothing else, we hope that it will bring home to the student that race is not a static thing at all, but that new races are constantly being formed. . . ."

Can Racial Factors Account for Backwardness? The question is often raised as to whether the technological backwardness of the Negroes of Africa and of the South Sea Islanders in modern times can be regarded as evidence of racial inferiority. Actually the culture of a people at any specific time or place cannot be regarded as an index of its hereditary potentialities. There are, to be sure, impressive differences in technological achievement, in material progress and comforts, in physical conditions of living, and in complexity of economy and societal structure among people dwelling in different parts of the world. The problem is to determine the causes of these differences. If they are not due to racial differences, what accounts for them? Variations in geography or climate are not adequate explanations. Britain has had the same climate for two thousand years past but has exhibited great changes in culture. The tremendous achievements of Egyptians and Mesopotamians in pre-Christian millennia contrasted with their way of life in more recent times suggest that factors of a non-geographic kind must have been operative. The differences of cultural achievement in Peru, Mexico, Japan, India, Sumatra, or Nigeria in different centuries indicate too that climate and geographic environment cannot have been the dynamic factor responsible for divergent cultural manifestations in successive centuries. Geography and climate made possible important features of these cultures, but clearly did not cause cultural changes.

Queries regarding the contribution to civilization of the African Negro or the South Sea Islander are best although not completely explained by an examination of the historical consequences of certain basic advances in food-producing methods. In the period from 12,000 B.C. to 8000 B.C. the culture of all populations was based upon hunting, fishing, food-gathering techniques. The tempo of cultural change in different parts of the world could not then have been as uneven as it is now among the different modern peoples.

When, however, members of what was probably a Caucasoid population then resident in districts of central western Asia bred up some wild grasses to domesticated plants (see p. 95), and when Indians of South America, who were of Mongoloid affinity, independently domesticated maize, potatoes, and manioc (see p. 96), the resultant primitive agricultural procedure was so infinitely more productive that it was adopted by others. The fact that agriculture developed independently both in the Old World and the New World among peoples of different races is evidence that this momentous discovery was not dependent upon the unique racial characteristics of its innovators. Moreover, American Indians are all so similar in genetic heritage that the change to agriculture in one or two areas cannot be ascribed to superior genes in those areas.

Peoples who learned agricultural techniques from their neighbors increased in numbers, acquired food surpluses, released many persons for specialized skills and crafts, and developed commerce and trade. The racial characteristics of these peoples could not have changed significantly, but by the accident of geographic propinquity, the populations close to the districts where primitive agriculture and, shortly after, primitive pastoralism were first hit upon were first enabled to create superior techniques and more complex social systems. Populations many thousands of miles away from these technologically favored western or southwestern Asian districts acquired the new techniques thousands of years later, and hence were enabled to build culturally and in a comparable fashion only at a much later time. Populations farthest from the initial Asian centers of agriculture and pastoralism were the last to acquire those techniques.

The development of agriculture and of pastoralism, which permitted complex economies and social systems, has thus been the strategic factor which accounts for progressiveness or backwardness in various regions of the Old World. Populations south of the Sahara or out in Oceania are still backward materially, technologically, economically, and in certain complexities of social structure, because of the accident of remoteness of geographic location, certainly not because of hereditary inferiority. Whereas the Old World populations resident in the areas of great civilizations have had agriculture and pastoralism for a long time, peoples of the Gulf of Guinea Coast and the Congo of central Africa, and peoples of Melanesia, have had these advanced techniques for only a few thousand years. Large populations, wealth, surpluses, specialization of labor, commerce, and trade have never developed overnight. The differential in favor of the Western World has been increased in consequence of the commercial and industrial revolutions of recent centuries.

Similarly in the New World where primitive agriculture developed independently, the spread of agriculture from South to Central America and Mexico and the fact that it had not yet spread to northern California, Idaho, or British Columbia account in general terms for the material advances of the Mayan and Aztec Indians and the simple material achievements of the nonagricultural Hupa, Nez Percé, and Nootka Indians. Certainly no claim can be made for important differences in heredity between the Indians of these districts. Moreover, in terms of climate the Mayan architects, masons, and sculptors undoubtedly were much more handicapped than were their technologically primitive northern cousins. Neither race nor geography is thus strategic for technological and material advance, whereas food-producing techniques are.

The further argument that the dark-skinned peoples are racially inferior because of their meagre scientific, technological, or cultural contributions in the last four centuries has no validity. Slaves, peons, unskilled wage laborers, and other economically submerged populations are rarely permitted to receive the specialized education and opportunities requisite to make noteworthy creative work possible.

The Plasticity of Human Behavior. Scientific genetics has too limited a knowledge of the process of inheritance in relation to the central nervous system to change the genetic inheritance for mind and personality through selective breeding. We know too little to breed successfully for a population with innate potentialities for higher I.Q.'s.

However, the mental and emotional manifestations of any large population are extraordinarily variable. That this is so can be demonstrated by historical changes in the mental and emotional behavior of a population. Note, e.g., the six thousand years of recorded Egyptian history, during which genetic changes were negligible, and the three thousand years of Greek history. The same people who developed mathematics, philosophy, logic, and science, and who created the drama as well as the superb sculptures and architectural treasures of pre-Christian Greece, functioned differently in later centuries. Arabic-speaking Mediterranean peoples who were creative in philosophy, mathematics, and art forms in earlier Christian centuries have lost pre-eminence in these fields during recent centuries.

Changes in mind, in temperament, and in personality in England during the last six centuries and in Germany especially during the last fifty years are familiar to all who know history. The mental behavior of the Mayan Indians who developed architectural and sculptural arts, astronomical knowledge, and a technique of writing early in the Christian era had changed before and changed again after the Spanish Conquest. These changes must have been due to historical causes and not to changes in genetic inheritance.

The potential range of mental behavior of a geographical population is also suggested by the various cultures it has developed. A population as homogeneous as the American Indians exhibits widely diversified cultures such as those of the Pacific Northwest Coast, California, the Pueblos of the southwest United States, the Mayan and Aztec agricultural civilizations, the simple socio-economic systems of the Basin Shoshoneans in the western states, and the wealthy Chibcha and Inca civilizations of the Andean highlands. The Malay cultures of the Dutch East Indies run another gamut from the economically lowly islands southwest of Sumatra and the comparably simple social structures in the interior of Celebes and Borneo to wealthy and complex social systems in Java and the Philippines. African Negroids also display cultures of great variety from Senegal to the Anglo-Egyptian Sudan and from Timbuktu south to the Cape.

The potential range of the behavior of American Indians, Malay Mongoloids, or African Negroids is not indicated merely by all their past achievements, and by the varied personality types that have developed among each of these populations. With the introduction of industrialization, new types of education, and universal literacy, further changes in mental behavior have occurred and no one can now estimate the ceiling of potential creativity. This can be raised without significant changes in genetic inheritance. Historical conditions and circumstances, not genes, are therefore the immediate determinants of a people's cultural achievements. The central nervous system of each population offers possibilities of a tremendous range of cultural expressions, but relatively few of these possibilities develop in any one period of history.

The biological nature and genetic heritage of man has not been shown to have changed significantly for thousands of years, but the cultural and mental manifestations of that inherited nature are very varied and have no measurable or definable limits. In this sense human nature is infinitely malleable, plastic, or changeable in its social, ideological, and temperamental expressions. Since the potentialities of all human populations are much greater than is indicated by any inventory of their specific achievements, the biological or genetic improvement of the human race would not be the immediate issue even if scientific knowledge were available to make that possible. On the other hand, broader economic opportunities and better education are known to make possible the creative development of people otherwise backward. Present inability to improve our genetic inheritance is no justification for pessimism regarding human nature because it is already rich in the options it accords each population. Science has not revealed a difference in potential between populations.

The Life Cycle. Except in the case of differences in physical growth, which seem to be due primarily to dietary factors, no evidence is available that differences between populations in the behavior, thinking, or feeling of children are determined by biological factors. Such differences as are found seem entirely explicable in terms of parental and community behavior towards the child. Psychologists and anthropologists have collaborated in attempting to trace the variable consequences of early or later weaning, kinds of cradling, methods of toilet training, forms of reward and punishment, and other babyhood experiences. Whether or not these experiences are decisive or minor factors in personality, in temperament and character formation, and also in culture formation, is still in the realm of controversy. An earlier body of opinion rated them as decisive, and there are still many protagonists of this point of view. Others contend, however, that the social experiences and the features of the cultural heritage encountered in the years immediately following babyhood are more influential in the shaping of the adult psyche. While the answer to this question is moot, both groups of scientists eschew a theory that differences in biological heredity—that is, in gene frequencies—have any effect upon differences in the behavior pattern of childhood in different cultures.

Cultural differences in childhood living and thinking are very great. Weaning occurs early in some areas but is often delayed until three years of age in other areas. Babies or young children play with dolls in some parts of the world but not in others. Animistic personalizing of objects is found among some or most youngsters the world over, but it is reported as absent among the youngsters of a New Guinean community studied by Margaret Mead. Babies have the same central nervous systems in all populations but what they later do, think, and become seems to depend entirely on custom and on familial or socio-economic environment.

Childhood play and activities also vary from culture to culture. Among peoples of primitive economy the play of youngsters in the years from six or seven to puberty involves much more experimentation with and learning of adult techniques and ways than in our social system. The child looks forward to early participation as an adult in these cultures and prepares accordingly. In our society, on the other hand, the awareness and expectancy of, as well as active preparation for, adult participation often develop later in the adolescent years, especially in the white-collar class, and so there are more years of relatively irresponsible activity. Children in non-European societies play and have games, but play and games may continue into adult life without the abrupt halt or change at puberty that occurs in our society. In a primitive economy, therefore, the way of life and not hereditary difference makes for an earlier maturity in temperament, personality, and character than among European Caucasians.

Notable differences in rates of physical growth and time of puberty occur between segments of any population. There are such differences between youth of different socio-economic levels, and between rural and urban youth, where no important differences in heredity can be claimed. Hence the observed differences in physical growth and development between populations whose heredity is different warrant no inference that heredity has been the crucial factor in determining these differences. It is not necessary to suppose that racial difference accounts for an earlier or later onset of puberty, because diet and other environmental factors may be primary. All populations might have identical physiological manifestations were identical conditions of diet and environment to be found, but at present such identity exists nowhere.

Race differences in blood pressure and basal metabolism appear also to be primarily determined by different cultural heritages and modes of living, and by external factors such as climate or altitude, and possibly little or not at all by differences in gene frequencies.

Although physiological changes of one and the same kind occur at puberty among all peoples, the social and psychological behavior at puberty varies from culture to culture. In Western European society the physical change at puberty may often be accompanied by emotional conflicts, but it is not proved that such conflicts are determined solely by innately caused physiological changes. The main predisposing cause for emotional disturbance or turbulence at puberty may be the change in social status which the society has created at that age level. Evidence is not available from a sufficient number of societies, as to the kinds or degrees of emotional change found in early adolescence, to make generalizations in this field.

The menopause or climacteric is also a physiological change characteristic of every people. Although many physicians have thought that most instances of emotional disturbance at the climacteric were directly traceable to hormone changes, the frequency and degree of disturbance must also be determined to a certain extent by the customary social change which occurs for women at that age. Where women's participation in the community increases at about the time of the climacteric, or where there is no lowering of social status about that time, they are less often likely to become the victims of emotional disturbances. Many peoples with primitive economies accord more opportunities for socially significant work to older than to younger women. Where the climacteric age level means a lessening of social opportunities and participations, as is characteristic of Western European society, women tend to be more often subject to such disturbances.

Intelligence Test Results. Within each population the physical traits of the residents of one district, or of one social class, when measured, invariably display averages different from those of other areas or strata of the community. Populations which differ in other respects may also exhibit different average results in so-called intelligence tests. Increasing evidence substantiates the judgment that the test scores do not reveal the inherited intelligence of such groups, but reflect influences arising from social status, background, and education. Scores on intelligence tests are therefore not valid measures of group differences in native ability.

Where the group tested has a culturally sanctioned etiquette that disapproves of rapid oral responses, the scores obtained will be affected accordingly. Where the group is not interested in the kinds of test questions asked or judges them to be foolish, the results will suffer. The alien physique, dress, speech, or identification of the tester may cause resentment and unco-operativeness. People unused to pencil and paper, such as Australian Blackfellows, obviously cannot be expected to react as we do, and questions about arithmetic, color distinctions, large houses, garments, or the larger domestic animals may involve materials beyond the experience of some peoples. A test that is usually graded according to speed of completion is not applicable among peoples who are not interested in speed of performance. In short, a test whose content and method of scoring were developed by the carriers of one cultural heritage appears to be valueless for any determination of the native ability of the groups who have other cultures. Even slight dialect differences in the language employed by the tester and the subjects sometimes seem to lessen the value of the results, because of unfamiliarity with the terms used in giving the test instructions or test material; where the tester uses a foreign language, the test given appears entirely valueless. Within a socially stratified population, economically and educationally handicapped groups do not do so well on the tests as those who are better off. Rather notable improvements are shown by foster children after they have been placed in excellent homes and have lived there for some years, which indicates an important degree of malleability within limits still undetermined. No one knows how high an intelligence test score of groups or individuals may rise after protracted enjoyment of a change to optimal conditions of living. The length of schooling, the time spent each year in classrooms, and the quality of school equipment and personnel also affect the results.

Intelligence testing of racially disparate groups therefore lacks validity except where the groups compared are equal in language, culture, education, socio-economic background, and expectancies regarding their participation in the world about them. A comparison of American Negroes with American whites is a doubtful procedure because of the impossibility of controlling various factors which may influence the results. Intelligence tests may therefore not be used as measures of differences in native ability between these groups. When comparisons are made within the same race or group, it can also be demonstrated that there are very marked differences depending upon variations in cultural background. It has been found, for example, that the test scores of northern Negro children are much higher than those of southern Negro children. Investigation has shown that this difference cannot be explained in terms of selective migration of superior Negroes to the North, but is attributable to the superior economic, educational, and social opportunities afforded the northern Negro. The superiority in World War I army intelligence test scores of northern urban American Negro groups as compared to some southern rural whites is to be interpreted as evidence of the importance of environmental opportunity and not as proof of the innate mental superiority of northern Negroes to some southern whites. During World War II, the learning accomplishment of scores of thousands of Negroes from all sections of the country, in the United States Army Special Training Units for functional illiterates, where educational inequalities existing in civilian life were eliminated, compares favorably with that attained by scores of thousands of similarly diversified whites. Superiority in test scores of urban white to rural white groups likewise gives no evidence of selective migration of natively superior rural dwellers into urban districts, but indicates the cultural advantages of urban life.

Sense Perceptions and Special Aptitudes. There have been many claims that dark-skinned people have superior visual or auditory acuity, but upon investigation every instance of such acuity has been shown to be explicable in terms of the longer period of practice these peoples have had in noting or discriminating sensory cues. As far as hereditary equipment goes, general vision, olfactory and auditory acuity appear to be the same for all populations. Reports that some peoples are less sensitive to pain may be to a degree correct, but the explanation does not lie in a difference in heredity. Childhood conditioning and various cultural and ethical factors are undoubtedly decisive in these matters.

There is no convincing evidence of race or other group differences in character or personality, or in innate abilities of kinds such as music or dancing. Neither special tests nor other pertinent considerations give the slightest warrant for the popular belief that Negroes are innately more given to rhythmic or musical expression than other peoples. The creativity in music and dance as well as the success in athletics of American Negroes are demonstrably the result not of genetic factors but of relatively greater approval and wider opportunities accorded this minority in such fields and of their exclusion from participation in many other forms of activity permitted non-Negroes. American Indians invented many things before and few following the Conquest, but it cannot be said that they first possessed and later lacked a specific and distinctive sort of inventive talent that is gene-determined. There is no evidence of a genetic proclivity for specific forms of expression such as Maori wood carving in New Zealand, Navajo blankets in Arizona, voodoo rites in Haiti, impressionistic Bushman rock painting in South Africa, initiation ceremonies in central Australia, bronze sculpture in Negro Benin, architecture in marble in ancient Greece, writing for pulp magazines, swimming, violin playing, jitterbugging, shopkeeping, or salesmanship.

As far as is known all peoples are able to share creatively in all known cultures and to transmit them through education to their offspring. The specific forms of creative expression of a people at any period, whether they be in speechmaking, music, dance, bricklaying, science, or poetry, are in each instance to be explained in terms of the dynamics of the existing cultural heritage—that is, in historical terms and not in terms of race differences. Historical factors, not race factors, determine the nature and degree of special achievement of a people.

Mental Pathology. Present-day psychiatric science is as yet too undeveloped to ascertain the causes and forms of mental pathology among peoples who are outside the orbit of Western civilization. The causes and categories of neurotic and psychotic types among such peoples are not yet sufficiently defined to permit analysis.

Ethnologists are agreed that although mental pathology is found in individuals in all races and cultures, the forms or patterns of emotional disturbance, ideological disorientation, and socially intolerable behavior vary from culture to culture. Therefore the main problem is to correlate social or cultural patterns on the one hand with specific forms of mental pathology on the other. Some forms of mental pathology must also be due to peculiarities of diet, to special drugs used, and to other more easily traceable physical causes.

There exist among different peoples forms of aberrant but socially approved mental behavior. Among these are the waxlike postures and trance states achieved by southern Asiatic mystics; the institutionalized adoption of the manner of living of the opposite sex (transvestitism) and guardian spirit visitations among American Indians; the hypnotic and imitative behavior of Siberians in the throes of "arctic hysteria"; the imitative mania termed *lattah* and the phenomenon of running amuck among Malaysians. These are not racially determined mental states, because in each instance other sections of the same population do not manifest the type of aberrant behavior indicated. In other words, factors of cultural heritage rather than genetic inheritance are decisive in the determination of these behavior patterns. The classification of mental abnormalities which will eventually be developed for modern Europeans will need to be supplemented with portrayals of patterns of mental abnormality such as are found in the peoples who have other kinds of cultures. But there is no warrant for believing that distinctive genetic factors in one or another non-European population were or are determinative of specific mental manifestations, whether normal or abnormal. The causal factors reside in the conditions of living.

Crime. Statistics regarding the frequency or nature of crimes in various racial groups are worthless as indices of criminal proclivities. In the United States, for example, Negroes are arrested and convicted with less evidence and justice than is accorded other groups and therefore the statistics regarding the degree and rate of crime among American Negroes reveal nothing about race as such.

Proof that a group lacks innate propensity for one or another specific crime is found in the change in the frequency of that type of crime in successive generations. First or second generation American-born descendants of some immigrants, for example, may show an increase in burglaries whereas the immigrants themselves displayed a small incidence of that type of crime. Students of the question therefore agree that racial heritage or national origin does not directly determine either the crime rate or the specific types of crimes. These are influenced wholly by circumstances of the group's socio-economic environment.

At present there is a high rate of crimes among most American Indian groups. The explanation lies in the effects of the rapid disintegration of Indian socio-economic ways of life and culture, in rural racism, and in the lack of opportunity for social recognition and job acceptance for Indians except in communities remote from the home territory. Indians are so demoralized, hopeless, and untrained, as well as so enveloped by the most backward members of the Caucasian group, that carousing and brawling constitute channels of escape and release. The heritage of high evaluation of intense emotional experiences in pre-Caucasian era religions also carries over as reinforcement for those who indulge in alcoholic or other excess. But Indians who have participated on a basis of equality with Caucasian Americans are no more addicted to alcoholism or crime than are those among whom they live.

Is There a "Primitive Mind"? There is widespread belief among laymen that economically primitive, dark-skinned populations are characterized by fickleness, impulsiveness, lack of restraint, and improvidence. Such belief is not supported by the testimony of scientific observers. The socio-economic systems and cultural heritages of non-Europeans afford many varied situations which involve restraint, reflection, concentration, and the resourceful employment of knowledge and skill.

At the same time the acceptance by some peoples of premises and associations of ideas which are untenable to persons educated in Western culture is no indication of childish responses and thinking. Rather, it indicates that the influence of the technological, scientific, or philosophical heritage of the modern world has not displaced the premises in their culture regarding magical processes and supernaturalism. The French philosopher Lévy-Bruhl suggested that "primitive" people thought "prelogically"—that is to say, they were incapable of clear definition and setting apart of logically unconnected or unrelated phenomena. This suggestion has been widely misinterpreted. Although belief in causation of one or another kind is universal, categorizations of experiences and things and ascriptions of causal interrelationships are often inaccurate in the absence of a scientific method for checking and rechecking. Preliterate and pre-scientific people are constitutionally as capable of clear definition or of logic as are the inheritors of European civilization. However, the cultural heritage of the Europeans, because of its wealth and special-ization of skills, has facilitated the devising of a set of canons of logic, methods of scientific procedure, and premises freed of animistic or other forms of supernatural associations. These methods and ideas have now diffused widely.

Scientists who know non-European languages vouch for the se-quential, logical, and alert thinking of any peoples, granted their magical, animistic, supernatural, or other incorrect premises. The distinction between prelogical and logical made by Lévy-Bruhl does not set Europeans or Caucasoids apart from others so much as it sets apart a small group of highly skilled and literate persons with educa-tional, scientific, or technological backgrounds from the masses of human beings, Caucasoids and others, who have lacked such back-grounds, which are made possible by industrialization and universal secularized education.

Anthropologists are agreed that inventiveness, insight, originality, and creativity are found in every population. People are stimulated to invent or create in that arena of conventional interests or produc-tive work which because of its complexities and importance chal-lenges them. When the motivation is present, technical mastery leads to free play with the technique or field of interest and then to original achievement. In other words, genius or unique creativity is a function not of rare genes but of opportunity and of drive to master a complex technical, aesthetic, or other heritage. The inter-ests of many darker-skinned peoples and hence their creative ac-tivities are centered not around structural steel, organic chemistry, or atom splitting but around bamboo houses, fish nets, or pottery making, or around song cycles, dance patterns, magical devices, ritual, or cosmological theory. Original achievements in such matters usually do not leave permanent results whereas in the case of cutting tools and food-producing techniques advances are cumulative. For this reason it is difficult to find surviving testimonies for frequency and degree of originality except among contemporary and literate peoples. However, ethnographic research among peoples of primitive economy has everywhere revealed originality in material and in ideological and aesthetic forms certainly not less than that found among the peoples of the Western World.

Racism. Although race prejudice supported by false data has a long history, modern racism has developed recently among Europeans as a rationalization of conquest, chattel slavery, and imperialist expansion. It has been used to justify predatory behavior toward darker-skinned peoples who have simpler technologies and hence have been regarded as mentally inferior. In Germany, the creed of Aryan superiority among the Nazis led to the extermination of millions of Jews and helped to incite World War II. In the United States, racism serves primarily to sanction and to perpetuate discrimination against Negroes and other dark-skinned peoples. In colonial areas it has impeded the efforts of submerged peoples in their struggle towards equal opportunities, justice, and independence.

Contrary to the findings of anthropology, racism holds that each population is characterized by a cluster of inherited physical, mental, and temperamental features peculiar to itself, which are relatively unaffected by social, educational, or other environmental influences; that there are innately superior and inferior races and ethnic subdivisions, and that hereditary factors determine every phase of a people's cultural life. Overt forms of snobbish, discriminatory, and irrational behavior follow upon the uncritical acceptance of these unscientific premises. There has been a marked intensification of racism recently, largely because of the widespread activities of antidemocratic agencies. This fact presents a crucial challenge to the effective functioning of the ideals of democracy.

Since social scientists are agreed that young children do not become racist minded until older children or elders influence them in that direction, education can play a significant role in combating racism. The situations which breed racism can also be changed by democratic legislation outlawing discriminatory practices and by giving all people, irrespective of race, equality of opportunity. The rapidity with which modern racism developed suggests that racism can be attenuated if democratic programs of legislation, education, and community action are vitalized and enforced.

The Jewish Peoples. Although, as will be shown, the Jews are not a race, they have recently been singled out for special attack in most racist propaganda, and it is therefore desirable to summarize historical and anthropological findings concerning them here.

In pre-Christian and early Christian eras, Jews in Palestine were linguistically, culturally, and religiously but not anatomically distinctive. They were in all physical respects identical with other eastern Mediterranean Caucasoids. In the almost thousand-year period from the sixth century B.C. until the collapse of the Roman Empire they are known by historical records to have traveled, proselytized, intermarried, and enjoyed relatively complete freedom of social movement in all countries between France and Spain in the west, India in the east, Russia in the north, and Ethiopia in the south. The groups therefore which maintained the Jewish religio-cultural heritage were in every country in process of becoming physically indistinguishable from the non-Jews of that country. In some northern districts of Europe, for example, the percentage of blondness increased and approximated that of the rest of the population. In some central and southeasterly districts of Europe the percentage of nasal convexity among Jews also increased until it also approximated that of the rest of the population. There followed, however, after about A.D. 1100 seven or eight centuries during which most Jews in Europe were restricted in their movement and social participation, were denied the ownership of land, and were confined to urban ghettos. Although restrictions curtailed intermarriage with non-Jews, previous intermarriages and conversions during fifteen hundred years preceding had already made each group of Jews anatomically similar to the peoples of the region in which it had long resided. There is therefore no more a Jewish race or ethnic subdivision than there is a Catholic, Mormon, or Methodist race or ethnic subdivision. The physical and cultural types found among Jews vary widely, as widely in fact as the types found among the non-Jews in the lands where Jews dwell. The Jews of Abyssinia have a distinctive religio-cultural heritage, but in other aspects of culture and anatomically they are Abyssinians. Chinese Jews are identical in all respects with other

Chinese, except for their religious heritage and associated customs. The same is true of European Jews, particularly in the years following the removal of ghetto restrictions. Higher percentages of nasal convexity can be found in Yugoslav (so-called Dinaric) and Armenian districts, or of curliness of hair in other regions, than in any Jewish groups except in the case of those Jews who have lived for centuries among peoples with such anatomical characteristics. Yiddish, which is spoken only by Jewish groups which have been segregated in eastern and central European countries and by some of their descendants, is not Semitic or Hebrew except in some vocabulary words, but is basically a standard High German dialect from medieval west-central Germany.

If a strictly or narrowly anthropological rather than one or another popular concept of culture is employed, it follows that there is neither a general nor a localized specifically Jewish culture, and there has been none since Roman times. However, although there are millions of persons of Jewish religious ancestry who have become almost perfectly integrated in the cultural environments of the industrialized nations in which they now dwell, there are other millions of Jews both in industrialized nations and elsewhere who adhere to religio-cultural heritages which are specifically Jewish. The Jewish religio-cultural heritages comprise aggregates of cultural traits and themes (see pp. 76–78) which are of several kinds. One kind, for example, is a product of the way of life of Spanish-speaking Jews resident, since 1492, in Greek- and Turkish-speaking districts. Another is a product of severely isolated ghetto groups resident in central and eastern Europe. A third is in process of development by several hundred thousand European Jewish immigrants who have settled in Palestine since 1880. The distinctively Jewish cultural traits and themes of such populations, which in no instance comprise notably extensive lists, differ markedly in the several Jewish religio-cultural groups which live in countries such as Morocco, Romania, Poland, Turkey, and Greece. In the highly industrialized countries such as England and the United States where first and second generation Jews have participated in social and economic life with relatively free mobility, the always small lists of specifically Jewish cultural features which their ancestors had brought have become negligible or have vanished. To speak either of a Jewish culture or of a Jewish religio-cultural heritage for many Jewish individuals long resident and thoroughly integrated in such countries is erroneous.

Group cohesion among Jews, when it exists, may be largely explained as a form of counterassertion against prolonged and recurrent discriminations against them. In a democratic and urbanized country, social distance between Jews and non-Jews tends to disappear wherever discriminatory practices and social antagonisms expressed by the dominant group cease.

Assertions regarding the higher average native intelligence of Jews cannot be substantiated because their biological ancestry always appears to be indistinguishable from that of the groups among whom they have long dwelt. It is because Jews have long been established as an urban group that they score high ratings on mental tests. Moreover, the religious heritage and ghetto way of life in Europe have elicited especial respect among Jews for education and professional attainment, just as the Negro people of the United States, long deprived of educational opportunities, now tend to admire educated Negroes.

The concept or stereotype of Jews as a racial group is on the whole a development of only the past century. Anti-Semitism used to constitute essentially an ideology and pattern of behavior directed against an isolated urban group and its religion, not against a pseudo-race. Contemporary anti-Semitic stereotypes, such as the belief that Jews constitute an anatomically distinctive population and have a racial nose, head hair, or temperament, are precisely on the level of a belief that there is a Baptist chin, form of head hair, and racially determined temperament. Such stereotypes would also have evolved had Baptists been comparably segregated in ghettos, maltreated, or socially humiliated for centuries.

The American Negro People. Racism in the United States is primarily directed against the Negro people, whose low social status is associated with the fact they were brought to this country as slaves and more lately have constituted an unskilled labor and servant class. More than 80 per cent of the slaves brought to the Americas between 1530 and 1860 were bought or captured in coastal Nigeria or in the adjacent western African districts; that is, they were from the ethnic subdivision of the African Negroids least hybridized with other African populations. The slaves were therefore not typical of African Negroes in general, but only of the Gulf of Guinea coastal peoples west of the Cameroons.

Neither were they culturally typical. Over 80 per cent of them came from the economically most advanced, artistic, and socially complex areas of Negroid Africa. The economic, organizational, and aesthetic levels of these districts were in general comparable to the slave empires of Egypt, Mesopotamia, Greece, and Rome. The widespread notion that the Negro slaves were taken from "darkest Africa" and were devoid of culture before being brought to this country serves only to attempt to justify slavery or later forms of discrimination against Negroes as inferiors.

Small numbers of slaves were taken to America from the Congo, Angola, Mozambique channel districts, and other places where the cultures were quite different from Nigeria and the socio-economic patterns somewhat less complex.

The fact that Nigeria and other parts of Africa were the main sources of a cheap labor supply for the Americas is explained by African proximity by sea voyage to the West Indies or eastern coasts of America, and by the inability or reluctance on the part of the Europeans to incur the expense in men, military equipment, and ships that would have been necessitated had slaves been gotten in other areas such as India, Indonesia, Mexico, and Peru that at the time also were potential reservoirs of cheap labor.

Throughout the history of slavery in America there were countless slave uprisings. Only in the Guianas, however, were the slaves so numerous and well organized that they succeeded in establishing free and independent groups. Significantly, these free peoples are the only descendants of African slaves who have maintained African languages and cultures to any degree. All others were either creolized (see p. 293) or Europeanized. A prolonged era of enslavement is everywhere characterized by progressive loss of native language and culture and progressive development of new patterns of speech and living.

The first Negro slaves in the thirteen colonies were brought into Virginia in 1619 and the slave traffic continued in the colonies and later in the United States for another 250 years. Throughout this period slave women had little to say regarding the paternity of their offspring, and so rapid hybridization occurred and the genes of Englishmen, Scotchmen, and other northwestern Europeans were dispersed through the slave population. The gradual rise in status and the improvement in the living conditions of the Negro people during the last eighty years have been accompanied by a progressive decline in further accretions of Caucasoid genes.

Very few Negro people of the United States today can prove, by means of names and dates of arrival of slave ancestors, that they are of pure African ancestry. Estimates vary from 30 to only 2 or 3 per cent who are entirely of African ancestors. All others of the fifteen million Negro people of the United States are hybrids who vary from an almost nonvisible component of African ancestry to a non-visible component of northwestern European Caucasoid. In addition a few million have some Choctaw, Cherokee, or other American Indian genes. In general, the Negro people of the United States are anatomically no longer typical of any part of Africa.

An undeterminable number of offspring of Negro-white inter-marriages either fled from slavery before 1861 or have withdrawn from the Negro group since 1865. In this fashion they and their descendants have gained freedom of movement in the white community, equal opportunity in jobs, education, and housing, and surcease from social humiliations. The dispersion of their genes has therefore been such that some millions of "white" Americans have a minute component of recent African source in their genetic composition, are unaware of the fact, and can never by any device now known to science or to bureaus of investigation ascertain the fact. This process of "passing" by at most a few thousand largely "white" persons each year will certainly produce no perceptible darkening of the "white" population at the end of a period of centuries. The entry of Caucasoid genes into the Negro group is at present also proceeding so slowly as to warrant no likelihood of perceptible lightening of that group during a comparable era.

The rise in economic and social status of the American Negro people during the last eighty years has been accompanied by progressive lessening of exchange of genes between the two groups. If present social trends continue, the two groups may remain relatively unchanged in average color. However, the Negro group may become more homogeneous in color as its now darkest segment diminishes in size with disappearance of all persons of pure recent African ancestry.

Linguistic, cultural, and temperamental traits which are associated with Negro people of the United States are in most instances not of African origin, although they are widely supposed to be.

Linguistic features traceable to African origins are negligible. A few African words may survive among small numbers of rural Negroes but probably no features of grammatical structure and no sounds or sound units as such survive. Minor African tonal features of sentence melody may be present and may have affected the tonal patterns of the white population of the Deep South. The distinctive content in southern rural Negro speech seems, however, to be largely a product of an American slavery rather than that of Africa. It evolved when the slaves adopted English sounds, words, and forms, and from early creolization of such borrowings (see p. 293).

Cultural features traceable directly to African origins are difficult to discover. The technological heritages and manual processes of African cultures were entirely replaced by the tools and hand movements required of slavery in America. Social relationship patterns such as the family, community, clan, class station, and government disappeared and new patterns developed, determined by slave status. Religious ideologies and rituals also disappeared, although magical assumptions, objects, and procedures together with some magical practitioners maintained an uneven survival. The evangelicalism and passion of Christianity among Negroes have been patently forms of expression of slaves rather than vestigial carry-overs from Africa. The music of the plantation Negroes is basically derived from English hymns and folk songs, but the poetic lines of the songs together with some stylistic features are the creative expression of slaves or later plantation menials. The manner of employment of the voice in song is partially African, but the origin of the solo-chorus pattern is uncertain. African plastic and graphic art heritages vanished under the conditions of American slavery. No dance patterns or body movements have been traced to African dances. American Negro dancing like American Negro religious manifestations and music is essentially a creative achievement and symbolic expression of a people burdened by their low status. Small sections of African folklore have survived but these are now told in an extremely changed form. The search for African cultural survivals has therefore led to the discovery of a few vestigial features which are now completely rewoven into new patterns, some of which constitute notable creative achievements.

The posture, walking gait, speed of movement, temperament, sense of humor, and patterns of laughter of American Negroes are often supposed to be African in source. However, each of these features of behavior is also essentially or wholly a development of the American environment. Generations of deliberate slow-down tactics by the slaves in plantation labor, consciously resorted to in order to produce as little as possible without incurring reprisals from white overseers or owners, together with hopelessness, resulted in a characteristic posture, gait, and speed of motion as long as incentives were absent. However, such physical habits have repeatedly been transformed overnight upon acquisition by Negroes of independent farms or of other enterprises, upon their receipt of wages that make a high standard of living possible, or upon their entry into remunerative specialized or technical work. The caricature of the slow-moving, poverty-stricken southern Negro is not the representation of a transplanted African but of an American slave or menial Negro. Native Africans bear no resemblance in temperament, posture, or voice to this stereotype. Just as plantation work habits and social relationships effected a posture and gait, so too did they shape the patterns of temperament, mood, and humor of the slaves and of southern Negroes since the Civil War. African origins do not account for these distinctive features of many rural, or recently rural, Negro people.

African survivals are much more numerous among some Negro and part Negro peoples in Latin American countries. Entire languages and cultures survived among the now long-independent descendants of escaped slaves in the Guianas. Many features of language, religious ideology and ceremonial, magic, music, dance, and folklore can be found for example in the West Indies and Brazil. The explanation for the many survivals in these countries and for the nearly absolute shattering of African heritages in the United

States lies primarily in the greater intensity and degree of exploitation of Negroes in the cotton, tobacco, and sugar cane plantations of the United States, in the outnumbering of the Negroes by the whites, and in the manner of integration of Negro people in American economic life.

The Integration of the Negro People into American Life. Complete and democratic integration of American Negroes as unsegregated and unharassed citizens of this country today depends upon equality in employment opportunities—that is, the end of discrimination and exclusion on a basis of color and granting of jobs on a basis solely of ability to do the job; upon equality in educational opportunities and a cessation of humiliating Jim Crow customs of segregated schools and public facilities; upon cessation of restrictive rental and house-purchasing real estate covenants, and equal opportunity to secure proper housing; upon just and equitable land and tenancy laws in the southern states; upon the elimination of poll taxes and legal and administrative hindrances to the full participaion of Negroes in political life; and upon the elimination of racist and other social humiliations of many kinds through education and through proper legislative action and efficient administrative enrorcement of antidiscrimination laws on local, state, and federal levels. The issue is not whether intermarriage shall occur, which is a bogey often raised, but whether democracy is going to become a reality in this country for all its peoples.

Summary. In order to give scientific answers to the question as to whether or not there are significant differences in the hereditary endowment of the human populations, relevant evidence has been evaluated. Supplementary data will be appraised in later chapters. The evidence which is to be considered in this connection may be classified as (1) comparative skeletal anatomy; (2) comparative anatomy of external features such as hair texture, skin color, and nasal breadth; (3) comparative anatomy of the brain and central nervous system; (4) comparative anatomy of internal organs such as the heart, lungs, and glands; (5) comparative study of blood types; (6) comparative physiology; (7) comparative study of physical growth and development; (8) comparisons of intelligence test results; (9) comparative study of mental pathology; (10) comparative study of crime; (11) study of the time, nature, and significance of the process of domestication of our ancestors during the Pliocene and Pleistocene eras; (12) the determination of the degree of plasticity, inventiveness, or potential creativity in diverse populations; (13) study of the nature of social and cultural historical processes; (14) study of the influence of geographic factors upon achievement; (15) the concrete testimony from cultural and social anthropology as to the achievements of the populations; (16) comparative linguistics. No valid judgment can be made as to the relative significance of any single type of evidence.

SELECTED READINGS

Alpenfels, E. J. *Sense and Nonsense about Race*. New York: Friendship Press, 1946.

Ashley Montagu, M. F. *An Introduction to Physical Anthropology*. Springfield: C. C. Thomas, 1960 (3rd. ed.).

——. *Man's Most Dangerous Myth*. New York: Columbia Univ. Press, 1945 (rev. ed.).

Barzun, J. *Race: A Study in Modern Superstition*. New York: Harcourt, Brace, 1937.

Benedict, R. *Race: Science and Politics*. New York: Viking, 1945 (rev. ed.).

——, and G. Weltfish. *The Races of Mankind*. New York: Public Affairs Committee, 1943.

Boas, F. *Anthropology and Modern Life*. New York: Norton, 1932 (rev. ed.).

——. *The Mind of Primitive Man*. New York: Macmillan, 1938 (rev. ed.).

——. "Race," in *Encyclopedia of the Social Sciences*, XIII (1934), 25–34.

——. *Race and Democratic Society*. New York: Augustin, 1945.

——. *Race, Language, and Culture*. New York: Macmillan, 1942, Pp. 3–195.

Boyd, W. C. *Genetics and the Races of Man*. Boston: Heath, 1950.

Comas, J. *Manual of Physical Anthropology*. Springfield: C. C. Thomas, 1960.

Coon, C. S. *The Origin of Races*. New York: Knopf, 1962.

——, S. M. Garn, and J. B. Birdsell. *Races . . . A Study of the Problems of Race Formation in Man*. Springfield: C. C. Thomas, 1950.

Count, E. W., ed. *This Is Race*. New York: Schuman, 1950.

Davie, M. R. *Negroes in American Society*. New York: McGraw-Hill, 1949.

Dobzhansky, T. *Genetics and the Origin of Species*. New York: Columbia Univ. Press, 1941 (2nd ed.).

Drake, S., and H. R. Clayton. *Black Metropolis*. New York: Harcourt, Brace, 1945.

Dunn, L. C., and T. Dobzhansky. *Heredity, Race, and Society*. New York: Penguin Books, 946.

Eells, K., A. Davis, R. J. Havighurst, V. E. Herrick, and R. Tyler. *Intelligence and Cultural Differences*. Chicago: Univ. of Chicago Press, 1951.

Frazier, E. F. *The Negro in the United States*. New York: Macmillan, 1949.

Garn, S. M. *Human Races*. Springfield: C. C Thomas, 1961.

Herskovits, M. J. *The American Negro*. New York: Knopf, 1928.

——. *The Myth of the Negro Past*. New York: Harper, 1941.

Hulse, F. S. *The Human Species*. New York: Random House, 1963.

——. *Physical Anthropology*. New York: Random House, 1963.

Human Origins: An Introduction to Anthropology. Selected Readings. Series I. Chicago: Univ. of Chicago Bookstore, 1945. *Passim*.

Huxley, J. S. and A. C. Haddon. *We Europeans*. New York: Harper, 1936.

Johnson, C. S. *Patterns of Negro Segregation*. New York: Harper, 1942.

Klineberg, O., ed. *Characteristics of the American Negro*. New York: Harper, 1944.

——. *Race Differences*. New York: Harper, 1935.

Kluckhohn, C. *Mirror for Man*. New York: Whittlesey, 1949. Pp. 78–144.

Kroeber, A. L., and T. T. Waterman, ed. *Source Book in Anthropology*. New York: Harcourt, 1931 (rev. ed.). Pp. 17–32, 77–174.

Lasker, G. W. *The Evolution of Man*. New York: Holt, Rinehart and Winston, 1961.

Linton, R., ed. *The Science of Man in the World Crisis*. New York: Columbia Univ. Press, 1945. Pp. 19–77.

Locke, A., and B. J. Stern, ed. *When Peoples Meet*. New York: Barnes & Noble, Inc., 1946.

McWilliams, C. *Brothers under the Skin*. Boston: Little, Brown, 1943.

——. *Prejudice. Japanese-Americans: a Symbol of Racial Intolerance*. Boston: Little, Brown, 1944.

Myrdal, G. *An American Dilemma. The Negro Problem and Modern Democracy*. New York: Harper, 1944 (2 vols.).

Powdermaker, H. *Probing Our Prejudices*. New York: Harper, 1944.

Shapiro, H. L. *Migration and Environment*. New York: Oxford Univ. Press, 1939.

——. *Race Mixture*. Paris: UNESCO, 1953.

Stern, C. *Principles of Human Genetics*. San Francisco: Freeman, 1949.

The Race Concept: Results of an Inquiry. Paris: UNESCO, 1952.

CHAPTER FOUR

PREHISTORY

The Primitive Beginnings of Culture. When the *Dryopithecus*
populations of the Late Miocene period, devoid of artifacts, language,
and culture, had lived on earth 3,000,000 to 5,000,000 years, their central nervous systems had developed a degree of complexity and potentialities never previously attained by any animal. A much superior
brain, freed forearms, ground locomotion, and experience in adapting themselves to new ways of living in tropical areas led to new
kinds of customary responses to situations. In the epoch of the Middle
Pliocene to Late Pliocene periods, these populations had therefore
changed into what may be called prehuman populations who were
utilizing crude tools, weapons, utensils, or other artifacts to supplement the use of their toes, fingers, and teeth. Sharp-edged stones and
shells were used for some kinds of cutting, but the greater availability of usable sticks, poles, creepers, leaves, grasses, and other decayable substances and the difficulty in fashioning cutting tools of
stone warrant the assumption that the first level of culture was essentially one in which decayable artifacts were used. It was not a Stone
Age. In fact, at no time have the majority of artifacts been made of
stone. During most of the Pleistocene period the basic artifact was
of stone, but it was a cutting tool which was used to manufacture
many other artifacts. Correlated with the crude artifacts of the first
culture epoch of the Middle Pliocene to Late Pliocene periods were
the primitive beginnings of true languages and of human-like work
groups, family clusters or bands, and other forms of social organization.

The Methods of Archeology. The scientific methods used by
archeologists attempt to reveal concrete evidence of the course of
human history from the Pliocene era of decavable artifacts through

a million or more years up to the time when peoples recorded their history in writing. A major problem for research workers seeking evidence of the cultures of earlier Pleistocene times is to know where to dig. Paleontologists, who know the kinds of fauna and flora that were present in Pleistocene regions and epochs, suggest sites where artifacts may be found. Geologists with a knowledge of Pleistocene strata provide similar leads. These scientists co-operate with archeologists in the dating of the artifacts that are uncovered. Although as noted previously (p. 27) caves were not abodes until later periods, they were frequently visited by people during all Pleistocene epochs and the indestructible artifacts which these people lost or discarded in the caves are easiest for the archeologists to uncover by digging. Likewise, wherever the remains of habitations, or rubbish heaps and shell mounds, are visible they may be expected to reveal materials left by Pleistocene communities.

Generally archeologists do not dig up an entire cave or other site because scientific workers are aware that later developments in scientific methods, techniques, or equipment may produce superior results. Sometimes the choice is to dig trenches which will not remove more than 10 to 20 per cent of the site and the remainder is left for later excavations. Careful workers photograph what they are doing at every important stage of the excavation, make minute notations of depths, distances, and artifacts found, and handle uncovered artifacts of a decayable or fragile kind with the utmost care.

The archeologist always seeks to dig in a site where strata deposited during successive epochs will be exposed to view in the walls of the trench. When as many as three or four or five superimposed strata are found, each several feet thick, with distinctive artifacts in each lying at about where they were originally dropped, the archeologist has the basis for comparative and historical studies, and for relative if not approximate dating of everything that is found. It is important that the site must have remained undisturbed during all earlier eras, and not many sites are found in so desirable a condition.

Objects found on the top of the ground cannot be easily dated or arranged chronologically in relation to other objects found in the ground. But in the case of superimposed strata the stratum that is underneath and the artifacts that repose in it must be older, and relative dating therefore offers little difficulty. Absolute dating in terms of thousands of years is possible only for the most recent 15,000 years and then only in a few regions. Datings for earlier finds are always approximate and the older the epoch, the greater the probable error.

An interesting method of dating basketry materials, pottery, and other prehistoric artifacts which permits the chronological classification of deposits since the beginning of the Christian era, with margins of probable error of not more than a generation or two, has been developed by scientists working in Arizona and New Mexico. Trees cut and employed by Indians in ancient times for roof timbers have been examined for their annual growth rings. Since the quantity of rainfall varies from year to year, the concentric circles in the trunks of trees are spaced unevenly, with larger spaces between adjacent circles signifying rainier years. Through their study of these tree rings scientists know the relative amounts of annual rain in the Southwest for almost 2000 years. The outside ring tells the approximate year when the tree died or was felled. Artifacts found in a stratum or site that includes part of such a tree can be dated as roughly a generation or two younger than the tree. In this way many pots and other artifacts used by the Southwest Indians before the coming of the whites have been dated fairly accurately. Wherever an already known and dated type of prehistoric pot is found, it in turn dates other objects found in association with it.

Annual deposits of silt from streams vary in much the same way as do the growth rings of trees and leave irregular termini called varves. Series of such varves of silt have been dated accurately into a period many thousands of years before the Roman Empire. Where an artifact is found, the associated varve dates the artifact.

The use of tree rings for dating deposits is limited by the fact that old trees have resisted decay only in desert areas, and there serve only for the last few thousands of years. In areas where there is an even growth all the year round, the tree ring technique cannot be used. It works only where there are sharply defined rings due to a growing season alternating with a dormant season. In most regions and epochs the strata of archeological artifacts cannot be dated with exactness because no tree ring or varve calendar is available.

The Eolithic Age. As hundreds of thousands of years went by, prehuman and then progressively near-human populations who were employing decayable artifacts gained increasing familiarity with types of stones available, an increasing control of the eye and hand co-ordinations involved in hitting stone with stone, and an increasing knowledge of what could be done with given sizes, shapes, and edges of stones. Progressive changes were made in the direction of a more frequent and efficient utilization of stones, especially flints, that were deliberately chipped and shaped. Almost all chipped stones made into artifacts lack a crystalline structure, and because they have an amor· phous structure like glass, they fracture conchoidally. This very quality renders them especially suitable as a material which will produce sharp edges and points. In the final Pliocene and very Early Pleistocene epochs the use of cutting tools made of flint became ever more strategic. However, very crudely chipped flints that also could have been made by prehuman or near-human hands have been found in the Miocene, Pliocene, and the earliest of Pleistocene deposits of Europe. A majority if not all of these claimed artifacts, termed eoliths or "dawn stones," could have been chipped by falling trees, by the heavy tread of large animals, or in other accidental ways, rather than by human hands. Irrespective of the manner by which they were chipped, sharp-edged stones must have been increasingly often utilized in the Eolithic Age, and were increasingly often shaped in order to secure better cutting tools and to make superior artifacts of decayable materials. The most important conclusion regarding the Eolithic Age is that during its progress, cutting tools of stone were never basic or decisive artifacts, and the prehumans or near-humans were only familiarizing themselves with the simplest methods of fracturing stone.

The Paleolithic or Old Stone Age. The Eolithic Age character-ized by decayable artifacts was followed by an era during which a large number of stone artifacts were utilized whose manufacture by near-humans cannot be doubted. Fairly early in the Pleistocene deposits of the Old World several kinds of such flint artifacts are found. One is the clumsy hand axe or fist hatchet (French, *coup de poing;* German, *Faustkeil*), especially large numbers of which have been found in western and central Europe. The fist hatchet continued to be used, largely in western Europe and in adjacent areas and on into India, during hundreds of thousands of years of the Early Pleistocene to Middle Pleistocene epochs. Its uses are in doubt. In deposits in many other parts of the world few or no fist hatchets are found but there are crudely chipped flint flakes which served, along with shells, for scraping and cutting softer woods or other materials during most of the Pleistocene epoch. The techniques for fashioning flakes were constantly improved, and although archeologists once regarded the fist hatchet as an important tool, the evidence indicates that chipped flakes that had been broken from larger cores were the basic cutting tools throughout the Old Stone Age, and may have been supplemented by several inferior cutting tools such as shells.

The progressive development of Pleistocene flint work is thoroughly documented by hundreds of thousands of flints of varying ages. No inventions which effected notable improvement in technology and hence in conditions of living were ever abandoned until they were superseded by other and superior inventions, and each invention was in turn sooner or later improved upon. Only those inventions which were not immediately or notably useful were ever surrendered. Chipped flints or flakes were useful at once and since these basic cutting tools progressed steadily in efficiency through the Pleistocene epoch, increasingly efficient weapons, tools, and containers made from decayable materials were probably devised throughout that era. Progress in cutting tools therefore led to the improvement of many or most of the other artifacts.

The Paleolithic era of primitive but ever improving stone-chipping techniques continued from the early Pleistocene or first glacial (or pluvial) period until about 8000 to 12,000 years ago—that is, for a period of 500,000 to 900,000 years. The era may be subdivided for successive levels of stone-chipping techniques. However, in contrast with human biological development, in the case of which many or most Old World populations may have advanced almost as a unit, the chipped-stone forms took on individual characteristics in different areas, and the cultures also assumed many distinctive features from area to area. For this reason, archeologists interest themselves justifiably in differences between areas within each given developmental level of techniques.

Glacial and interglacial periods	Techno-logical levels		Core biface work	Flake work	Blade work	
					western	eastern
Würm	Paleolithic	Upper			Magdalenian Solutrean Gravettian Aurignacian Chatelperronian	Hamburgian Gravettian
		Middle	Mousterian	Tayacian		
3rd interglacial			Acheulean	Levalloisian		
Riss		Lower				
2nd interglacial				Clactonian		
Mindel						
1st interglacial			Abbevillian	? Clactonian		
Gunz						

FIG. 5. Paleolithic "industries."

European archeologists long denoted six levels of Paleolithic tech-nology for European areas. The earliest was designated Chellean, and the others Acheulean, Mousterian, Aurignacian, Solutrean, and Magdalenian in the order given. These names came from French excavations where the pioneering researches in Paleolithic strata were conducted. The Chellean and Acheulean were termed Lower

Paleolithic; the Mousterian, Middle Paleolithic; and the Aurignacian, Solutrean, and Magdalenian. Upper Paleolithic. Present
usage of these terms is quite different, and is briefly described in the
next paragraphs.

The Lower Paleolithic Technological Level. In western Europe
this includes two contrasted but largely contemporaneous types of
work or "industries" with flint, from the first interglacial until during the third interglacial. One is of basic tools of core-biface type, the
other of basic tools of large flakes. In France, crude biface chippings
of flint hand-axes of a type termed Abbevillian are first interglacial;
they are supplemented by chips and flakes perhaps for use as cutting
tools and scrapers. Sometimes finer because retouched core-biface
work, termed Acheulean, is found throughout the long eras of the
second to the end of the third interglacial. Basic tools of large flakes,
struck off from cores and retouched on one side, occur in the second
interglacial as Clactonian; from the middle of the second interglacial
on into the fourth glacial as Levalloisian; during the third interglacial as Tayacian. The Chinese Lower Paleolithic has bipolar flakes
with bevelled edge, generally termed "chopper" tools. There have
been claims that some later Acheulean tools were hafted on to a
wooden handle.

Sinanthropus deposits have suggested that second interglacial populations may have had control and use of fire. The use of fire, which
served for warmth, safety, health, and comfort, and which increased
the numbers, palatability, and digestibility of foods, perhaps diffused
far and wide. *Sinanthropus* bands may not have been among the
earliest to use fire. At present the first real evidence for European
use of fire is third interglacial.

Claims of perforated flints and shells as ornaments have been made
for Lower Paleolithic populations. Assertions have been published
that there were wooden handles and mallets or strikers for chipping
flints. The technical literature has contained suggestions that splinters and pointed pieces of bone were used, and that these may have
facilitated some early kinds of sewing and fiber work. In spite of
frequency of report, this has not been established as fact. If bone
was employed at all in Lower Paleolithic times, it was not widely
or often resorted to as far as is now known and a true "industry"

of bone implements appears to come first in Middle Paleolithic eras.

The evidence of cannibalism in the Lower Paleolithic deposits of the *Sinanthropus* caves does not provide any important additional information (see p. 20), since this trait reveals little or nothing regarding other features of culture. The sum total of knowledge regarding the Lower Paleolithic is very slight. The archeologists' discoveries of control of fire and of basic cutting tools and their progressive improvements are momentous, but the remaining items that have been discovered are minor features of Lower Paleolithic cultures. Much remains to be learned of the way of life of such hunting and food-gathering populations.

The Middle Paleolithic Technological Level. This era may be timed for the latter part of the third interglacial until sixty thousand or more years ago, during the last Ice Age. It witnessed significant improvements in the manufacture of cutting tools of stone. One tool technique, Mousterian, ranges from western Europe to western China. A contemporary technique, Middle-Upper Levalloisian, is found from western Europe to western India and most of Africa. These two flint "industries" meet, influence each other, overlap, or even commingle. Edges of flakes were sometimes skillfully retouched both by striking and by pressure with a pointed tool. The variety and sharpness of such cutting tools may have permitted many improvements in other artifacts. Careful burials have been interpreted as indications of ideologies premised upon beliefs in the supernatural and in a life after death, concepts which of course may have been developed much earlier.

The Upper Paleolithic Technological Level. The sequence of Upper Paleolithic blade "industries" in Europe is at present termed Chatelperronian, Aurignacian, Gravettian, Solutrean, and Magdalenian. The first three appear to be separate technological diffusions to western Europe from origin points to the east. Solutrean and Magdalenian workmanship may not appear in central and eastern Europe; there the eastern Gravettian parallels them and later develops into the Hamburgian of northern Germany. Chatelperronian and Aurignacian flint work have been estimated as fifty-five thousand to almost seventy thousand years old. Gravettian in France and Spain appears to be a little later and short lived. Solutrean may date from sixty-seven thousand to about fifty-five thousand years ago. Magdalenian may have endured from about fifty thousand to perhaps as late as ten thousand years ago. In central and eastern Europe the Gravettian may also have lasted until the period of about twenty thousand years ago, changed to Hamburgian, and then paralleled the later Magdalenian. Changes from Ice Age subarctic conditions occurred in the later Magdalenian and Hamburgian levels.

In Upper Paleolithic times, pressure flaking and hence the efficiency of the basic cutting tools advanced notably, presumably effecting important advances in other artifacts. Bone and perhaps ivory were used for handles, harpoon points, and other objects. Splinters of bone were perforated to make eyed needles, so that excellently sewed garments could now be made. The bow and arrow may have developed in the latter part of the era. Some drawings of western Europe, found in caves, may be as much as sixty to seventy thousand years old. Fine paintings of game animals, in polychrome and with shading to indicate depth perspective, are Magdalenian and perhaps twenty to twenty-five thousand years of age. Another Upper Paleolithic art is in small stone and ivory figurines from Central Europe; they portray female nudes in a highly stylized manner. Pieces of bone and ivory were tastefully carved or incised. There are also bas-reliefs on cave walls and animals modelled of clay. Additional Upper Paleolithic arts will doubtless be uncovered in various parts of the world when further excavations are made. In later Magdalenian times flint, bone, and ivory work continued to improve and to display more varied and more efficient forms. The bow and arrow may have spread to many areas and the spear-thrower, which probably preceded the bow, was also widespread. Fish hooks and harpoons with detachable points were widely used. Although the first direct evidences of domesticated dogs are later, the end of the Magdalenian may have witnessed the very first selective breeding of a wild jackal or related form. Some Upper Paleolithic cultures, that were contemporaneous with the later Magdalenian, could have advanced to a technological level and a complexity of social organization in most respects like that of the advanced food-gathering Indian communities of the Pacific Northwest Coast (see p. 133).

A remarkable impressionistic and silhouette-painting art on rocks, representing game animals and also persons, is found in western Mediterranean borderlands associated with some distinctive features of technology and culture. These findings are dated as contemporaneous with Magdalenian and later levels and are designated Capsian.

The Mesolithic, Epipaleolithic, or Transitional Level. In a period of several thousand years, called the Mesolithic, which followed immediately after the Magdalenian Upper Paleolithic, and dated roughly between 8000 and 13,000 years ago, pressure-flaked and other flints were manufactured that were exquisitely refined and diminutive in size. They are termed *microliths*. A wooden sled and a few other wooden artifacts have been found in Danish sites termed *kitchen middens*. Large numbers of painted pebbles and some bone wands, the use of which is not known, have been uncovered in European deposits. The stone technology of the Magdalenian level was surpassed in the Mesolithic level, and social conditions developed which made possible the extraordinary advances of the Neolithic era immediately following. Since the Mesolithic period had not yet developed agriculture and since this was the last epoch of a food-gathering type of economy, the term *Epipaleolithic* has appropriately been applied to it. Since the period marked the achievement of those conditions which made an advance to agriculture possible, the term *Transitional* is also fitting.

The Neolithic Period of the Old World: Agricultural Crops and Their Diffusion. Although the first agriculture may have been the planting of cuttings of wild banana trees in India, botanical and other considerations suggest a more likely origin or origins for agriculture somewhere between the Caucasus districts and India. There one or more of the wild cereal mountain grasses or grains such as wheat and perhaps barley were earliest to be seeded and bred up. The technique of developing domesticated and more productive grains from wild and less productive plants diffused widely, and many other plants were soon bred. Those of economic importance were millet, rice (probably an Indonesian domestication), cabbage, turnips, peas, parsnips, carrots, beets, lettuce, onions, soy beans, pears, plums, celery, cherries, grapes, peaches, olives, figs, dates, melons, cucumbers, coconuts, oranges, and breadfruit. Cotton and flax were domesticated for spinning and weaving.

The Neolithic Period of the New World. Some 4000 to 8000 years following the domestication of wild cereal grasses in western Asia, social conditions broadly similar to those which had led to the first domestication of plants in the Old World had developed in the Andean valleys or in the near-Andean uplands of west-central South America. A wild pod corn was bred to a domesticated maize, a wild root to a domesticated potato, and in Amazonia a tuber was bred to a domesticated manioc or cassava. Beans became an economically important domesticated plant in Central America. The date for the domestication of plants in America may be anywhere from 4000 B.C. to 2000 B.C. Scores of additional American plants were domesticated in the millennia following. They include the sweet potato, pepper, squashes, tomato, pineapple, cacao, tobacco, and cotton.

About as many plants were domesticated in the Americas as in the entire Old World. The inventories are so different as to give proof of the lack of contacts between the Old and New World by ocean routes until the time of Columbus and of the independent development of agriculture in the two hemispheres.

The Origin of Primitive Agriculture. The consequences of agriculture have been so momentous in human affairs that discussions regarding the time, place, and manner of origin of agriculture, as well as the reasons why it did not appear in some other way and at another time and place, have been extensive. An answer can be given to this query as to why agriculture appeared where and when it did, if a basic feature of all true inventions or important changes in procedures with materials is comprehended. Such inventions or changes follow upon long and intensive working with certain materials and techniques, and upon mastery of them. All Paleolithic peoples collected many kinds of self-seeded plants. But they did not work intensively with those plants for, since they simply collected, they had no need to master a technique of controlling the seeding and growth of plants. They worked intensively only with the usable plant products. If an insufficient number of plants grew, the Paleolithic bands resorted to magic alone. They concentrated their energies and ingenuity on the mastery or further elaboration of intricate and intriguing techniques of magic rather than on the simpler tasks of seeding, watering, and weeding. Something other than the possession of creative imaginaticn was needed to develop an interest in or intense preoccupation with seeding and plant tending. The procedures of plant tending, watering, weeding, and selection of seeds are so much less challenging and indicative of imagination, creativity, or inventiveness than are the procedures involved in a thousand other inventions, that a claim that the advance to agriculture correlates with genius is poorly founded. The New World and Old World changes to procedures of plant tending and selection must be ascribed to nothing more than changes in the daily habits of productive work of food gatherers. These changes may well have been of the kind exemplified by the unusually careful plant-tending habits of the tidewater food-gathering communities of the Pacific Northwest Coast (see p. 133). Such habits were apparently developed when specific bands claimed ownership of holdings of wild-plant sites, within a food-gathering social system which had developed social strata differentiated by wealth, only possible with the advanced cutting tools and other technological features of a Magdalenian or Mesolithic level.

Unprecedented social conditions, not genius or imagination, thus brought about the first careful selection of seeds, the first extensive seeding, and the first watering, weeding, or fertilization of soil. A series of advances in cutting tools, in pressure flaking, and consequently in techniques of other kinds during the Upper Paleolithic period was ultimately responsible for these beginnings of agriculture. Such technological advances increased the size of the population, produced food surpluses, led to property in slaves and in hunting and fishing districts and plant sites, and developed specialization of labor. For the first time in history, wild cereal grass areas or fruit trees were zealously and intensively tended. In a sense, therefore, agriculture was less an invention than it was a change of procedures of work in relation to food plant sites because of changed social conditions. Because research in Magdalenian and Mesolithic archeology is still in a pioneer stage, it is still impossible to determine why a few districts in the Old World and in the New World rather than other districts were the first to attain the advanced technological levels and social forms essential to the development of agriculture.

But the consequences of agricultural production were greater than any other advances of the Neolithic period and made possible other advances. The Neolithic period starts, then, with the first true agriculture, with a revolution in work procedures in the realm of plant foods.

The Consequences of Primitive Agriculture. Wherever the newly domesticated food plants diffused, whether in the Old World or New World, the size of the population vastly increased. Land suitable for primitive agriculture went progressively into the hands of a few wealthy owners, especially in the areas that were most productive and populous. Large numbers of persons were released from food production for specialized work of many kinds, for the manufacture of pottery, for weaving, basketry, hide and leather work, carpentry, boat making, fishing, trade and government, and religious activities. This specialization of labor resulted in many inventions. Year-round habitations came to be more solidly constructed. The houses of the wealthy, as well as the buildings of the government and those used for religious exercises, were built painstakingly. The specialists who performed or supervised the work made advances in the techniques of architecture. In both hemispheres bricks were made and later improved. Stone house construction also developed. The wealthy acquired ever larger armed forces and governmental bureaucracies. They engaged in large-scale predatory warfare, and captured peoples were forced to labor in the fields or on construction projects. Specialized villages or castes developed, and they sent their products as commodities into larger market villages or market places for sale. Money developed and facilitated commerce. Specialists in stone worked with harder stones, and superior cutting tools were made by grinding and polishing. These tools in their turn made possible finer and more varied manufacture of all sorts of products. The tremendous growth in population soon made hunting inadequate and new kinds of specialists developed pastoralism.

The Second Neolithic Revolution: Pastoralism. At one time it was thought that pastoralism preceded primitive agriculture, but now many scientists incline to the belief that pastoralism followed the earliest agriculture. In fact, it is likely that a major consequence of the agricultural revolution in the Old World was the assignment of specialists to the confining or guarding, tending, and selective breeding of those wild animals which were economically most important. As a result the following animals were domesticated: cattle, sheep, goats, and swine from 8000 to 6000 B.C. or shortly thereafter; the horse, possibly as early as 3000 B.C.; the camel, donkey, and cat, about 3000 B.C.; water buffalo and poultry sometime before 1000 B.C. in southern or southeastern Asia; and the reindeer, about 500 A.D. in northern Asia.

In the New World the priority of agriculture in relation to pastoralism is clear. Here pastoralism is demonstrably a consequence of the social systems effected by New World agriculture. Specialists were assigned to care for wild creatures which were domesticated not very long before the Spanish Conquest. The most important of these were the llama and alpaca in the Peruvian highlands. Also domesticated were the guinea pig, in the Andean highlands; and the honey bee, in Central America. Two of three types of wild turkey were partially domesticated.

Not all animals were domesticated for purely utilitarian considerations. Nevertheless those animals which are now economically important were in all probability originally domesticated because of their use for foods, wool, or hides or as dray animals. Cats and a few other animals may have been initially domesticated by people of leisure who amused themselves with certain tamed animals, or by priesthoods who worked intensively with economically useless creatures that were thought to possess supernatural power.

The consequences of pastoralism were in general comparable to those attributed to agriculture. Agricultural advances were further intensified in areas that remained primarily agricultural, by the utilization of the new productive resource of pastoralism. But in districts such as northern Asia and East Africa, domesticated herds became more productive than the primitive agricultural techniques and the strategic economic resource came to be the domesticated animals—cattle, sheep, and later in parts of Asia, horses. When Spanish horses were taken over by some American Indian primitive agricultural peoples in the Mississippi valley, the horse became the most strategic resource and sometimes, although rarely, agriculture was even given up. Comparable economic transformations appear to have occurred in several other parts of the Old World during the Neolithic period.

Neolithic Cutting Tools. The earliest Neolithic communities continued to chip and flake by pressure in order to make cutting tools. But during the Neolithic period in the Old World the already long-known techniques for grinding and polishing wood, bone, and stone came to be applied extensively to the cutting tools, some of which began to be manufactured from harder kinds of stones which could not be chipped or flaked. Thus the later Neolithic peoples developed cutting tools and other artifacts which were unprecedentedly hard and durable. So efficient were the ground and polished stone tools, most of them of compacted granular rather than amorphous substances, that they diffused rapidly to all parts of the world except to Tasmania. The consequences of such superior artifacts were significant in those regions which had specialized carpenters and other technicians who were able to utilize the more efficient tools in order to fashion better houses, boats, weapons, and other products. Such highly important inventions as the plough and the wheel, which appeared towards the end of the Neolithic period, were facilitated by the availability of cutting tools made of ground stone.

Pottery. Pottery was undoubtedly invented and developed independently at least twice, once in the Old World and once in the New World, and perhaps several times in each hemisphere. In the New World pottery was fashioned without the aid of the potter's wheel, which was utilized for the production of pottery in Neolithic and wealthier districts of the Old World. The people of the Aurignacian period had modelled in clay, and modern food-gathering peoples such as the Aleuts, the Eskimos, and the Andamanese also made pots. But not until the development of Neolithic agriculture did social conditions permit a high level of pottery craftsmanship. The first use of a "slip" or wash before firing, to produce a red ware, and the use of a brush and paints to make geometric or other symbolic designs on the surface, occurred during the early Neolithic period of the Near East. Not till later Neolithic times in the

Near East, and in Europe after 1000 B.C. and during the Iron Age, did people build kilns or ovens, which permitted a higher temperature when firing and more efficient painting on pottery surfaces. Glazes were made possible by these more efficient firing techniques, which were developed in the Old World and in the New World from Peru to New Mexico. A glazed or vitreous surface seals a pot, prevents seepage or evaporation, and provides a superior storing vessel.

The shapes of the earliest pots imitated baskets, gourds, and other containers of preagricultural times. Later the potentialities of pottery materials and techniques were exploited and objects which were made no longer resembled the earlier containers. As specialists increased their technical skills, the shapes and painting of pottery became ever more varied until in the Bronze and Iron Age realistic representations were achieved.

An analogous sequence of technological developments and of ever more skillfully made and varied forms of pottery occurred in the agricultural districts of the New World. Here as in the Old World, pots which were fragile, but rapidly produced, progressively replaced baskets and other containers which were sturdier but took longer to produce. Pottery in a sense tended to follow agriculture as the latter diffused into regions that had had food-gathering economies.

Since pots can be made very much more rapidly than baskets or wooden containers, many persons who had labored steadily at the fabrication of perishable containers in preagricultural times were now released to do other work, and a few persons could produce surplus pots to be sold as commodities in market centers. Pottery therefore not only increased material comforts and opened up opportunities for aesthetic achievement, but its surplus production also stimulated trade.

Textiles. Like some modern nonagriculturalists, Upper Paleolithic peoples may have twisted or spun wild mountain sheep, goat, dog, or other animal fibers into coarse threads, and may have woven them to make belts, head bands, or even rough blankets. Very likely some primitive spindles and the simplest of looms were made in pre-Neolithic areas. But the release of the energies of many persons in a Neolithic economy, the advance in cutting tools and technology in general, and Old World Neolithic domestications of flax, cotton, and hemp, were some of the changes which account for the further development of spindles and looms in Neolithic times and for the quantitative and qualitative advances in woven stuffs which are characteristic of Neolithic areas. Cotton was independently domesticated in the New World, and there too the agricultural peoples developed along the general path trod somewhat earlier by Old World spinners and weavers. Surplus woven stuffs became commodities. They were sold in the markets, and they stimulated other production and trade by specialists. In central Asia pastoralism was followed by the invention of felting of wools, and such material became an important commodity over tremendous areas of Asia.

Copper Work. Paleolithic peoples used only those metals that were available without mining or chemical change—that is, rare pieces of meteoric iron, gold, silver, and copper. These were either too meagre in quantity or too soft to be used for cutting tools that could be of any consequence in production over a period of time. Only a few ornaments and sharp or pointed instruments shaped with stone hammers were possible. For a few centuries before the Spanish Conquest the agricultural Aztecs hammered copper for some of their ornaments, needles, and axes. They had also borrowed from Central America methods of gilding copper and mixing gold with copper and they cast copper as well as gold ornaments by means of the "lost wax" (*cire perdue*) method. In the case of the latter invention, which was achieved independently in the Old World and the New World, the craftsman sculptures a wax model of the metal object desired, makes a coating or mold of clay, pours molten metal into a hole in the mold, breaks away the clay, and finally smooths and polishes the metal object.

The earliest heating and reduction of copper ores, or the smelting and fusing of copper, occurred in or near Egypt about 4000 B.C. That area was then probably the most wealthy of all later Neolithic areas, because of the agricultural productivity of the alluvial Nile, the supplementary production from herds, the use of slave war-captives, and the degree of specialization of labor. Ornament inlays and jewelry were made by specialists who used malachite, which is a soft copper carbonate, and turquoise, the ores of which yield copper when heated in contact with charcoal. Malachite powder was also used by wealthy Egyptians after 4000 B.C., as a green cosmetic paste. Clay molds for casting copper objects antedated 3000 B.C., and in general it is clear that the wealth and specialists of the region established the pre-requisites for the development of new specialties such as the mining of cuprous earths, their reduction with charcoal, and the control of the techniques of production of copper ornaments and other arti-facts. Thus the so-called Copper Age of the Near East dates from 4000 B.C. to sometime before 3000 B.C.

Bronze Metallurgy. The Near Eastern specialists in copper metal-lurgy soon learned how to reduce another kind of ore, cassiterite, which gave tin. This metal, mixed in a proportion of one of tin to nine or ten of copper, gave bronze. Bronze metallurgy was under the control of specialists just before 3000 B.C. in Egypt, and shortly thereafter in Mesopotamia and northwestern India. The specialists' knowledge of ores, methods of reduction, alloys, and castings con-tinually advanced in these districts. From 3000 B.C. to about 1000 B.C. the Near East was in what may be termed a Bronze Age. Cutting tools of bronze and other bronze artifacts were much harder, sharper, and more durable than most of those made of stone, and they progressively replaced stone. Above all, the cutting tools of bronze permitted a variety of advances in carpentry, boat build-ing, and construction of wheels, chariots, carts, weapons, and a thousand other objects of economic importance. Wherever bronze artifacts were used in considerable numbers important economic, social, and cultural changes occurred.

The control of the metallurgy of bronze was only in its initial stages in Inca Peru at the time of Columbus, and so neither Peru nor other American areas advanced to a Bronze Age in the sense of enjoying the socio-economic and cultural consequences of the re-placement of cutting tools of stone by those of bronze.

Ferrous Metallurgy. The reduction of ferrous earths followed soon after bronze metallurgy. There is evidence that it was achieved about 2800 B.C. in northern Syria and perhaps elsewhere in Mesopo-tamia. Bronze everywhere remained dominant for tools, however, until after 1400 B.C. in the Near East and until 1200 B.C. in Egypt, because the wrought iron that the metallurgists knew how to make before that time was definitely inferior to tools made of bronze. Only a rare piece of iron or steel was made by smelting during sixteen hundred years and until about 1400 B.C. when extensive production of iron and steel started in the Near East, and after 1200 B.C. in Egypt. The New World never advanced beyond Peru's level of bronze metallurgy; it is merely a matter of curious interest that a few Aztec chiefs had knives hammered from meteoric iron. But in the Near East efficient artifacts of iron and steel, metal for which had been reduced from ferrous earths, gradually displaced bronze artifacts, and ferrous metallurgy eventually caught up with bronze work in most other parts of the Old World. By 800 B.C. bronze was giving way to the more efficient metal in Greece.

In a few regions, notably in Africa south of the Sahara, the peoples borrowed from one community to another the simpler techniques of reducing ferrous ores and of making iron and steel tools, and for this reason almost all of the Negroid peoples had iron tools. They also had a well-established lower caste of metallurgical specialists by the time of the white economic envelopment of Africa. These peoples south of the Sahara never reduced tin or copper ores or made bronze. As Neolithic agriculturalists and pastoralists they simply changed from their earlier technology based on cutting tools of stone to a much superior and borrowed technology for the manufacture of iron and steel tools.

The claim that Negroids invented ferrous metallurgy is now seen to be unfounded. Only specialists in the mining of various ores, in the actual process of reduction, and in the construction of pottery-making kilns or other enclosed chambers where high temperatures were attained could have brought about the development of ferrous metallurgy. Archeological and historical evidence as well as these theoretic considerations agree in pointing to Egypt or near-by countries shortly after 3000 B.C. as the place and time of this strategic technological advance. It seems to have occurred only once in history, and it then diffused to all other districts that have had it.

Bronze metallurgy had spread by way of the Danube and other routes into central and northern Europe before 1000 B.C. and had played a decisive role for a number of centuries in transforming the socio-economic systems of those Neolithic areas. After 1000 B.C. ferrous metallurgy in its turn proceeded west and north in Europe, and advanced the economic levels of the peoples further. Some of the wealth and predatory habits of the Celtic and Germanic peoples during the centuries of the Roman Empire are to be laid to their recent acquisition of ferrous artifacts.

The Interpretation of Archeological Findings. Because of the vast quantities of Paleolithic and Neolithic Old World artifacts, it is usually assumed that such concrete evidence illustrates particular features of these ancient cultures. However, only in the case of some Upper Paleolithic artifacts and many of the Neolithic artifacts can the uses and functions of these artifacts among the people who made them be indicated with anything approaching exactness. For example, a Magdalenian harpoon point of bone twelve thousand years old is identified perfectly and ethnographers know the possible uses of such points. An eighty-thousand-year-old leaf-shaped Mousterian flake of flint is not familiar to ethnographers from their study of modern peoples and the functions of the flake among the Mousterians who made it are therefore subject to varied interpretations. It looks like a cutting tool or scraper or both, and it may have been utilized in some such ways, but one cannot be as certain as in the case of the Magdalenian harpoon point. The interpretation of the uses and functions of the Lower Paleolithic fist hatchet of 600,000 years ago is even more uncertain. Knowledge of the particular features of a culture becomes increasingly meagre the farther back into the past one ventures, not only because the surviving items of culture of remoter eras are fewer, but because the interpretation of those samples gives at best only general rather than specific information.

For the Lower Paleolithic period one can assert that there were cutting tools of chipped stone flakes, but the nature of the artifacts of decayable materials that were made by those stone tools cannot be ascertained. Knowledge of the Lower Paleolithic epoch therefore includes generalized information regarding the probable efficiency of cutting tools, but not a particularized inventory of specific uses and functions of the hatchets and flakes. Knowledge of the Lower Paleolithic period also includes generalized knowledge of the presence of hunting and food-gathering techniques, but not of the specific techniques utilized. It is clear, however, that they were in general less efficient, because of the primitive level of the cutting tools, than were the techniques of production of Upper Paleolithic peoples, whose cutting tools were much sharper. It is clear also that populations were sparser in the Lower Paleolithic period than in later eras of superior productivity and that in social organization there could have been only very small bands composed of family groups. The fist hatchets and flakes of the Lower Paleolithic period therefore serve primarily not as samples of ancient cultural traits of a specific kind, but as leads to general formulations such as low productive level, sparse numbers, and tiny bands composed of family groups.

In the archeology of the Old World of Paleolithic times broad generalizations on the relative socio-economic levels, the forms of community and band, and the size of the population are made on a basis of the characteristics of the stone tools which have been found. To arrive at such formulations archeology must employ the method of analogy. It must resort to an analysis of the general features of the social pattern of surviving food-gathering peoples, and must cautiously read some of these general features into Paleolithic epochs. The earlier the Paleolithic epoch the more dependence there is upon analogy. For later periods, however, available information becomes more detailed and general formulations more probable because the uses and functions of the artifacts of that time are indicated by the virtually identical artifacts found among some technically backward peoples of modern times. Generalizations are even more reliable regarding the social patterns, the religion, and other aspects of the cultures of Neolithic ages because so much is known about modern peoples on the level of primitive agriculture. Moreover, the uses and functions of Neolithic artifacts are also exemplified by such artifacts as are in use today among some peoples on a low level of economic development.

The Revolution in Perspectives of History. A century ago the only available secular perspective of the human past involved meagre glimpses of Near Eastern and Asiatic empires, and detailed histories of classical Greece and Rome. Nothing was known of human origins and of the nature of culture even shortly before the Egyptian, Mesopotamian, and Persian empires. No one dared to think in terms of cultures hundreds of thousands of years old all over the Old World.

Now ever larger numbers of people are learning that near-human beings employed crude cutting tools of stone, roasted meats, and warmed their habitations with hearth fires well over 400,000 years ago, and that during the years that followed the cutting tools were progressively improved. Students of art now know that superb paintings and carvings were created in Europe 20,000 years in the past. Eight thousand or more years ago agriculture began to spread and revolutionized thousands of food-gathering communities; the new mode of production formed the basis of new patterns of living. Pastoralism had comparable spread and influence. Wars on a large scale began only in the Neolithic epoch. New forms of specialization of labor dovetailed with technological advances and material progress occurred ever more rapidly.

Whereas most of the Old World has been inhabited by preagricultural peoples for 1,000,000 years, people have lived in America only about 20,000 years. All America was still uninhabited during much of the Wisconsin glaciation, and the largely or wholly postglacial peopling of the American continents with Paleasiatic food-gathering bands continued until agricultural techniques spread among them from west-central South America and prepared the conditions within which the wealthier and more spectacular American civilizations developed.

In spite of the tremendous perspectives which prehistory has lately opened up, they are only bare beginnings. African and Asian prehistory is still sketchy and much more remains to be discovered about Europe's prehistory. Science is only in the initial stages of orienting humans historically.

SELECTED READINGS

Braidwood, R. J. *Prehistoric Men*. Chicago: Chicago Natural History Museum, Popular Series, Anthropology, No. 37, 1948.

Clark, G. *Archeology and Society*. New York: Barnes & Noble, 1960 (3rd ed.).

Clark, G. *World Prehistory: An Outline*. New York: Cambridge Univ. Press, 1961.

Clark, G. and S. Piggott. *Prehistoric Societies*. New York: Knopf, 1965.

Coon, C. S. *The Story of Man: From the First Human to Primitive Culture and Beyond.* New York: Knopf, 1962.

Curwen, E. C. *Plough and Pasture.* London: Cobbett, 1947.

Daniel, G. E. *A Hundred Years of Archeology.* London: Duckworth, 1950.

Forde, C. D. *Habitat, Economy, and Society; a Geographical Introduction to Ethnology.* New York: Harcourt, Brace, 1934.

Haring, D. G.. and M. E. Johnson. *Order and Possibility in Social Life.* New York: R. R. Smith, 1940. Pp. 461–507.

Hawkes, C. F. C. *The Prehistoric Foundations of Europe.* London: Methuen, 1940.

Human Origins: An Introduction to Anthropology. Selected Readings. Series I. Chicago: Univ. of Chicago Bookstore, 1945. *Passim.*

Kluckhohn, C. *Mirror for Man.* New York: Whittlesey, 1949. Pp. 45–77.

Kroeber, A. L., and T. T. Waterman, ed. *Source Book in Anthropology.* New York: Harcourt, Brace, 1931 (rev. ed.). Pp. 175–201, 227–244, 472–489, 512–524, 535–545.

Libby, W. F. *Radiocarbon Dating.* Chicago: Univ. of Chicago Press, 1952.

Martin, P. S., G. I. Quimby, and D. Collier. *Indians before Columbus: Twenty Thousand Years of North American History as Revealed by Archeology.* Chicago: Univ. of Chicago Press, 1947.

McGregor, J. C. *Southwestern Archeology.* New York: Wiley, 1941. Pt. I.

Rickard, T. A. *Man and Metals.* New York: McGraw-Hill, 1932 (2 vols.). *Passim.*

Willey, G. R. and P. Phillips. *Method and Theory in American Archeology.* Chicago, Univ. of Chicago Press (Phoenix), 1962.

Wright, W. B. *Tools and the Man.* London: Bell, 1939.

CHAPTER FIVE

RESEARCH AND THEORY IN CULTURAL ANTHROPOLOGY

Research Method in Cultural Anthropology. The science of cultural anthropology is still in its formative period. The descriptions and analyses available of the economies, families, clans, classes, governments, and other institutions of peoples living in primitive economies are still uneven and inadequate even in the reports of trained anthropologists. Moreover, theories as to the dynamic processes of development and change of these features of social life are still for the most part undeveloped.

There are many reasons for this immaturity of cultural anthropology. Among them are (1) the fact that it has but recently emerged as a science; (2) the heritage of European ethnocentrism, racist conceits, and notions of cultural superiority, which have resulted in distortions of descriptions and interpretations; (3) the lack of adequate funds to support sufficient numbers of observers, to maintain them during long sessions of field research, and to provide them with permanent professional careers; (4) the barrier of language, which makes field observations difficult; (5) the heritage among most non-Europeans of misunderstanding, distrust, or hate toward European observers, which prevents such rapport as would permit rapid, intimate, and thorough observation by the research worker; (6) the almost complete absence of anthropologically trained personnel recruited from the natives themselves, except in a few Latin American countries and in the Soviet Union; (7) the extent of recent change or destruction that has occurred in most native cultures.

The development of theory regarding processes of origin and change in cultural phenomena has been hampered by these and a variety of other factors, among them some naive and mechanical forms of evolutionary theory; some equally mechanical forms of diffusionist theory; the dogma that there could be no laws of cultural development with the result that none were sought; and the preoccupation of many recent cultural anthropologists with psychological processes which has diverted attention from other problems of accounting for cultural patterns.

The fieldworker's first task is to obtain accurate descriptions of cultural phenomena. Whereas the subjects of the physical and biological sciences are wholly unaffected by the age, sex, race, temperament, or prejudices of the investigators, the subjects of cultural anthropology are human beings who are influenced by these factors. Moreover, these subjects also are of a specific age, sex, race, and temperament and have sets of prejudices as well as sharply defined views on what the Europeans have done to them and to their cultures. The human subjects of cultural anthropology possess beliefs, values, choices, and procedures that make the research of the most well-meaning and most skillful of cultural anthropologists difficult.

Apart from other differences in the type of materials observed, the number of units studied by cultural anthropology differs so markedly from that of those studied by the physical and biological sciences that the research problems, procedures, and theoretical generalizations are of necessity entirely different.

Physicists observe the mass average behavior of billions of ions. They are wholly satisfied with theoretic formulations that are basically statistical and that disregard special or aberrant forms of behavior that conceivably are present in small clusters of those ions. But the cultural anthropologist tries to observe, for example, the special features of a clan system in which clusters of only a few hundreds, not billions, of units participate. The formulations of the cultural anthropologist regarding the processes that bring about or change cultural patterns cannot, therefore, be statistically exact like a physicist's formulations regarding the behavior of vast numbers of ions. Similarly, the bacteriologist reports on the mass average chemical behavior of a bacterial strain sampled by hundreds of thousands of members, none of which are inheritors of a complex central nervous system or of the variable technological, economic, social, religious, or artistic features of culture. But the cultural anthropologist is asked to report on a complex cultural-historical product such as a kinship system peculiar to only several hundred persons.

Physical and biological sciences are thus interested in and are characterized by generalizations regarding the average structure and average manner of change of enormous numbers of individual entities. The focus of cultural anthropology is entirely different. Its task is to formulate the social patternings, origins, histories, and manner of change of the variable behavior of humans; it is also to consider the significance of every special patterning that is localized in time and place. That is why cultural anthropology cannot give mathematical formulations—that is, mass averages—as solutions except for a few problems that arise in the most economically advanced areas where populations are large. The laboratories in which the physical and biological sciences observe great masses of units are in marked contrast with the special or circumscribed periods of time, geographical locations, and historically determined situations within which cultural anthropology must conduct its laboratory observations on the most recalcitrant, tendentious, and subtly variable of all animal species.

The pooled experience of cultural anthropologists has shown that the most effective initial approaches to peoples who are the subjects of observation are through a study of their technology or material culture and related features of economic life and through their language. All persons take pride in their skilled handiwork. No matter what their previous experience with Europeans may have been, they rarely refuse to explain how artifacts are made or how their people carry on their economic activities. Similarly, very few peoples will refuse to help in the pronunciation and translation of their language.

The cautious cultural anthropologist therefore usually initiates his field studies with a period of many weeks of notations of material culture or language or both. He tactfully avoids prying into intimate features of social life, religion, or other aspects of culture unless such information is voluntarily offered by the people. If this procedure is observed, the researcher is more likely to develop a relationship with the people he is studying which is not weighted with fears or suspicions. Intimate details of the culture of a people will be discussed most often and most quickly with outsiders with whom people have been long acquainted and with whom a relationship has been maintained on a level of mutual respect and forbearance. As a rule the more haste there is in field observations in cultural anthropology, the less is achieved.

Although observations of technology, material objects, and economics in general can be recorded in the observer's language, concepts of the natives regarding their social patterns, emotions, magicoreligious entities, and ideologies are often barely translatable. In consequence the observer usually obtains much more accurate data if he employs the words of the natives and their context in native speech. Some cultural anthropologists have written texts, that is, phonetic transcriptions with interlinear translations, which describe features of social, religious, or psychological phenomena that are otherwise difficult to render in their own European vocabularies. In recent decades the value of full-length autobiographic texts dictated by natives has been recognized.

Culture Traits or Elements. Just as chemistry has been long in process of working out and utilizing concepts such as neutrons, ions, atoms, molecules, and compounds, so too cultural anthropology on its level has developed and is using an inventory of concepts in discussing cultural phenomena. It is indisputably convenient for scientific purposes to employ such concepts and terms as *geographical population, band, village,* and *community,* but there are additional and more formal concepts that are also serviceable.

The ultimate conceptual units, efficient for the various purposes of cultural anthropology, in addition to individual persons are those minimal material, ideological, artistic, linguistic, and social organizational features of a human way of life which have been created and transmitted by persons since their Pliocene development into humanlike beings. These ultimate units of social or cultural heritage have been termed culture elements or culture traits. To give but few examples: they may be a type of chipped flints, a technique such as pressure flaking, coiling in basketry, the bull-roarer, a language sound or grammatical feature, a folkloristic theme, a rhythm in music, woodpecker scalps used as decorations on headbands, a guardian spirit, a kinship term for nephews, a clan custom, or permissible polygamy. Culture elements or traits may thus be defined as those invented and transmitted units of culture which for particular purposes of description and theoretical treatment need not be subjected to further subdivision.

Any aggregate of persons who live in a community, no matter how small it may be, possesses a heritage of culture elements which always numbers in the tens of thousands. The elements of the linguistic facet of this heritage alone may number many thousands. There are at least some hundreds of culture elements of technology or material culture. There are also at least hundreds of minimal features or elements of the musical portion of the heritage and of social organizational traits. All cultures and communities are over a million years removed from the Pliocene era of prehumans who had no culture elements whatever, but the smallest modern inventory of elements, presumably that of the now extinct Tasmanians, would have displayed an impressively large total.

The convenience of conceptual discreteness, for purposes of analysis, of each of the thousands of culture elements of a community does not mean that each element functions anarchically. Just as there is no such thing as a completely free ion, proton, or neutron unrelated to all other particles, so too culture elements are never unrelated one to another. Neither on the level of physical phenomena nor on that of the phenomena of cultural life do the ultimate units circulate capriciously in a vacuum as isolated units. The interrelationships or interconnections of culture elements must be assumed as axiomatic if scientific method is to be utilized. The identification of such elements in time and place, as well as the analysis of their manner of operation or functioning, constitutes much of cultural anthropology. It must be presumed, as in physics, that these conceptual units stand for real entities that also have their patterns of interrelationship. Culture elements interconnect in innumerable patterns within the community and also with elements and patterns of elements found in contiguous or even distant communities.

Cultural anthropology is therefore a study not only of the cultural content, structure, and functioning of communities, but also of the interconnections between communities. It is therefore historical and geographical as well as sociological and psychological.

Some theoreticians in anthropology have seen fit to deny the value of the study of historical and geographical interconnections. Others have been uninterested in psychological functions and interrelationships. Still others have believed that psychological aspects of cultural phenomena are the most deserving of study. Each of these partial views or preferences may do injustice to the science of anthropology if it is urged to the exclusion of all other possible approaches.

The terms cultural anthropology, or social anthropology, or simply the study of culture, stand for a science whose task it is to study the presence of, origins of, changes in, and interconnections between all culture elements. However, this is an excessively abstract, mechanistic, overschematic definition, and actually it is of little help as a guide towards what to study or what is most important for study. The associations of culture elements, not the discrete elements, pose the main problems for scientific treatment.

The functioning patterns and interconnections of culture elements are many and complex. Cultural anthropologists have therefore resorted to the employment of additional concepts to designate some of the patterned interconnections or meshings of culture elements.

Culture Complexes. One of these additional concepts is termed culture complex. In a mechanical or schematic sense it is an identifiable pattern of culture elements. More accurately it is only a larger segment of the cultural phenomena peculiar to a community or larger area of communities. For example, the many material manifestations of poverty such as the poorer houses and garments of the "pitiable" or poor class of the Pacific Northwest Coast communities; the mythological beliefs that the natives had concerning this hereditary class of people; the special kinds of participation of the poorer class in food collecting, in the acquisition of supernatural power, and in social gatherings; the exclusion of poor people from government; the psychological and personality concomitants of low class status; and a thousand other features of the way of life and mentality of poor people constitute a complex of material, social, ideological, and psychological items of a special kind. If it were convenient, these interconnected features could be considered as a culture complex. Similarly, the many traits of culture that developed in the Plains following the modern acquisition of horse pastoralism:

the methods of corraling, tending, and harnessing horses; the customs of ownership and use of horses; the features of predatory behavior, warfare, and the like; and the psychological and personality features which developed in connection with all these new features of culture following the acquisition of horses, constitute a modernly developed segment of Plains culture termed the *horse complex*.

Themes or Elementary Ideas.   A concept which is closely related to the concept of a culture trait or element, and which also shares the characteristics of a culture complex in the importance of its functioning, has been described in various fashions by a number of anthropological writers since Bastian's work of the later nineteenth century. According to this concept, each community has not only thousands of unit traits of culture and a number of trait aggregates or complexes, but also a small number of features of culture of largely ideological form. They are value-attitudes, or fundamental ideas, or simply themes. They are the people's most basic ideological premises, whether implicit or explicit, and they exert historical influences second only to the most fundamental technological or material factors. For example, the several value-attitudes or themes of democracy, of fair play and sportsmanship, may be regarded as important features of modern American culture in addition to the most basic technological factors, social patterns, stratifications, and customs which shape that culture.

The analysis of a culture into myriad minimal units termed culture elements or traits is of course easier than the analysis of a complex ideological and value-attitude heritage into its most basic themes. In fact very little scientific work has been done on methods of classifying culture content into basic themes.

Culture Areas.   Just as scientific procedure in race classification has warranted the use of classifications of a continuum of minutely intergrading forms of physical anatomy, so too is it desirable to classify the minutely intergrading culture elements and complexes into large and useful groupings.

For example, it would be valuable if sufficient knowledge were available of the musical styles of peoples in primitive economies to draw broad lines between each of the areas which appeared to have a cluster of distinctive musical features. It would also be useful to delimit regions each of which had a number of distinctive sounds in its respective languages. This would permit the tentative mapping of tens or scores of musical areas the world over, and tens or scores of phonetic areas. Anthropology has not yet ventured to any extent in the direction of even a pioneer sketching of such musical or phonetic areas. But if and when they are mapped out, their utility may become at least as great for study of historical processes in music or phonetics as is the utility of race classification for study of processes of biological change in races. Archeologists have already been able to map technological areas for distinctive artifacts of the Paleolithic, Epipaleolithic, and Neolithic periods.

Intergrading and contrastable features of technology and material culture, together with features of economic, social, religious, and artistic life, have been classified into larger conceptual units termed culture areas through ethnographic researches in North America during the past decades. The peoples in each so-called culture area have displayed gradually changing as well as intergrading forms of culture from one group to another.

Some of the traits and culture complexes have seemed to be especially elaborated in what are called culture centers or focal districts of the culture areas. Here were what are conceived to be the culturally typical tribes. Their several especially distinctive traits and complexes have attenuated and faded towards the geographical or cultural margins of the areas. It cannot be assumed, as some writers have done, that the culture centers are necessarily the points of origin of the culture traits or complexes.

Very wide boundary belts rather than knife-edged boundary lines have to be drawn around each culture area. The cultures of communities located in or near such wide boundaries have been termed marginal cultures. There has not been general agreement as to the precise locations of the broad belt boundaries of culture areas. There has also been no fixed body of opinion as to the cluster of most distinctive culture complexes and traits which characterize the culture center of each area and which radiate in varying degrees of attenuation out to the area's marginal cultures.

Some examples of what are characterized as culture areas in North America will illustrate the use of the concept. A broad stretch of northern North America along the Arctic coast together with some adjacent districts is delimited as the Eskimo culture area. Some of the traits and complexes which are employed to characterize it are its seal hunting, caribou hunting, dogsled, tailored fur garment, bone-ivory work, shamanistic and mythological complexes, the Eskimo languages as such, and several features such as the semispherical snow house which are exclusively Eskimo developments but which are found in only a part of the area. In the culture area of the Pacific Northwest Coast are found hereditary classes including slaves, market centers, money, secret societies, a special clan complex, a characteristic basketry, long houses made of adzed planks of soft woods, ocean-going large canoes of a special kind, and a style of abstract art applied to wooden boxes, rattles, house posts, masks, and other ceremonial regalia.

Additional culture areas of America are the Mackenzie, Northeast Woodlands, Southeast Woodlands, Plains, Basin-Desert, Californian, Southwest, West Indian, Amazonian, Chibchan, Incan, Araucanian, Mayan, and a few others. Each has been portrayed in terms of a distinctive cluster of ten to fifteen culture complexes or traits. The cluster includes features of technology and material culture, and features of social patterning, religion, and art.

The pioneer mapping of North America into culture areas has been followed by attempts to map other large regions in terms of distinctive culture complexes and traits in the same fashion. An analogous classification of Africa into large culture areas, for example, gives Mediterranean, Egyptian, Guinea-Sudan, Nilotic Sudan, Abyssinian, Northeast Horn, Congo, Eastern African Cattle, Hottentot, Bushman, Madagascan, and other areal divisions.

The value of culture area concepts for the segregation of ethnographical specimens for museum halls and for introductory survey teaching purposes has been considerable. They are simple and vivid, and exhibit some sharp and arresting contrasts in ways of living. But their value as conceptual tools for the scientific and historical purposes of pointing to processes of origin, change, diffusion, and interconnections of the many facets and features of culture is limited. Each culture area as now denoted covers too many different processes and features of culture, and each usually lumps together too many differ-

ing kinds of socio-economic systems to be of much utility. For purposes of scientific analysis, the present portrayals of the main features
of culture areas greatly oversimplify the cultural situation.

The structures and functionings of the several kinds of socio-
economic systems and governments found within the so-called Pacific Northwest Coast, Guinea-Sudan, and East African Cattle areas,
for example, are so different that any scientific identification and
interpretation of the processes of development and change in the
features of economy and government within each area demands a
further segmenting of the area into a number of subareas. The same
must be done with any research problem of like kind in the Plains,
Southwest, Amazonian, and other large areas. Actually each scientific worker has already tended to limit his analysis to the structure
and functioning of a subarea whose cultures were relatively uniform,
rather than to all the cultures of the larger culture area.

However, the most important defect in the characterizations of
culture areas employed in recent decades, and therefore the main
barrier to their efficient use as scientific tools, is the absence of weight-
ing of the significance of the complexes and traits that are listed for
each area. For example, the Eskimo shamanistic complex is important for comprehension of the Eskimo way of life, but it is by no
means so important or strategic a feature of that way of life as is the
seal-hunting complex. The latter feature is decisive, and lacking it
there would have been few or no residents of the Canadian Arctic
shoreline. The former feature is important, but lacking it there could
still have been an Eskimo-like way of life. The listing of a characteristic type of wood carving in the inventory of notable features of
the Northwest Coast area, and the lack of mention of surpluses which
were taken over by the hereditary nobility, is another example of
the failure to distinguish between what was merely incidental and
what was a decisive or essential feature in that area.

If all culture area and subarea characterizations were to be revised and the most distinctive features of each area pointedly weighted
according to their historical, social, and other interrelations or functions, culture area and subarea classifications could be transformed
into a tool of first importance for analysis of the processes of culture
and culture change.

Independent Invention and Parallels. The culture element, culture complex, culture area, subarea, culture center, marginal culture, and other widely used classificatory concepts of cultural or social anthropology are employed in connection with the following basic concepts of dynamic processes of change: invention, diffusion, and patterning or functional integration.

Independent invention is the term used in cultural anthropology for the idea that all cultures have witnessed creative changes or inventions in every aspect of culture. Anthropologists speak of parallel inventions where the same change or invention has occurred in disparate groups. Agriculture, pastoralism, the concept of the zero, astronomical calculations, bronze, the "lost wax" method, and writing are parallelisms which have each appeared at least twice, once or more in the Old World, and once in the New World.

Some of the social or other causes for inventions have already been suggested (see p. 74). In summary it may be said that inventions appear most often when a change in social conditions has permitted an intensification of specialized preoccupation with certain older features of the culture. Any theory which favors spontaneity, capriciousness, or pure chance in inventions impedes scientific analysis. It discourages research which might reveal changes in preceding social or cultural conditions that facilitated or tended to bring about inventions. Completely chance or accidental inventions cannot ever have occurred, because some portions of past heritages have always been components of the situations wherein the inventions have appeared. The study of invention in cultural anthropology must take the form of determining the kinds and frequencies of objects and methods created in each type of socio-economic life or culture area and the special social situations that facilitated such inventions in each of these types.

Specific inventions usually cannot be studied in general terms to exemplify all sorts of inventions. The social processes which have brought about inventions have varied from invention to invention and also from cultural type to cultural type. For example, it is clear that writing was never invented and never could have been devised under the social conditions prevailing in any of the food-gathering economies or areas. This invention was made possible, or actually determined, by social conditions of an entirely new kind which appeared only in types of economy and advanced agricultural culture areas of the Late Neolithic period. In culture areas where there is advanced agriculture, large market or urban centers may be found which support so many specialists that a large number of inventions are made. Influences radiate out from such culture centers which may have a much deeper effect than have the fewer and scattered inventions made in districts outside of the culture centers.

Diffusion. The diffusion of features of culture or of new traits is also a major dynamic process in cultural change. While diffusion is as universal as invention, the forms which diffusion takes, the varying speeds with which different features of culture spread, and the social conditions which impose obstacles to or facilitate diffusion vary from one to another cultural type. For example, language sounds probably spread rapidly from one language stock to another in culture areas which have food-gathering economies because the number of people is sparse and bilingualism is frequent. On the other hand, the relatively smaller percentage of bilinguals in economically advanced and densely populated areas probably results in fewer or rare instances of the spread of sounds across language stock lines. This illustration suggests that it is necessary to be cautious regarding formulations of the dynamics of diffusion in general, and that the specific dynamic processes of diffusion in each type of culture must be examined.

Comparisons of lists of culture traits obtained from many communities or tribes in an area show that most of the culture traits of any one community cannot have been invented by members of that community but were borrowed from adjacent communities. No community has created more than a very small per cent of all its culture traits. The process of borrowing or diffusion has therefore certainly been much more decisive in almost every community's history than has the process of invention.

The manner in which diffused features are changed when they are accepted by the borrowing community also cannot be studied in general terms. Borrowings by one type of culture are probably influenced in ways different from borrowings by other types of culture. Considerable research is needed along these lines. The reasons why objects, ideas, and institutions spread also need to be clarified by research. Traits of certain cultures diffuse into other areas with much greater alacrity than do those of other cultures.

One group of English diffusionists, led by the anatomist G. Eliot Smith, has supposed that whenever massive stone sculpture or architecture, mummification, hieroglyph writing, and a number of ideological, aesthetic, and other features of culture which were developed in Egypt are found in regions outside of Egypt, they have diffused from the Nile. This school of thought has not interested itself in the details and patterns of culture which have appeared in other culture areas and which can easily be shown not to have originated in Egypt.

Pattern, or Integration. Every culture element or complex that is borrowed is taken into an at least slightly different cultural setting. The borrowers modify and reinterpret what they have taken over. They also readjust and modify their own heritage in the process. The same process of readjustment and modification occurs following an invention or change in their own society.

The process of readjustment may be brief or lengthy depending on the type of innovation. The introduction of European shirts, for example, has usually had slight if any effects upon the receiving culture. Similarly the introduction of European folk tales usually has had little or no effect upon the culture to which they have diffused, which has simply changed the folk tales, added them to its list of tales, and told them according to unchanged canons of style. On the other hand, every introduction of steel knives has resulted in drastic economic, social, and cultural changes.

No culture is characterized by perfect integration or a static equilibrium of its component traits and complexes, because inventions and diffusions are in continual process of development and movement. However, food-gathering societies have been more integrated and unchanging in their patterning than were the advanced agricultural and pastoral societies whose very wealth, surpluses, specialists, commerce, and predatory features made for more frequent inventions and borrowing and more frequent internal modifications, conflicts, or readjustments of fundamental kinds. In the present period of history no societies can be found that are not in process of profound disturbance of earlier patterning. Older features of social relationships, religious organization, ideological heritage, and the like are in conflict with or inconsistent with newly introduced or developed social relationships and beliefs, and the processes of readjustment are legion.

A somewhat different concept of culture pattern has been introduced into cultural anthropology by Ruth Benedict. She has utilized the term to refer to a basic ideological heritage and set of values which constantly and directly influence social behavior. However, this special concept of cultural pattern (pp. 115–116) refers only to one, and an essentially ideological, facet of the larger cultural pattern of the society as a whole.

Evolutionism. Some cultural anthropologists from the 1860's to about 1900 believed that a major dynamic process in cultural history was a tendency for communities to progress from lower to ever higher stages. It was thought, therefore, that the proper sphere of cultural anthropology was to portray each of these stages, by examples from living peoples on low technological levels who were presumably in such stages. Although oversimplifications as well as errors were made by many evolutionists, there has been a tendency on the part of critics to distort the general purpose and method of the best of the classical social evolutionists. For example, Lewis H. Morgan, the noted American social evolutionist, did not conceive of his function as that of a cultural historian who must trace specific historical events as inevitable sequences. He was concerned with classifying types of societies on the basis of distinguishing social characteristics that people shared at certain levels of social organization and with noting the sequences in the development of these types. Moreover, he recognized that regular trends or sequences within any culture area are disturbed by borrowings from other cultures. But other influential social evolutionists did accept the incorrect premise that the degree of diffusion of traits was not such as to affect the major dynamism of isolated, progressive, and inherent tendency to advance from stage to stage of social organization.

Protagonists of evolutionism often directed their attention to special facets of cultural anthropology. For example, Edward B. Tylor argued that an initial stage of religious ideology characterized by individual spiritual beings tended to change and be succeeded by a higher and polytheistic ideology, which in its turn later evolved into a kind of monotheism (see p. 201). Lewis H. Morgan formulated a series of successive stages, from low to high, in familial patterns: these were promiscuity, group marriage, matrilineal reckoning, patrilineal reckoning, and the bilateral family (see p. 157). A. C. Haddon argued that an early stage of realistic representation in art tended to be succeeded by a later stage of geometric, symbolic, or abstract representation (see p. 218). Comparative linguists contended that polysynthetic languages were examples of a primitive stage of evolutionary development, and that such languages passed through successive stages to a high culmination in inflectional languages (see p. 288).

The contributions of these and other protagonists of evolutionism applied to cultural anthropology have been many and important. Many of them assembled considerable data in convenient readable forms, popularized the scientific study of culture, did yeoman service in their implicit acceptance of an antiracist point of view, and noted the importance of many hitherto unrecognized social and cultural phenomena such as clan patterns, kinship relationships, and animistic religious beliefs. Among them were the great pioneers of scientific cultural anthropology. Moreover, they had the great virtue of being concerned, as scientists, with the discovery of the dynamic processes of historic change as well as with accurate analyses of social systems and cultures of the modern period.

A portrayal of stages for the technological aspects of culture history is by and large correct. Archeology has given the documentary proof for such sequences. Food-gathering economies universally preceded agriculture and pastoralism. Some other stage sequences are certainly correct if qualified by reservations. For example, shamanism in preagricultural societies was followed by priesthoods in economically advanced societies, and folklores and mythologies appear to have preceded theologies.

Many of the special stage sequences suggested by individual evolutionists, however, no longer can be regarded as tenable. Among the most serious inadequacies in the writings of some evolutionists were an excessive preoccupation with stage sequences which precluded interest in other theoretical pursuits; a failure to conduct intensive field ethnographic researches; an uncritical acceptance of poorly conducted observations of non-European cultures; a degree of ethnocentric conviction that resulted in unjust evaluations of non-European features of culture; and sometimes an underestimation of the degree to which cultural borrowing has occurred and its significance.

The Kulturkreis School.   A number of German-speaking scholars, among them Graebner, Ankermann, Wilhelm Schmidt, and Menghin, have since about 1910 been in process of weaving a complicated fabric of theory for social anthropology which combines some premises of evolutionism with others of diffusionism. According to the *Kulturkreis* scholars, different culture complexes or types of culture, each characterized by a number of essential and minor features, developed in one or another part of the world in successive epochs, and each complex or type subsequently diffused over indicated portions of the world. The *Kulturkreis* writers have therefore tried to show that an analysis of any one community will reveal the complexes or culture types which diffused to it in ancient times, and which are now present in it, layer upon layer.

The principal criticisms of this school have been that it has assumed widespread diffusion of some traits and trait complexes which have not been sufficiently proved to have taken place, and that it has sometimes unwarrantably presumed too great a degree of adhesion between the traits of an expanding cluster of traits. The members of the school have also not always carefully evaluated the relative significance of the trait components of an expanding culture type—that is, whether the traits played an essential or superficial role in social life. The members of the *Kulturkreis* school of thought have agreed with the other anthropological schools in their rejection of racism.

Functionalism.   Unlike followers of evolutionism, diffusionism, and *Kulturkreislehre,* protagonists of functionalism in cultural anthropology have tended to deny interest in formulating the theories and in pursuing the difficult inquiries required to reveal the dynamic historical processes in the development of culture. Functionalists appear to wish to restrict cultural anthropology to a painstaking study of the dynamic, functional interconnections between the many features of living cultures. Radcliffe-Brown, a leading theoretician of functionalism, has resorted to a tenuous biological analogy. He has suggested that a culture resembles a complex biological organism, and that the proper sphere of the cultural anthropologist is the study not of the growth or evolution of social organisms but only of their present structure and physiology.

The avowed members of the functionalist school such as Radcliffe-Brown and Malinowski were anticipated by other anthropologists who had also stressed the need to study the structure and functioning of societies and the interrelationships within them. It is true, however, that functionalists focussed their attention directly and exclusively on that task. They have spent little or no time in the analysis of historical origins or changes, or of the interconnections of features of specific cultures with those of other areas. Their work has led to some relatively intensive studies of cultural behavior in selected communities. But these studies have been merely cross-sectional and their value has been limited by the fact that they have lacked historical perspectives and have not been placed in the setting of the cultures of their areas. Functionalism has been a kind of social anatomy and physiology without genetics. But just as botany without genetics is hardly adequate as a science, so too anthropology must take historical factors into consideration.

Another basic inadequacy of functionalists in anthropology is their failure to evaluate what is strategic or essential in societal functioning and what is incidental or peripheral. For example, some functionalists have given the impression that the interrelationships of clans and kinship systems with other features of social organization are more central for analysis than is the daily agricultural or pastoral work of the people.

Correct weightings or evaluations of that which is significant are indispensable in every science. If the functionalists would develop a theory as to what is essential and what is incidental in cultures of one or another type, they would at once be forced to deal with the dynamic processes of change, and they would then be obliged to consider historical and areal interrelationships.

In fact the very nature of their main interest, which is in social physiology, ought to lead them to valuable formulations regarding the relative weightings to be given to different aspects of culture. Individual functionalists, however, have so far avoided even some problems of historical processes that were actually indispensable for the understanding of the dynamics of living cultures. In castigating evolutionist and diffusionist attempts to obtain historical and genetic solutions, the functionalists often pointed correctly to over-hasty historical formulations, but they have offered no alternatives.

Psychoanalytic and Related Theories. Cultural anthropologists have recently become increasingly interested in studying the determinants of the basic or modal personality, variability in personality, and the definitely aberrant types found in different societies. In order to pursue such interests many or most of these workers have operated with Freudian psychoanalytic premises, or with the premises of later revisions offered by schools of thought which have evolved from Freudian origins. Almost all anthropological workers who have accepted these premises have presumed that the experiences, conditionings, and traumas of the first years of life are the most important of all factors in the shaping of normal as well as abnormal patterns of adult personality. In consequence, intensive study is made of customs regarding nursing, weaning, toilet training, infant feeding, and the factors in infancy that make for ego security or insecurity. A few scholars have even suggested that the basic features of social systems, religions, and arts have developed from such determinants.

An immediate consequence of this interest in personality has been the accumulation of fuller ethnographic and photographic data on infancy among a few peoples with primitive economies than had previously been acquired by cultural anthropologists. The technique of the psychoanalytic interview has also stimulated these workers to secure recordings of dreams, full-length autobiographies, and other data which had rarely or only casually been noted by earlier ethnologists. Among the main values of the psychological emphasis in cultural anthropology is, therefore, that it produces descriptions of facets of human life which other anthropologists have not stressed. Moreover, it has revealed psychological behavior which the sciences of psychology and psychiatry had not previously observed because they restricted their researches to the members of only one or two cultural heritages.

Some axioms of the psychoanalytic groups, such as the strategic importance of the years of infancy in the formation of adult personality, have developed from interpretations of clinical researches on members of our own society. It would be regrettable if the loyalty of cultural anthropologists to such axioms should cause them to neglect to make exhaustive observations, in their field work in non-European cultures, of the childhood years from five or six years of age and up to puberty. The very tenability of psychoanalytic axioms or premises must be tested through scientific field work of the cultural anthropologists. Their task is to describe and interpret dynamic psychological processes on all age levels and in all areas of experience, whether or not they have as yet been discussed at length by the psychoanalytic schools.

Acculturation. Until recently most cultural anthropologists excluded from the scope of their researches the influence of European civilization upon the native cultures they were studying. Their concern was with description and analysis of the cultures that were rapidly becoming extinct. The inadequacy of this approach from the point of view of anthropology as a science is now almost universally accepted. It is recognized that no contemporary cultures, however isolated they may be, can be studied without consideration of the impact of the economically more advanced cultures upon them.

This change of emphasis in anthropological research has occurred not only because of the realization of the theoretical inadequacy of the earlier approach, but because of the increasing use of anthropologists by governments. When the destruction of the cultures and economies of native people had proved to be politically and economically unwise, some of the major colonial powers began a policy of indirect rule through partial if sometimes grudging acknowledgment of the cultures of their subject peoples. To do this it became necessary to have anthropologists as experts to facilitate the work of administrators. Such anthropologists took over practical roles and important social responsibilities relatively new to persons working in this science. At times they have been utilized merely to direct the more effective control of colonial peoples. In other cases the data they have provided have been of scientific value, have served the critics of colonial control, and have been helpful in various ways to the natives themselves.

Irrespective of the social consequences of research in acculturation, the enlarged horizons it has afforded have enriched the subject matter and the methodology of anthropology. Acculturation studies have shown the causes for the selective receptivity of cultures, that is, why some culture traits are readily accepted and others rejected; have tested previously unsupported generalizations as to the rate of change of material culture as compared to other aspects of culture; have evaluated the effect of cultural disorganization on personality; and have studied the processes and forms of cultural change and cultural integration after cultural contacts have occurred. These studies produce results which compare in many respects with what has been ascertained by students of diffusion. However, the contacts of modern advanced economies with primitive economies create special methodological and theoretical problems. All in all it is much too early for significant generalizations to have emerged from acculturation studies.

The Applied Science of Human Relations. Anthropology is capable of making several significant contributions to an applied science of human relations. The theory of interviewing and observation, which is implicit rather than fully discussed in anthropological writings but which is used by creative and mature fieldworkers, is based upon the assumption that culture is a pattern of a dynamic kind rather than merely a composite of traits. The ideal of absence of specialization and compartmentalization in the anthropologist's approach to the study of culture, and the fact that he deals with widely variable human behavior, many types of social adjustment, and different kinds of cultures, are conducive to the development of objectivity. Because of the recognition of the fruitfulness of this peculiarly broad theory and approach, interest in the science of anthropology as applied to our own society has been increasing not only among historians, sociologists, psychologists, psychiatrists, and economists, but also among practical men in the fields of business and administration. Except for arenas of practical work such as race relations, intercultural education, and administrative policies in economically backward parts of the world, the trends toward an applied anthropology are, however, as yet amorphous.

SELECTED READINGS

Barnett, H. G. *Innovation.* New York: McGraw-Hill, 1953.

Benedict, R. *Patterns of Culture.* Boston: Houghton Mifflin, 1934. New York: Penguin, 1946.

——. *The Chrysanthemum and the Sword.* Boston: Houghton Mifflin, 1946.

Boas, F. "Anthropology," in *Encyclopedia of the Social Sciences,* II, 73–110.

——. *Mind of Primitive Man.* New York: Macmillan, 1938 (rev. ed.).

——. *Race, Language, and Culture.* New: Macmillan, 1940. Pp. 243–311.

Childe, V. G. *Social Evolution.* New York: Schuman, 1951.

Evans-Pritchard, E. E. *Social Anthropology.* Glencoe: Free Press, 1951.

Firth, R. *Elements of Social Organization.* New York: Philosopical Library, 1951.

——. *Human Types: An Introduction to Social Anthropology.* London: Thomas Nelson, 1956.

Goldenweiser, A. A. *Anthropology.* New York: Crofts, 1937. Pt. III *et passim.*

——. *History, Psychology, and Culture.* New York: Knopf, 1933. Pp. 1–208.

Goldschmidt, W. *Man's Way.* Cleveland: World Pub. Co., 1959.

Hallowell, A. I. *Culture and Experience.* Philadelphia: Univ. of Penn. Press, 1955.

Herskovits, M. J. *Acculturation. The Study of Culture Contact.* New York: Augustin, 1938.

Human Origins: An Introduction to Anthropology. Selected Readings. Series I. Chicago: Univ. of Chicago Bookstore, 1945. Nos. 20, 21.

Kardiner, A. *The Individual and His Society.* New York: Columbia Univ. Press, 1939.

——. *The Psychological Frontiers of Society.* New York: Columbia Univ. Press, 1945.

Kluckhohn, C. *Mirror for Man.* New York: Whittlesey, 1949. Pp. 17–44, 196–289.

Kroeber, A. L. *Cultural and Natural Areas of Native North America.* Berkeley: Univ. of California Press, 1939 (Univ. Cal. Pubs. Amer. Arch. and Ethnol., Vol. 38).

——, and C. Kluckhohn. *Culture: A Critical Review of Concepts and Definitions.* Cambridge, Mass.: Peabody Museum, 1952.

LaBarre, W. *The Human Animal.* Chicago: Univ. of Chicago Press, 1954.

La Farge, Oliver, ed. *The Changing Indian.* Norman: Univ. of Oklahoma Press, 1942.

Linton, R., ed. *Acculturation in Seven American Indian Tribes.* New York: Appleton-Century, 1940.

——. *The Tree of Culture.* New York: Knopf, 1955.

——. *The Cultural Background of Personality.* New York: Appleton-Century, 1945.

——. *The Study of Man.* New York: Appleton-Century, 1936. Pp. 80–112, 271–421.

——, ed. *The Science of Man in the World Crisis.* New York: Columbia Univ. Press, 1945. Pp. 78–200.

Lowie, R. H. *The History of Ethnological Theory*. New York: Farrar and Rinehart, 1937.

Malinowski, Bronislaw. "Culture," in *Encyclopedia of the Social Sciences,* IV, 621–645.

——. *The Dynamics of Culture Change*. New Haven: Yale Univ. Press, 1945.

Mead, M. *The Changing Culture of an Indian Tribe*. New York: Columbia Univ. Press, 1932.

Nadel, S. F. *The Foundations of Social Anthropology*. Glencoe: Free Press, 1951.

Opler, M. K., ed. *Culture and Mental Health*. New York: Macmillan, 1959.

——. *Culture, Psychiatry, and Human Values: The Methods and Values of a Social Psychiatry*. Springfield: C. C. Thomas, 1956.

Piddington, R. *An Introduction to Social Anthropology*. Vol. I. Edinburgh: Oliver and Boyd, 1950. Pp. 3–29. Vol. II. 1957. *Passim.*

Radin, P. *The Method and Theory of Ethnology*. New York: McGraw-Hill, 1933.

——. *Social Anthropology*. New York: McGraw-Hill, 1932. Pp. 1–26.

Redfield, R. *The Little Community*. Chicago: Univ. of Chicago Press, 1955.

——. *Peasant Society and Culture: An Anthropological Approach to Civilization*. Chicago: Univ. of Chicago Press, 1956.

——. *The Primitive World and Its Transformations*. Ithaca: Cornell Univ. Press, 1953.

Sapir, E. "Custom," in *Encyclopedia of the Social Sciences,* IV, 658–662.

——. *Time Perspective in Aboriginal American Culture*. Ottawa: Geol. Survey, Dept. Mines, 1916.

——. "The Unconscious Patterning of Behavior in Society," in *The Unconscious*. New York: Knopf, 1929. Pp. 114–142.

Schmidt, W. *The Culture Historical Method of Ethnology*. New York: Fortuny's, 1939.

Steward, J. H. *Theory of Culture Change*. Urbana: Univ. of Illinois, 1955.

Thomas, W. I. *Primitive Behavior*. New York: McGraw-Hill, 1937. Pp. 1–48, 610–747.

Wilson, G. and M. *The Analysis of Social Change*. Cambridge: Cambridge Univ. Press, 1954.

CHAPTER SIX

PRIMITIVE ECONOMICS

Types of Primitive Economic Systems. Few anthropologists have attempted even the sketchiest sort of study of the economics of the cultures they have reported upon after their field trips. A scientific presentation of the economic systems of the technologically inferior and nonliterate peoples is therefore handicapped by the extreme paucity of field observations. The knowledge, as well as the space, is not available to analyze here each of hundreds of the relatively diverse primitive economic systems. Any two of these systems, like geographical populations and ethnic subdivisions, may differ only in minute respects. As in race classifications or culture area classifications or any other series of intergrading phenomena, it is necessary, however, for the scientist to point tentatively to a small number of what he judges to be the high or "ideal" points in the intergrading continuum of forms. Each of these high points may then be considered as constituting a type of economic system whose dynamic processes contrast with the processes of the other types noted. This classificatory or taxonomic approach is a helpful and even indispensable device for both scientific and pedagogic purposes.

A limited number of generalized types of primitive economic systems are given in the following classification. It is somewhat less specific than various typologies that have been suggested by earlier writers. Its central feature is that it contrasts economic systems which produce small surpluses with those that achieve large surpluses. This is done because the amount of surplus produced is a crucial determinant of many other aspects of the economy and social system of a people. It plays a significant part in deciding the density of the population; the complexity of the social organization; the division of labor and degree of specialization; the form of ownership, exchange, and inheritance of property; and the amount of leisure time and the potential for development of arts, crafts, and ceremonies. Major types of primitive economies are:

1. Hunting, fishing, food-gathering economies
   a. that lacked exchangeable surpluses. These will be designated as simple food-gathering economies.
   b. that produced small exchangeable surpluses. These will be referred to as advanced food-gathering economies.
2. Economies based on primitive agriculture, or on pastoralism, or on primitive agriculture and pastoralism
   a. that lacked pastoralism and produced small surpluses. These will be referred to as simple agricultural economies.
   b. with or without pastoralism and that produced large surpluses. These will be referred to as advanced agricultural or agricultural-pastoral economies.

Simple Food-gathering Economies (1a). Societies lately existing that may be classified as simple food-gathering economies, although their economies and cultures differ in very many details, include: Tasmanians, Australians, Toala of Celebes, Pygmies of the Philippines, Pygmies of the Malay Peninsula, Andaman Islanders, Veddas of Ceylon, Ainus, some non-reindeer-owning Siberian Arctic peoples, the Bushmen of South Africa, South American Indians of southern Chile and Argentina, and the Indians dwelling in the vast and continuous area of North America from the peninsula of Southern California north to and including Aleuts and all Eskimos, east in the United States and Canada to districts where primitive agriculture was practiced, and excluding only the tidewater and lower river villages of the Pacific Northwest Coast from the Klamath River to the Tlingits of southern Alaska.

Only a few hundreds of thousands of persons the world over, most of them Australians or western North American Indians, lived in this type of economy before the modern expansion of European civilization. Every society in this category did not engage in fishing or gathering of wild plants; nor was the hunting which every one of these societies featured necessarily the most strategic form of production.

In spite of diversities when specific cultures are compared, the main general economic features found in all these societies were as follows:

1. With the exception of some parts of California, populations were sparse.

2. The self-sufficient economic units were bands or communities that averaged less than forty persons and rarely exceeded seventy-five or eighty. Assemblages of many hundreds were temporary and brief.

3. Economically strategic food collection was usually undertaken by democratically conducted work parties or band organizations of either sex. Usually a party, squad, or group of adolescent and older males hunted and fished; usually a party, squad, or group of adolescent and older females carried on all other economically strategic production. The entire community usually made seasonal moves for the sake of obtaining the major food supply. Minor and incidental production was by parties or individuals.

4. Distribution of economically strategic products was always potentially shared although not necessarily frequently so in practice. Incidental production by individuals was less often shared.

5. There was a simple sexual division of labor and no further specialization.

6. There were no economically significant surplus products, no money, commerce, trade, or markets. Exchanges were almost entirely of gifts or presents.

7. Strategic resources, which were mainly fishing areas, hunting districts, or wild-plant-collecting sites, were owned not by individuals or lineages but by the entire band or community, and usually could be utilized for production by any member of the community.

8. There were no significant inequalities in ownership of wealth since the most productive resources were not individually owned. There could be wide differences in ownership of personal effects but these were of minor social, not major economic, significance.

Advanced Food-gathering Economies (1b). Only one area that exemplifies this type of economy has survived into modern times. It includes all lower coastal river and tidewater villages of American Indians from northwestern California to the Tlingits of Alaska.

In spite of diversities of specific societies, the central features of economy in these societies, which embraced a few hundred thousand persons in all, were as follows:

1. Populations were many times denser than in the simpler food-gathering societies.

2. Self-sufficient village communities may have averaged forty or fifty persons each, but market villages numbered many hundreds of persons, sometimes reaching as high as approximately 1500 or even 2000 persons.

3. Economically strategic food getting was by work parties of either sex. Parties of males hunted and fished and parties of females did other forms of economically strategic work. A great deal of incidental food getting was by individuals. But the work parties were recruited, organized, and led by hereditary headmen or headwomen, who could control incidental or individualistic production too. Only a part of the village made seasonal moves to obtain the major food supply. The village was maintained the year round.

4. Distribution of work party products was unequal, for the hereditarily wealthy received a better and larger portion and only the remainder was usually shared. All other products were kept by their individual producers, who often took care, however, to give a token gift of the product to the wealthy village headmen.

5. There was some slight specialization over and above the primary sexual division of labor. Northwest Coast specialists included slaves who did menial work, carvers, weavers, canoe makers, basket makers, and a very few others. Only one or two of each type of specialist were to be found in a single village except for slaves, who were numerous in some of the northerly villages.

There were also some primitive beginnings of village or district specialization. One district tended to specialize to such a degree as to produce small surpluses of furs, another of pounded dried salmon, another of slaves, and another of sea shells for ornamentation and money.

6. A small number of economically significant surplus products or commodities were sold. Trading was facilitated by sea shell money, and was especially intensive in market villages.

7. Some strategic resources were privately owned by lineage head-

men who were wealthy through heredity. These resources included slaves, ocean fishing areas, shellfish beaches, river fishing spots, fish-spearing rocks, and hunting districts. Productive resources thus owned could be utilized only by permission of their headman owner.

8. There were inequalities in ownership of productive resources; hence there were class strata such as the nobility, the well-to-do who were related to the noble lineage, the poor, and the raid captives or other slaves. These classes were hereditary.

9. Nobles received tribute from relatives, fellow clan members, or fellow villagers. They were also supported and made wealthier by the labor of slaves and by free persons who were attached to the noble household. They exacted fines from offenders, took a cut from other payments that were made, and profited from the sale of commodities produced by specialists attached to their household. Nobles and their armed followers also raided distant villages, taking slaves, money, or other valuable products. These were primitive beginnings of predatory warfare for the sake of accumulation of further wealth.

A variety of other exchanges were associated with the economic processes of the tidewater and lower coastal river villages of the Northwest Coast of America. Best known is the spectacular potlatch, which was a highly ceremonialized feast at which a lineage headman gave away tremendous quantities of commodities to invited guests of rank in a kind of gambler's investment that involved a possible return of greater amounts at later potlatches given by such guests.

Simple Agricultural Economies (2a). Wherever primitive agriculture diffused into a district marked by simple food-gathering economies which had no exchangeable surpluses, from the beginnings of Old World agriculture 8000 or more years ago and down to the centuries just preceding Columbus, agriculture rapidly became the strategic form of production and the most decisive of the various determinants of the economy. In a few areas, as in Oceania, any agricultural techniques brought by colonists to a previously uninhabited coral atoll inevitably resulted in a primitive agricultural economy with only very small surpluses because larger surpluses could not be produced on the meagre acreage cultivable. On continental mainlands or larger islands this type of economy did not always long continue. Improvements in the agricultural techniques effected increased production, and in areas at all fertile this eventually caused a shift in the direction of a more developed type of agricultural economy. The economies described in this section were therefore relatively transitory except in sub-desert or coral atoll locales.

This type of economy is identifiable in a number of New World districts such as in the northeastern portions of North America, along the upper Missouri, in Arizona and New Mexico, and in Brazil. It is rare in Eurasia or Africa, perhaps because of the longer establishment of agriculture there and also because of the surpluses effected by domesticated animals and plow techniques that early supplemented primitive agriculture. There are, however, primitive agricultural economies which produce small surpluses in limited districts of Malaysia, Micronesia, Polynesia, and Melanesia.

Probably as many as a few million persons all over the world lived in such economic systems before the time of Columbus. Their principal economic features were:

1. Populations were not much if at all denser than in the advanced food-gathering systems.

2. Self-sufficient economic units were usually villages of scores or hundreds of persons; rarely if ever was a village as large as 2000.

3. The economically strategic garden work could be carried on by individuals, but sometimes the community joined in harvesting or other farm work. Democratically run work parties of one or the other sex fished, hunted, and collected wild plants much as in the simple food-gathering societies.

4. Distribution of economically strategic products was potentially shared though not necessarily often in practice. Garden produce was kept by its individual producers and shared only in time of community need. What individuals produced they usually retained.

5. The surpluses consequent upon garden work and also upon fishing hauls in Oceania, the speed with which pottery could be made for containers, and the all-year-round habitations permitted enough leisure to release many individuals for specialized work or craftsmanship in basketry, pottery, weaving, carving, and other pur-

suits. The primary sexual division of labor was therefore supplemented by many individuals who were free to enjoy long hours at crafts and ceremonial or other specialized interests.

6. The release of many persons for specialized work resulted in economically significant surplus products which were given away as gifts or bartered from community to community. True money was absent or was only in its primitive beginnings, and no true markets had evolved.

7. Strategic resources such as hunting, fishing, and wild plant locales, and garden plots, were owned by the community. However, the garden was cultivated on land assigned democratically by the community, and for long terms, to lineages or individuals. Private ownership of cultivated land tended to develop out of such long-term assignments, but the community assignment of such land need not mean that it was true private property.

8. There were no economically important inequalities in the ownership of productive resources; hence there were no noteworthy inequalities in wealth or in class status. There were wide but economically nonsignificant variations in ownership of personal effects.

9. No self-perpetuating hereditary leaders were present, and there were no forms of taxation or tribute. Fighting was not predatory but in the nature of retaliatory slaughters or feud-vendettas, or in self-defense.

No one community probably ever exhibited all of the foregoing generalized features exactly. For example, a number of the features noted are found in the Pueblos of Arizona and New Mexico, but in other respects the Pueblos were already well advanced in a process of metamorphosis away from this type of economy in the direction of a more advanced one. Agricultural food-producing techniques yielded more and more products as they were mastered and improved and socio-economic changes followed. Few of these societies were, therefore, relatively as static as were the preagricultural types.

Advanced Agricultural-pastoral Economies (2b). Hundreds of millions of people of nonliterate heritages and backward economies fit into the category of advanced agricultural-pastoral economies. They constitute over 95 per cent of the living peoples dealt with by anthropology. They had evolved directly from earlier hunting, fishing, food-gathering economies to which agriculture, pastoralism, or both had diffused during the last 3000 or 4000 years; or they had developed from primitive agricultural economies that produced small surpluses after their techniques of production had long achieved larger surpluses; or they had taken over the socio-economic patterns of technologically more advanced neighbors. All African peoples except the Bushmen were pastoralists or agriculturalists who produced large surpluses, as were all groups on larger or volcanic Polynesian-Micronesian islands, most of the Melanesian and Malaysian peoples, and in the Americas the Aztecs, Mayas, Chibchas, and Incas.

Pastoralism of a pure kind, that is to say, economically self-sufficient and unconnected with societies that had agriculture, has been rare. It is best exemplified by the cattle- and sheep-owning Hottentots of South Africa and by some of the reindeer-owning groups of northern and far eastern Siberia. Because the socio-economic patterns of such economies, as well as of all combined agricultural-pastoral groups, were fundamentally comparable to the patterns of pure agriculturalists like the Mayas or Aztecs, it is correct to consider them together as a single economic category.

The basic and typical features of these otherwise tremendously variable economies were as follows:

1. Except for a few pure pastoralists, desert dwellers, and inhabitants of other geographically inhospitable districts, populations were dense.

2. There were, in addition to villages, towns and sometimes cities numbering many thousands of persons.

3. Strategic production was by individuals, or by war-captive or servile labor owned by nobles, chiefs, or monarchs. Important production was also carried on for market sale by specialists and specialist village or larger groups, such as the specialist villages in Central America, and specialist areas as in the Anglo-Egyptian Sudan. Specialists were more often men than women.

4. Distribution was unequal and the owners of lands, herds, or slaves received most. Nobles or monarchs also exacted taxation or tribute from free producers.

5. Large numbers of commodities were sold, especially in the

larger market towns. Such trade was facilitated by sea shell or other forms of money, such as cowrie shells in West Africa and chocolate beans in Central America. Men tended to take over much of the trade.

6. Strategic resources were privately owned by the nobility and the well-to-do upper-class men. The resources included agricultural lands, herds, subject peoples, and slaves.

7. Since there were inequalities in ownership of productive resources there were classes, which sometimes tended to develop into specialized occupational strata or castes.

8. Nobles, monarchs, and chiefs were supported by serflike or slavelike forms of labor or by the labors of a large class of poor persons. The well-to-do were also supported by various sorts of assistants, retainers, tax, tribute, and fine collectors, and other government servants and by armed police or soldiery. The latter carried on war on a considerable scale and obtained money, lands, herds, or captives for their chiefs, who in this way accumulated further wealth.

Economies of this type tended to be less static and more rapidly changing than the other types. This was because of the greater production, the often considerable specialization of labor, the greater frequency of inventions, the greater degree of trade and intercommunication, or other factors.

The Effects of the Contact of Diverse Economies. Some economic and cultural heritages have continued to function partially in spite of their envelopment by more advanced economies. Only some features of a few simple food-gathering economies have survived when they have been thoroughly surrounded by economies capable of greater productivity. An example is that of the Congo Pygmies, who long ago changed into a lowly hunting caste within the Congo Negro communities, by becoming elephant-hunting specialists. A technique of hunting that was formerly basic to their economy and some correlated social patterns survived, but not their economic system as a whole. Likewise, when some groups of Algonkin Indians of central-eastern Canada found themselves on the periphery of Europe's economy with the setting up of French fur-trading posts in the sixteenth century and following, basic economic changes appear to have occurred rapidly. There seems some likelihood that hunting lands had been community property before the advent of Europeans, but became the private property of lineages of hunters and trappers who produced surpluses of furs for the French market. Each lineage hunted in its own district, or remembered its privately owned hunting territory. When in recent decades anthropologists studied the forms of land ownership in northeastern North America they found such private hunting land ownership wherever furs were produced for a European market. Indians in the area seem soon to have developed into hunting and trapping specialists within the pattern of European economy.

When some of the Indians of the Pacific Northwest Coast, who had advanced food-gathering economies, were rendered extraordinarily wealthy by sale of furs to early mariners who were plying the Pacific, and also by the acquisition of iron and steel tools from whites, their headmen seem to have become predatory and warlike to an unprecedented degree; some Tsimshian, Haida, and other noblemen acquired unusual numbers of raid-captives or slaves. The period of initial economic changes intensified the development of some features of their earlier economies, such as slavery. In the decades following, the whites came in in such numbers that the Pacific Northwest Coast Indian economies were overwhelmed and promptly crumbled and the people became either wage laborers or fishermen in the backwashes of our economy.

In modern centuries the fates of primitive pastoral and agricultural economies have, like that of the hunting, fishing, food-gathering economies, hinged on the manner of entry of Europeans, on their numbers, and on the kinds of economic developments brought about by them. Each modern region has therefore to be studied according to its special circumstances. European economy sought furs in one area, sent colonists into another, developed rubber plantations in another, secured dried coconut kernels in still another. With rare exceptions the peoples of non-European economies have tended to be reduced to the status of either lowly specialized castes or nonspecialist cheap-labor classes within the expanding arena of European economy.

The Community. The term *community* has shifting connotations and needs specific definition for each level of economy. Among peoples of the most primitive economies, that is, the peoples of food-gathering types, the community is that aggregate of persons which lives in a given territory and produces with its heritage of artifacts from the resources available in that territory. The members of such a community are mutually interdependent in production and distribution and have a common social, cultural, and linguistic heritage, as well as a government.

In simple food-gathering economies such communities are usually mere encampments or small bands, which move about seasonally within their community territory in order to produce sufficiently for survival.

The communities of advanced food-gathering economies are small villages, with a few larger market villages. These bands or villages are economically self-sufficient. They are also autonomous politically, although they visit and meet together upon occasion in a temporary constellation of communities. The use of the appellation *tribe* or *nation* to such minimal, economically self-sufficient, culturally uniform, and politically autonomous units of the size of a band or village seems not to be especially useful. However, where a cluster of such communities has developed ties of economic interdependence, or more likely has knit some sort of military or political organization for the sake of defense or united front against an enveloping economy like that of the Europeans, the term *tribe* or *nation* is applicable to the larger aggregate of communities.

In the case of simple agricultural economies, there are likewise small village communities. Although these villages may remain entirely self-sufficient for a period of time following their acquisition of primitive agriculture, the very presence of such a resource usually permits surpluses and specialization of labor in little time, and as a result intercommunity barter of surplus products often exists to a degree not found in the wealthiest food-gathering communities. Thus a network of intercommunity economic ties develops, and each village tends to become increasingly enmeshed in economic interrelationships with adjacent villages. A cluster of village communities which share a common territory, language, and culture, and are economically interwoven, is often also designated a tribe. Some individual simple agricultural villages are so large that each of them has been termed a tribe rather than a village as, for example, Zuñi and Acoma in New Mexico.

At the more advanced level of primitive agriculture or of pastoralism the term *community* has wider connotations. Here it may refer to an individual village, or to a small cluster of villages whose economic interdependence involves periodic recourse to a market village for barter or sale of surplus products. It may also mean a larger aggregate of such clusters, an aggregate possessed of a common territory, language, culture, and economic interdependence and self-sufficiency. This larger community has also been termed a tribe or nation.

The most central feature of a community is its economic self-sufficiency and the economic interdependence of its members. In primitive economies such an independent economic life is associated with a common territory, language, and cultural heritage. The initial Pliocene and Early Paleolithic simple food-gathering clusters of families were much more primitive in their technological and economic life than anything known through anthropological field research among modern communities. These prehistoric clusters of economically interdependent families, which were fundamentally economic or productive units and only secondarily lineage, kinship, or biological units, must have been the first communities.

Property.   Peoples of primitive economies have property in clothing, cooking utensils, hunting and fishing gear, houses, lands, herds, songs, fetishes, dances, and curing incantations. Lineage or individual private ownership of intangible or noncorporeal property, such as songs, dances, or incantations, is to be found in any type of economy, but from the point of view of scientific analysis of the functioning of the economy, such features are of minor importance. Only the most productive property needs to be discussed in an analysis of the fundamentals of an economic system.

Some writers have supposed that mankind evolved from early forms of community ownership of everything, up to the modern period of an elaborate development of forms of private ownership. In one sense such an evolution in the direction of more forms of private ownership is correct, but in another sense it is incorrect. It is not true that peoples on the lowest economic levels, exemplified in a general way by simple food-gathering economies, have community ownership of everything. Personal effects and hunting and fishing gear handled by individuals are in these economies as in all other economic systems owned by those who wear or manipulate them. Back scratchers, belts, spears, bows, sleds, cooking utensils, or baskets are also always owned by individuals.

It is true, however, that the most productive resources are always owned by the whole community on the lowest economic levels. Pastoral and primitive agricultural economies that produce large surpluses are, on the other hand, characterized by private ownership by a wealthy few of some of the economically decisive productive resources. Since these economies are developments of the Neolithic and later epochs, one can say that property ownership of decisive resources of production has tended to move into private hands during Neolithic and later eras. Only in the case of the most productive resources has there been an evolution from community to private ownership.

In simple food-gathering societies that have had no surpluses the economically strategic resources are hunting districts, wild animal herds, wild food-plant sites, fishing sites, and shellfish beaches. Ocean harbor or inlet districts where seals are speared are a strategic resource to Eskimos. So too are the summer-hunted caribou herds. Such districts or herds are the community property of a number of Eskimo families, who agree as to where to live separately and individually in winter and hunt seals from their community-owned resource, and where to meet together for the joint caribou hunt in the summer.

There may be a long-term hunting district assignment by the community or band to one of its families. This assignment may give the appearance of private hunting territory, and has been so reported for the Veddas of Ceylon, but the Vedda encampment may reassign these hunting districts. The report that the encampment sometimes does not reassign such districts over a period of decades does not contravene the fact of Vedda community ownership rather than private ownership, since any potential reassignment of productive property by the Vedda band is a certain indicator of community ownership rather than private ownership of such property.

If, as in northern Australia, a clan is reported as owning a hunting territory, this is again not private ownership but community ownership with clans assigned a permanent duty to produce from a given area for the sake of the community.

Reports of private ownership of fruit trees or honey sites in societies of the lowest economic level may be regarded as private ownership of relatively minor and economically not strategic forms of property. The over-all picture of property in such societies is community ownership of the most decisive forms of productive property, which were hunting lands, water areas for fishing, herds, and shellfish beaches.

The advanced food-gathering economies have private ownership by the hereditarily wealthy village headman of one or more of the following strategic resources: slaves, fish-spearing rocks, river banks, shellfish beaches, wild food-plant sites, ocean fishing areas, hunting territories, and perhaps some others. Most coastal groups of Oregon and Washington had only slaves as individually owned property of an economically productive kind. Wealthy headmen in the most northerly groups such as Kwakiutl, Haida, Tsimshian, and Tlingit owned several resources of the kind noted above.

In simple agricultural economies which have small surpluses the most strategic resource is tilled land. It is owned by the community but long-time assignments of specifically delimited plots to clans, lineages, or small families have often been misinterpreted as privately owned property. Wherever the community may reassign such plots the land is probably community property although it may be in an early period of change to private ownership. In these societies other strategic resources such as fishing and hunting locales are much more obviously the property of the community. The fact that all-year-round houses as well as all personal effects are privately owned is of little economic significance.

In pastoral and primitive agricultural economies which produce large surpluses some of the strategic resources are in wealthy persons' private hands. These resources may be slaves, agricultural lands, herds and horses, and hunting or fishing districts.

Sexual Division of Labor.   In every society there is a partitioning of work into tasks conventionally allotted men and tasks allotted women. In almost every society of the lowest economic level all men hunt, fish, and do a number of other things that constitute men's conventional work, while women gather plant foods, obtain firewood and water, cook, tend dependent offspring, and do a number of other things that constitute women's work. In other types of economy some specialized tasks are also reserved for men and others for women.

The origin and cause of such a sexual division of labor and its socio-economic consequences are subject to considerable controversy. Some anthropologists have argued that superior strength, speed, and agility have always been characteristic of men as compared to women and hence they have been assigned to hunting, fishing, or other physically more demanding tasks. While men may be somewhat stronger on the average, experience and skills rather than greater brute power determine success in hunting and fishing. Women could therefore perform as efficiently as men, wherever techniques had become as important as speed, strength, and endurance.

Others have argued that childbearing and menstruation constituted mysterious or magically feared physiological functions, and that because the conviction of women's greater magical danger was spread over most of the world, women were eliminated from participation in such economic, religious, and other work as was most important for the community. Proof that the exclusion of women from some most productive tasks was due to such belief in magical contamination has not been given. In some areas where men hunt and fish, feminine physiological traits are not associated with magical danger, and so the magical-danger theory does not explain the assignment of males to hunting and fishing work in such areas.

Still others have argued that since Neolithic plough agriculture and pastoralism were initially associated with men rather than women, the labor of men in advanced agricultural and pastoral societies remained associated with the henceforth most productive occupations, and women were excluded from them. This theory does not account, however, for the sexual division of labor in food-gathering societies.

A simple and plausible means of accounting for the universal sexual partitioning of labor lies in yet another quarter. In all societies females become pregnant, give birth to, and nurse dependent off-spring. The lower the technological level of the economy, the more important becomes the productive contribution of each person. Hence the more important is the one unique and natural contribution of pregnant women and nursing mothers, for the community must be replenished. The community recognizes that women must be accompanied by their babies wherever they go; hence they cannot hunt or fish as efficiently as can the unencumbered males. Males are therefore free to be mobile and active while females have been accorded, by nature, a prior responsibility or obligation to rear additional members of the community in the only way this can be done. Hence the community assigns work involving more mobility to men and work involving less mobility to women.

Where the factor of differential mobility is absent, all tasks may be assigned to either sex. For example, cooking is not often man's work but hunting is very rarely woman's work. Men prepare hides in one group, women in another. Men tend to manufacture and repair the equipment used by them in their major work, but there are innumerable minor tasks the assignment of which to one or the other sex can be accounted for only in terms of the history and culture of the area.

Apart from certain natural activities related to the welfare of infants, no labor is naturally masculine or feminine. The reactions or attitudes of people regarding man's proper work or woman's proper work are determined not by what is natural but by historical circumstances and cultural conditioning. In our society, for example, there is nothing natural about the feminine assignment to housework, which can be explained only in terms of the history of the sex division of labor in our culture.

There are important economic consequences of assignments of work to different sexes. In the food-gathering economies of the Pacific Northwest Coast, physically unhampered men were able to engage in predatory raids to secure slaves, who became the most decisive form of privately owned productive resource in the area. Men were also physically freer to travel to market villages to engage in profitable exchanges. Hence they achieved greater economic importance, took over productive private property, and rose to governing power. In advanced agricultural and pastoral societies the mobility of men likewise made possible their control of slave or other field labor, and their ability to carry on profitable commerce and fighting, their ownership of herds, and their assumption of governmental control.

Specialization of Labor. In simple food-gathering areas and societies specialized labor which facilitated production was a luxury that could not be permitted except for the crippled and aged. Everyone, from the time he mastered adult productive techniques, that is, from puberty on, had to work at major productive tasks. The techniques of production in these societies were so primitive that hunting, fishing, and wild-plant-collecting work had to be carried on largely by two work parties, one of males, the other of females who were accompanied by infants. In the case of most Eskimos who did not hunt seals in groups of men, food producing and work with equipment otherwise permitted little further specialization.

In the food-gathering societies of the Pacific Northwest Coast menial labor by slaves and the very abundant resources in fish released energies which allowed some specialization by a few persons who usually were attached to a wealthy nobleman's house. They made canoes, carved, fought, hunted, fished, or did other useful tasks. A few women were similarly released to devote their leisure time to basketry, weaving, making of extra garments, and comparable work. Surplus products made by such partially or wholly specialized workers could be sold in intercommunity commerce or served as gifts in the rival potlatches or giving-away feasts of the nobles.

A small degree of specialization of labor occurred in the simple agricultural societies, which resulted in production of some surplus products that tended to lead to commerce, the use of money, and other economic features that characterized the more advanced societies. On Oceanian atolls primitive agriculture, the permanent all-year-round residences, and also the vast resources of fish available were among the several factors that released energies so as to allow specialized craftsmanship such as carving. The pottery made in many early simple agricultural economies was produced so much more rapidly than were baskets that many women were released from considerable drudgery and freed for spinning and weaving.

In the more advanced economies the superior techniques in agri culture, the slaves or other laborers of lower-class status, and in the Old World the herds and horses were among the factors that permitted an unprecedented degree of specialization. Not only were there many kinds of individual specialists who produced for the wealthy or for the market. In many Old World and New World regions entire villages or communities adopted just one or two specialized occupations and sold surpluses to other communities which specialized in another sphere. Thus individuals of a village that was primarily engaged in making pottery sold to members of another village which was predominantly engaged in raising of fruit trees or cotton, or was occupied in weaving or basketry. Some larger villages specialized in two, three, or four crafts, whereas smaller villages specialized in only one. Areas of this type had markets and used money equivalents of the surplus products. Regional as well as village specializations are also found, as in the Anglo-Egyptian Sudan where one group of low-caste villagers made ferrous artifacts, which were bought by upper-caste cattle owners, and intermediate-caste river dwellers produced surplus fish. In such economies groups of specialists tended to become hereditary castes.

The main initiating factors in the development of extreme specialization of labor in human history were the agricultural and pastoral techniques of the Neolithic period. The specialization which was effected by the invention and diffusion of these techniques in its turn speeded new inventions, increased production and wealth, and made possible further types of specialization and additional wealth.

Money. True money is not confined to precious metals or to paper guarantees to pay in precious metal, but is a product which functions as an especially efficient equivalent for other commodities in the exchange of commodities. It is the most socially fluid, most neatly divisible, most portable, and least perishable of the surplus products which are sold in an economic system.

On the North Pacific Coast strings of clamshell disc beads and large valuable sea shells termed *dentalia* and gathered with much labor at especially low tides were used as money in the same way as paper dollars or coins are used today. Sea shells equated with and circulated freely as a value equivalent for any salable products such as slaves, blankets, furs, or beaten soft copper plates.

Where surplus products were few and interchanged sparingly true money did not develop; product exchanges in these societies were actually only gift exchanges. True money developed only in those food-gathering societies that had some surpluses, as on the Northwest Coast. In simple agricultural societies the numbers of surplus products exchanged became larger as techniques advanced and as numbers of specialists increased, and in consequence money developed.

Sea shells, teeth, or other forms of money were used before there was any extensive production of precious metals or of copper. Cowrie shells were employed in the agricultural-pastoral economies of West Africa and chocolate beans functioned as money in Central American agricultural economies at the time of the arrival of the Spaniards.

Trade and Markets. Trading of surplus products had virtually no economic significance in the simple food-gathering societies, where trading consisted only of the exchange of sea shells, pigments, and a few other things. There was also so-called silent trading in several regions, such as among the Eskimo and adjacent Indians of northern Canada, where members of one group placed a commodity at a site resorted to conventionally for trading, and returned to pick up the commodity placed there in exchange by the other group, without the traders' having spoken to or having seen one another.

The societies of the Pacific Northwest Coast traded in any village, but concentrated trading occurred in the larger and wealthy market villages such as Oregon City and the Dalles in the lower Columbia River valley. One village out of each regional group of twenty or more villages was a true market village. Any visitor could employ sea shell money or mere commodities for the purchase of slaves, furs, and a variety of artifacts. Bride purchase payments and gift giving were characteristic of the economy of the Pacific Northwest Coast area and functioned as a sort of trade or exchange that was of considerable economic importance.

True market villages were only in an incipient stage of development in those simple agricultural societies where relatively few sur plus products were made for sale, but there was some gift giving and exchange of products from village to village.

Market centers or towns developed to notable size in all more advanced agricultural and pastoral areas. To such markets journeyed the bearers of salable products such as woven stuffs, pots, fruits, basketry, and artifacts of many kinds. Markets were usually held periodically each third day or at other brief intervals. The nobleman whose governmental apparatus controlled a district might exact rentals from the sellers at the market, or might exact fees from those who used the roads leading to the market. Groups of merchants traveled with armed guards in the advanced agricultural areas of Central America and in some other parts of the world.

SELECTED READINGS

Barton, R. F. *Ifugao Economics*. Berkeley: Univ. of California Press, 1922 (Univ. Cal. Pubs. Amer. Arch. and Ethnol., Vol. XV, No. 5).

Firth, R. *Primitive Economics of the New Zealand Maori*. London: Routledge, 1929.

——. *Primitive Polynesian Economy*. London: Routledge, 1939.

Forde, C. D. *Habitat, Economy, and Society; a Geographical Introduction to Ethnology*. New York: Harcourt, Brace, 1934.

Foster, G. M. *A Primitive Mexican Economy*. New York: Augustin, 1942 (Monograph 5, Amer. Ethnol. Soc.).

Goldenweiser, A. A. *Anthropology*. New York: Crofts, 1937. Pt. 2, Sect. 1.

Herskovits, M. J. *Economic Anthropology*. New York: Knopf, 1952.

Hobhouse, L. T., G. C. Wheeler, and M. Ginsberg. *The Material Culture and Social Institutions of the Simpler Peoples*. London: Chapman Hall, 1915.

Lowie, R. H. *Primitive Society*. New York: Boni and Liveright, 1920. Pp. 205–256.

Malinowski, B. *Argonauts of the Western Pacific*. London: Routledge, 1922.

——. *Coral Gardens and Their Magic*. New York: Amer. Book Co., 1935 (2 vols.).

Mead, M., ed. *Co-operation and Competition among Primitive Peoples*. New York: McGraw-Hill, 1937.

Moore, W. E. *Economy and Society*. Garden City: Doubleday, 1955.

Notes and Queries on Anthropology. London: Royal Anthrop. Inst., 1929 (5th ed.). Pp. 122–142, 158–162, *et passim*.

Piddington, R. *An Introduction to Social Anthropology.* Vol. 1. Edinburgh: Oliver and Boyd, 1950. Pp. 256–317.

Polanyi, K., C. M. Arensberg and H. W. Person (eds.) *Trade and Market in the Early Empires.* Glencoe: Free Press, 1957.

Radin, P. *Social Anthropology.* New York: McGraw-Hill, 1932. Pp. 135–239.

Stern, B. J., ed. *The Family, Past and Present.* New York: Appleton-Century, 1938. Pp. 13–33.

Thurnwald, R. *Economics in Primitive Communities.* Oxford: Oxford Univ. Press, 1932.

Wagley, C. *Economics of a Guatemalan Village.* Menasha: Amer. Anthrop. Assoc., 1941 (Memoir 58).

CHAPTER SEVEN

FAMILY AND CLAN

Introduction. Every social system or community of primitive economic level has assigned to both sexes special sorts of essential work. The care of dependent offspring, especially those who are not yet weaned, is so taxing that work has always been assigned in such a way as to permit the mother to take care of her infant. Males naturally could not give birth to or nurse infants and as a result they could move about more freely in pursuit of foods to maintain survival of dependents, whereas women were relatively less able to do so. The biological role of woman was therefore a primary determinant of the family unit of husband, wife, and dependent offspring. The family as a social institution is thus not only universal now but it has been a universal feature of all human societies. It is likely that it has been a basic social relationship or "association" which has aided survival from Late Pliocene to modern times. The family has functioned not because it has been determined by instincts but because it has facilitated survival.

The precariousness and insecurities of living in societies with meager technology appear to have been such for long eras that several family units banded together both for more efficient defense and for more efficient production of food. Other persons, especially those who were kin, also helped in a variety of ways. Thus in addition to the small family unit the social relationship patterns of the small band or community, and the extended family or lineage, were present. These too could have been universal features of societies since the earliest times, again because they may have served so well for efficient survival. The clan, a lineage-like group, also appeared in various areas (see p. 173), but not everywhere because its functioning was very likely not indispensable for survival.

Special historical developments in the culture of different areas, their economic levels, and many other diverse conditions have resulted in strikingly variable manifestations of the small family, the extended family or lineage, and clan ties. The primary task of the present chapter is to outline some of the principal differences in the patterns of family, lineage, and clan structure and the possible causes for their formation and changes.

FAMILY PATTERNS AND CHILDHOOD

Monogamy. All available information on the way of life of peoples of simple food-gathering economies, as well as evidence of the kinds of families found in such societies, leads to the conclusion that a family composed of one male and one female, who cared for the needs of their immature offspring, may have afforded one of the most efficient ways of keeping down the mortality rate and facilitating community survival during the Pleistocene period. When a distinction is made between basic social relationships and relationships that are largely sexual, there is not a society in the world that is other than monogamous as far as the majority of its people go. The people in societies of low technological level cannot take care of unmarried adults who know only the skills of their own sex and not those of the other sex. All persons must therefore get married not long following puberty, or after the deaths of their mates, or after divorces; they would otherwise be a perpetual source of irritation or a burden to their relatives. Since every adult is usually married, most people must be monogamously married most of the time because the sexes are roughly equal in number.

However, a few people in every community can have and are allowed special privileges in marital relationships, if they wish them. The universal institution of the monogamous family therefore has interesting variants. There are polyandry or the polyandrous family, which has plural husbands, and polygamy or the polygamous family, more correctly termed polygyny, which is featured by plural wives. The controversy on whether the family patterns termed promiscuity and group marriage once existed will be discussed later.

Polyandry. A functioning family unit of one woman and plural husbands has long been supposed to occur in a small number of societies. In simple food-gathering economies it has been reported, for example, among Eskimos, Palawan Philippine Pygmies, and the western United States Shoshoneans. In wealthier agricultural-pastoral economies it has been said to have been present among Marquesans, some East Africans, Tibetans, the Todas of southern India, and a few others.

Polyandry has been admittedly rare. Claims for its presence suggest that less than 1 per cent of the peoples of the world's tribes or other politically independent units have permitted it. Moreover, where polyandry was permitted only some of the families were polyandrous while the majority of the persons in such societies lived in monogamous or polygynous families.

The evidence regarding polyandry among the Shoshoneans is that women had parity of status with men, and they therefore had freedom of choice to secure temporary support from other men during the absence of their own husbands. This was patently not polyandry in the sense of a familial pattern but was a special arrangement more or less required by severe conditions of living. A voluntary companionship with a temporary substitute for an absent husband is not a type of family unit or marital pattern. There may have been sexual consorting with more than one man, but that was not a form of marriage, and it has probably occurred in all societies in one way or another. The Shoshonean evidence has indicated only sexual, not marital or familial, polyandry.

Similarly a temporary stay of a man with an Eskimo couple was a matter of freedom of choice on the part of the latter. The sexual concomitants of his presence in the household did not transform the relationship into polyandry. It was still only a matter of permissible sexual behavior. Assistance rendered the boarder by the wife, in the form of cooking, sewing, or other services, was a matter of the hospitality and mutual aid which Eskimos rendered persons who were traveling or otherwise unable to secure such help. Comparable relationships are very likely found in other societies.

If long-standing domestic unions of one woman and two or more men are found, they may be termed polyandry. Such unions may have existed in societies where the technological level was so low that people lived with one another with a degree of mutual aid and good will rarely found in economically much more advanced societies. In these simple food-gathering societies mutual affection must have also developed to such a degree as to receive expression in terms of sex relations. Since in these societies freedom of choice was the same for both sexes, it may have been mutually agreed that several men should live in a functioning and long-term relationship with one wife. In other words, polyandry has not been well attested for simple food-gathering societies, but the kinds of social relationships found in them were such that evidences of a few relatively permanent polyandrous families may some day be found.

No polyandrous families have been reported for the advanced food-gathering societies nor are any well documented by writers on simple agricultural economies.

The reports of polyandry in Tibetan and East African agricultural-pastoral societies may only have been instances where male relatives in poorer families contributed to a bride purchase payment. These poor relations remained in the household of the married couple until they could leave after they themselves had finally acquired the wherewithal to purchase a wife. Before such leaving, a male relative may have had a temporary role in relation to his brother's property, that is, to the purchased wife, that simulated the role of the legal husband. This relationship may or may not be defined as polyandry. Since the third person left when he could afford his own wife, there is as good reason to characterize the family as monogamous with some temporary polyandrous concomitants, as to characterize it as an instance of true polyandry.

In southern India the Toda pattern was of another kind. Here a group of men owned cattle jointly and purchased wives who were each nominally married to only one man, who was to be the legal father of her children. But the wives and women of the Todas were on a very low-status level. They were little more than producers of children, and were handed about from member to member of the group of males that bought them. Again, the appellation of polyandry is subject to question, for in Toda society marriage was little more than a ritual device to denote a child's fictional paternity and a household unit of any kind at all barely functioned.

Marquesan polyandry appears to have been a matter of sexual

rights accorded other males by a wealthy husband. Again, this was sexual behavior of a special kind, not a marital or familial pattern.

The evidence for polyandry is therefore, all in all, extremely poor, although a very few and isolated instances of long-standing polyandrous unions may yet be found among a few families where the participants in the union all wished to have it so.

Polygyny. Polygyny, which means two or more wives living with one husband in a long-term marital union, has been forbidden in few societies other than our own.

In simple food-gathering economies polygyny was rare but permissible. Since the sexes were of equal status it was not often that a woman wanted another wife in her home. Occasionally, however, she asked her husband to take another wife, or she acceded to his wish for another. However, three or more wives were virtually never found in these societies, if for no other reason than because the lowly economy involved too much labor for the husband in fulfilling his portion of the household's productive work.

The advanced food-gathering societies of the Pacific Northwest Coast had hereditarily wealthy headmen who took it as a matter of social position to purchase from two to as many as five wives, but more than five were rarely found. A few well-to-do men who were related to headmen were also able to purchase second wives.

Simple agricultural societies with small surpluses were about as equalitarian as the simple food-gathering societies and therefore had the same sort of freedom of choice for both participants in marital relationships. Hence polygynous unions were extremely rare and they almost never consisted of more than two wives. A plural wife in these societies, as well as in the simple food-gathering societies, was free to leave the marriage when she found the husband to whom she wished to be married monogamously. This was not true in the case of the polygynous wife who was purchased by a wealthy headman on the Pacific Northwest Coast nor of the polygynous wives of the wealthy agricultural-pastoral societies.

All advanced agricultural-pastoral societies had polygyny among the wealthier classes, whose males could afford to buy plural wives. These societies were wealthy enough to permit the nobles or monarchs to exceed by far the maximum of five wives found in such families on the Pacific Northwest Coast. Some African monarchs, for example, have been reported to have had hundreds of wives.

Europeans have long thought that polygyny was degrading to its plural wives. However, in societies where plural wives freely choose to enter and remain in such unions, and the status of the sexes is equal, polygyny is not degrading. In societies where wives are purchased and the feminine sex is of inferior status, polygyny is not in itself degrading although it symbolizes the fact of lower status. It is the social system in these societies, not polygyny, that imposes degradation on all women. When Europeans forbid polygynous unions in such social systems, they are attacking the social system. The prohibition of polygynous unions assists women in raising their status because the whole system is being undermined. When European colonial governments have allowed a continuation of polygyny, they have done so in order to perpetuate a native social pattern that has facilitated their control of the native population.

The women who are plural wives in wealthy agricultural-pastoral societies are usually married to upper-class men; hence they are actually in a social position superior to the monogamously married women. Plural wives generally have easier domestic chores and are also better off in other respects. Humane and democratic persons are critical of polygyny because they cannot condone a system of wife purchase, nor an equation of human beings with commodities, nor a social system which places women on a status level inferior to men.

Little is known regarding consequences to personality formation due to the presence of plural wives and a large number of siblings. If the social system itself, rather than the polygynous household produced by the system, contains the ultimate determinants of personality formation, one may expect to find quite variable personality concomitants of upbringing in polygynous households, because polygyny occurs in many different types of social systems.

Promiscuity.   The absence of a stable family unit has been claimed for early Pleistocene eras, but no convincing arguments for such a stage in early human social evolution have been adduced. All of the economically most primitive societies known are characterized by monogamous families, with rare but permissible polygyny or polyandry. The lower the technological level, the greater need there appears to have been for a family of two persons, one a man who had relative freedom of movement, the other a woman who did not have to hunt or fish, and who could therefore bear and nurse her baby. It follows that monogamy may well have existed from the very beginnings of culture—that is to say, from Eolithic or earliest Paleolithic times. Promiscuous and brief unions would not have permitted the same degree of survival of dependent youngsters as did monogamous unions. The monogamous family and not promiscuity was, then, in all likelihood the earliest form of the family, and it has remained the dominant form in all societies.

Group Marriage. A functioning and stable marital union of a group of males with a group of females has never been found. The conditions of living in simple food-gathering economies were such that group marriage, if it ever existed, probably would not have worked out as efficiently in the tending of dependent youngsters as would the simple monogamous family. In any case there are no indications of anything that could be interpreted as group marriage in the known simple food-gathering societies. This evidence rules out the claim that any prehistoric eras witnessed a group marriage pattern, because no modern societies, whether of the food-gathering type or those economically more advanced, give evidence of group marriage.

Some evolutionists among anthropologists interpreted as evidences of group marriage the kinship terminologies of several regions which utilized the term *mother* to designate a number of maternal aunts, and the term *father* for a number of paternal uncles. If kinship nomenclature had actually survived from a stage of the evolution of the family characterized by group marriage, such kinship terms might be expected. However, this kind of terminology is plausibly explained not as a survival from an ancient stage of group marriage but rather as arising from the operation of a type of clan system (see pp. 173-175).

Endogamic and Exogamic Rules; Preferred Mates. Customs regarding persons whom one can or must marry and whom one should not marry are found everywhere. There is always a segment of the community from which no mate can be sought, involving exogamic rules, and a remaining portion from which the mate must be obtained, involving endogamic rules. The specific application of endogamic and exogamic rules varies from culture area to culture area. For example, rules of clan exogamy are often found under which a member of a clan cannot marry a member of his own clan without undergoing dire penalties. Sometimes one must not only marry outside of one's own clan but also outside a number of other clans, so that potential mates are perhaps to be found in only half the clans; that is, there is both clan and moiety exogamy. (For a discussion of clans and moieties see p. 173.) Encampment or village exogamy is found in a number of areas. Exogamic rules sometimes prohibit marriage between any known although distant relatives.

Brother and sister marriage is prohibited as incestuous, except in rare and especially wealthy societies (Hawaii, Inca, ancient Egypt, some Congo groups, and a few others) where royalty is expected to marry a sibling, perhaps to prevent a division of the royal properties. In these societies no one but the monarch is allowed such a marriage. Parent-child marriages are almost universally tabooed. Uncle-niece or aunt-nephew marriages occur in rare instances when the participants are regarded as hardly related because they are of different clans. The horror of incest is therefore not instinctive. It is a learned response, and the form and degree it assumes depends on the community's heritage of custom. This is shown by the fact that what is natural and a permissible marriage in one social system is unnatural and forbidden with aversion in another. On the other hand, rules of endogamy demand that the choice of a mate be within one's own class, caste, religious denomination, or racial group.

Sometimes a father's brother's or mother's sister's child or "parallel cousin" is taboo as a mate whereas a father's sister's or mother's brother's child or "cross-cousin" is a potential or preferred mate. Parallel cousins are sometimes given one kinship term, cross-cousins another; the former cousins are often felt to be more closely related, especially in areas where parallel cousins are members of the same clan and call one another brother or sister, and cross-cousins are of different clans and are not fictional siblings.

Customs are widely found according to which the deceased member of a marriage is at once replaced by a sibling or some other available relative. Where a husband is replaced by a brother or cousin it is called *levirate;* where a wife is replaced in analogous fashion it is called *sororate*. Such replacement was usually mildly insisted upon but still a matter of freedom of choice in simple food-gathering and simple agricultural economies. In the advanced food-gathering societies and in wealthier agricultural-pastoral societies where human beings have commodity value, great pressure is exerted by the lineage upon an unmarried member to replace the deceased in the marriage. Where polygyny is frequent an unmarried sister of the wife may choose, or be expected, to join her in the marriage. This practice is designated sororal polygyny. Another form of sororate is the marriage of the wife's daughter where the latter was born to a former husband.

Other customs are found where one or another relative is selected as a preferred mate. These kindred ties function in such a manner as to weld many persons into a large group, the members of which accord one another mutual aid. Societies of most advanced economies tend to weaken such heritages of extended relationship ties, because they are not especially useful when people have attained a degree of security by their numbers, wealth, and advanced technology. The more developed the economy becomes, the more attenuated the relationships between kindred outside of the small family unit tend to become.

Premarital Arrangements. The choice as to whom a person is to marry may be made exclusively by the two leading participants or, at the other extreme, exclusively by nonparticipants; that is, there may be the fullest freedom of choice or no freedom of choice whatsoever, as well as intermediate forms.

In both simple food-gathering and simple agricultural societies, the sexes are of equal status and no individuals are equated with commodities. The ultimate choice of a mate rests upon each individual within the prescribed limitations and the preferred patterns such as band, clan, or moiety exogamy, and levirate, sororate, and cross-cousin customs. A person may marry anyone who is his or her choice within that segment of the society open for choice. Since these communities are very small, lineages are closely knit in multitudinous interconnections of customary obligation and mutual aid,

and elders are deeply respected. The insistence, advice, and interests of many members of the community may serve as partial determinants of the choice made. Ultimately, however, persons are not forced to marry against their will in these societies and in this sense there is freedom of choice. Procedures and customs of this kind may therefore be regarded as marriage by affection or romance. It may not often be romantic love of the special type that has developed in Western civilization during the past 150 years, but in a very broad sense it nonetheless functions in a similar manner.

In technologically more advanced food-gathering and in wealthy agricultural-pastoral societies, the choice of the mate often depends upon the planning and decision of the parents or lineages, and the judgment of the two persons who are to be married is not sought. Usually a bride purchase price is paid by the boy's father or parents to the girl's father or parents. The girl is thus a unique sort of commodity bought by the boy's father, often with financial assistance from his lineage. The price paid may be divided by the girl's father among his relatives, with the former retaining a large share. The price may be in cattle as in Central Asia or East Africa, or in shell money and other valuables as on the Pacific Northwest Coast. The youngsters in lower classes in such societies may manage to have some indirect say in their marital fate, whereas those in the upper classes, who are much more valuable in monetary terms, may have less to say. Sometimes the bride of the upper class may not see her husband till the day of the marriage ceremony. Romantic love may, however, develop following the marriage.

In a number of regions of the wealthier agricultural-pastoral type, such as in eastern Siberia, a bride purchase payment in commodity wealth is the essential pattern but an actual payment in commodities is for some special reason not feasible. In such societies a groom may buy his future wife through labor service rendered over a period of months or years to his future father-in-law.

Marriage by capture is probably absent in simpler food-gathering and primitive agricultural societies, which are not predatory but feud or fight merely in self-defense or for revenge or to eradicate persons believed guilty of dangerous magic. In all probability the capture of either men or women occurred only at late periods of human history, in areas of more advanced economy and of predatory habits. Since sexually attractive women were especially valuable commodities in such societies, some of the more attractive captives might be freed and subsequently married. In other words marriage by capture is very likely not an ancient but a relatively modern premarital procedure. However, no large number of men in any community ever secured mates in such a fashion. Ceremonial or dramatic symbolization of capture may be found in a few regions but this does not imply an earlier stage of true marriage by capture.

Marriage as Secular.   The ceremonial by which two persons are joined in a marital unit is accompanied by a supernatural sanction in only a very few societies. In societies of low economic level the initiation of a new family unit is most often accompanied by ceremonial which symbolizes only the new productive, social, or interpersonal obligations assumed by the two main participants and by their kindred. A family unit functions in such a way as to divide the domestic duties of the two participants in both an efficient and a conventional manner. It lessens the wife's mobility so as to protect her when pregnant or when she is nursing her infant, and assigns special adults for the protection and care of growing youngsters. The family unit also serves to eliminate some of the burden of work and help that would otherwise be demanded from other relatives. The marital unit therefore functions as it does because of its efficiency as contrasted with any other sort of social unit devised for such purposes. That is why it is found at every economic level and is a feature of every community the world over. The social relationship of husband, wife, and dependent offspring also enables its members to develop a warmth in emotional ties, and a degree of emotional and ego security, which are highly pleasurable.

An important distinction must be made between the religious sanction for marriage of persons during the past centuries in our own culture and the essentially civil, contractual, or secular conception of mutual obligation and bonding in the marriage of persons in almost all other societies. In the latter, one of two families simply tendered one of their own members to the other family, in order to set up a new household unit whose functioning as such was necessary for community survival. The reciprocal obligations entered upon were not merely between husband and wife, but were also between the extended lineages from which each came. The attachment of supernatural sanction and religious rites to the declaration of such obligations and relationships can be accounted for only in terms of the special historical circumstances of our culture.

Age of Mates. The lower the economic level the more important it is that parents be soon released from the labor of taking care of children, so that they can devote their energies to infants or thoroughly dependent youngsters. If children practice at adult forms of work from the ages of six or seven till puberty, they can master techniques sufficiently well to become producers who can carry a fair share of community work. Boys therefore practice at the techniques of hunting and fishing, and learn to make the equipment and gear employed in such work, and girls learn what is defined by convention as woman's work. It is therefore intelligible that most societies the world over witness the marriage of youths not long following puberty. No exploitation of children is involved here, for the youths are ready for marriage in their own expectations, in the seriousness of their interests, and in maturity of temperament and judgment. In many economically primitive societies an unmarried person as old as seventeen or eighteen is *ipso facto* a person who must be in some manner sadly inadequate, for he or she would otherwise long since have been married. Furthermore, the very terms *bachelor* and *old maid* are likely, in the languages employed, to connote much more than the fact of never having been married. They may connote an entirely unattractive person, obviously one whom nobody would want in marriage. The lowlier the economy, the more necessary it is that everyone be married so as to function most effectively in productive work, and without being a burden to others. Persons long unmarried who are attached year in and year out to the households of married couples are rare among peoples of primitive economy, for the burden might be intolerable over any long time. Widows and widowers therefore manage to remarry with alacrity. Perhaps it is the conditions under which people live that make everyone a little more tolerant of others' foibles and inadequacies, and less encumbered by qualms at marrying other people. Perhaps also the people of societies with lowly economies are fond of one another as persons, to a degree not comprehended by many in our society. Economically backward peoples are not naturally more generous, affectionate, or loving, but their conditions of living effect lineage and community ties of great range and intensity. Few among us would be heard to say, "I dearly love all my in-laws." But something of the sort is not rare in an economically poor social system.

These are some of the factors that account for early marriages as well as for marriages between persons of markedly different age levels. In societies where there is full freedom of choice there is sometimes found, for example, a deeply romantic attachment that eventuates in a successful and long-sustained marriage between a man and a woman who is old enough to be his grandmother. The rare instances of such marriages in our society are viewed more or less askance, and it is unlikely that the marriage has been determined by romantic love. However, marriages of persons of disparate ages in some societies of low economic level quite often contain an important component of genuine and deep affection. All the emotional responses of people who live under entirely different conditions cannot be judged by the measuring rod of the emotional responses that are engendered by our own heritage of values and conditions of living. In other social systems the older people may attain such community stature and may be so successful in the pursuits most respected by the people, that grey hairs and wrinkled skin have different symbolic meaning from what they usually imply in our society. Old age is to all peoples tragic in certain ways, but it may also be esteemed because of the worth of those who have reached it.

The pattern of ideal age mates in our culture is of mates of identical age, or of a male not many years older than a female. But special historical circumstances and not a universal biological response have determined this cultural ideal. The past practice of a male's buying a physically fresh and young person of the opposite sex takes the form at present of a man's being expected to support a young and dependent woman. In simple food-gathering and simple agricultural societies there is no such heritage, and many marriages may thus be found where the female is somewhat older than the male, and not infrequently great disparity is found in the ages of husband and wife. Custom has made our values and emotional responses seem right and natural, but the customs of other peoples make their values and emotions seem just as right and natural to them.

Marital Residence. When the married couple go to live in the husband's community, this is termed *patrilocal residence;* when they go to the wife's community, this is termed *matrilocal residence.* In societies where the sexes are of equal status, the couple often have freedom of choice of residence and they may even reside apart from either parental community.

Matrilocal residence has been said to be a causal factor in elevating a woman's status, but there are usually other factors that are the decisive determinants of such status. The custom of patrilocal residence does not in itself lower the status of woman, but where there is such a custom, woman's status has generally long been low because of the operation of other determinants. (See pp. 181–184.)

Customs of matrilocal or patrilocal residence are to be explained in terms of the specific conditions and historical developments of the culture areas. Exclusively patrilocal residence usually indicates that the woman is purchased property. But there also may be good economic reasons in a few simple food-gathering societies for a woman's going to live in her husband's district. For example, he may be thought to have special supernatural ties with his own locale, and for the sake of efficient hunting, his presence there may be regarded as indispensable.

Stability of Marriages. Culture areas differ in the stability of marital unions. All peoples of primitive economy allow divorce under given circumstances.

Where marriages are by freedom of choice and the sexes are of equal status, divorces may be frequent until the first baby is born. But in such societies the family union is not lightly dissolved when the obligation to take care of an infant has developed. The general rule for such societies is that most unions remain permanent following the birth of infants. A period of years of caring for dependent children usually serves to cement the married couple, who often attain a ripe old age together.

Where marriages are by bride purchase or equivalent forms, divorces may tend to be infrequent at any time. This is because the monetary tie functions as a powerful agent to hold the couple together. The departure of the wife, even upon considerable provocation, would be resented by those who had bought her, for loss of valuable property is resented. The husband would have less occasion to choose to leave his wife because of his position as purchaser and hence controller of the familial situation. The wife would be deterred from leaving her husband because her own family would be reluctant to return part or all of the price that had been paid for her.

Barrenness is almost always judged as a most serious inadequacy in simpler economies, and it warrants either the separation of mates or the addition of a sister or cousin in the marriage. Ill treatment also warrants separation in societies with meagre surpluses but it constitutes less justification in societies of more advanced economy where women are bought in marriage.

The Child in the Family: Early and Late Childhood.   The forms and customs by which infants are cared for are diverse, although affection for them is usually deeply felt. In societies of primitive economic levels the resources in soft foods may be so few or the beliefs regarding infants may be such that mothers may nurse babies for a protracted period, sometimes for two or more years. If the mother cannot nurse the baby, some other woman may help out. Customs vary widely in relation to the frequency of nursing, the manner and age of weaning, and other forms of infant care.

Theories regarding temperament, character, and personality patterns consequent upon such customs are moot, as has already been noted (p. 126). At the present stage of psychological research such theories cannot be regarded as sufficiently documented to warrant the presumption of a causal connection, for example, between late weaning and one trend in personality in a social system, and early weaning and another or contrary trend observed in another social system. Customary forms of granting of oral or other physiological satisfactions to infants, and of withholding or frustration of infants' wants, have been claimed as basic determinants of the most central personality patterns of adults. Such claims have been made confidently by psychoanalysts on the premise that the infant years are of strategic importance in the development of the most decisive emotional and social responses. Such theorists claim that responses learned in later childhood years are in a sense secondary and fit into deeper and primary grooves that have been already cut in the earliest infant months.

The ultimate decision as to the relative importance of responses stimulated in the earliest months, by contrast with responses developed in other childhood years, depends upon many kinds of research which must still be undertaken. For example, one must ascertain whether or not features of emotional and social behavior of a one- or two-year-old infant can be replaced or superseded by entirely new and equally basic responses and behavior that are developed in the years immediately following. If the personality has been shaped and rendered relatively fixed by the vicissitudes of the first five or six years, the consequences of knowledge that that is so will be tremendous for education, psychiatry, and many other fields. But if the early child personality can be thoroughly revamped in the course of experiences of the years from six to puberty, the consequences of such knowledge will also be momentous. In the absence of sufficient evidence for either possibility, it would appear that the most fitting as well as cautious premise on which to proceed in present-day education or psychiatry would be to allow for a human nature so plastic, so constantly re-educable, and so full of ever new potentials for the fixing of deeper traits of personality, that the years following six may be thought of as years wherein the basic personality may remain quite malleable under favorable conditions. The question of plasticity of personality following puberty is also moot. It would in fact be hasty to presume any great degree of rigidity in emotional or social reactivity for any age level providing that the new kinds of stimuli were presented under favorable conditions.

Several important problems have been left unanswered by those psychoanalysts who insist that customs of infant nursing, weaning, cradling, feeding, the controlling of processes of elimination, and the like are the most decisive in the shaping of the social and other aspects of later adult personality, and that differences in the personality of peoples in different culture areas can be traced to such ultimate determinants. One untouched problem is to determine the historical and other causes for the development of different customs in the handling and disciplining of babies. Another problem, already indicated, is to determine whether or not the social and other aspects of later adult personality are more certainly traceable to the social conditioning of youngsters immediately after they have been weaned and are toddling and playing about.

The social environments of children following weaning and learning to walk vary remarkably the world over. For example, Eskimo toddlers are often devoid of an opportunity to play with other youngsters and they may be guarded and disciplined only by the two parents. On the other hand, in parts of western North America, Indian youngsters from three to puberty are said to have left the village houses shortly after dawn, not to return till sundown. They were tended by older children in a kind of jungle play area hundreds of yards from the adults. As far as is known they saw little of adults until evening, when they ate dinner, sat in utmost quiet, and listened respectfully to parents and other elders until sleep overtook them. Most disciplinings, admonitions, and care came from other children, not from their parents or other adults. The isolated child of an Eskimo household is therefore socially conditioned in a manner strikingly different from a child who enjoys the interpersonal relationships of a crowd of children of varying ages at play, supplemented by adult group contacts in the early evening and early morning. In fact, few societies have witnessed so constant a supervision by individual parents, and so meagre a degree of relationship with others, as do the Eskimos and many middle-class families of our own society. Most societies of primitive economy provided a kind of village playground for youngsters immediately following their weaning, an environment which seems to have been a primary factor in their social conditioning. The environment of contacts with their parents or other immediate relatives such as the paternal aunt, maternal uncle, or one or another grandparent was secondary to that of the village playground. The consequences to personality of one or the other pattern of childhood social relationship remain to be formulated. The task is formidable, and the ethnographic and comparative scientific research needed is so full of possible pitfalls as to warrant great caution before interconnections which are claimed between the social behavior of one or another type of childhood and one or another type of adult personality may be regarded as established.

Further caution must be observed, because of the possibility that the experiences and social conditioning of the years immediately preceding puberty may contain determinants of adult personality much more influential than some psychoanalysts are now inclined to allow. Up to the present, few well-controlled scientific observations of the behavior of children during these years have been conducted.

Youngsters of societies with primitive economies manifest intense interest in preparing themselves during the six to eight years preceding their puberty, for entry into marriage and for adult participation shortly following puberty. In simple food-gathering and agricultural societies all adults participate on a basis of parity in production and all other forms of work. In consequence the attitudes and behavior of adults toward six- or eight-year-olds exhibit a degree of respect for the individuality and maturity of the youngster which adults in our society often lack for their twenty-five-year-old sons and daughters. People in many such primitive economic systems tend to consider their prepubescent youngsters as equals, and there cannot fail to be distinctive consequences to personality and mental development when youth is treated in this way.

In advanced food-gathering and agricultural-pastoral societies where women are salable commodities and are not expected to participate as fully as men in economic, social, or political activities, the relation of adults to prepubescent children, especially female children, is likely to be less respectful and to operate on a presumption that a youth "is still only a child," as in our society.

Wherever older children do most of the tending of younger children, and the adult relationship to children is predicated upon respect for the will, independence, and worth of the child as a near-adult, one is not likely to find sadism or brutality in adult disciplining of children. Corporal punishment is often taboo, and rational, social, religious, or other sanctions are more likely to be used to secure desired behavior.

One of the most striking differences between our own society and the economically primitive societies is the degree to which prepubescents make their own contributions to the family and community. Among the peoples of backward economy, the placing of responsibility upon the shoulders of older children for the day care of younger children undoubtedly serves to mature the older children and to give them profound satisfaction in significant work well done. Hunting and fishing on a scale smaller than that of adults, the gathering of bark, firewood, berries, roots, and other objects by the girls, and the early ventures in making of gear, basketry, and pottery are likely to be commended with pride by older people, and they serve to mature the youngsters socially.

Puberty rituals or initiations are practiced in many regions. They are found for both sexes in many parts of Africa and Australia and for pubescent girls on the Pacific Northwest Coast. The approach of a puberty so ritualized probably engenders serious sentiments among children. At a comparable age in our society children are not often overly sobered by the proximity of an elementary school graduation program, but that is because our graduations do not function as symbols of acceptance of children as respected adults and full participants in the community. More comparable are the present-day communion and confirmation rites of religious groups. A transition rite, or *rite de passage* as termed by Van Gennep, must symbolize metamorphosis in important social relationships in order to make a profound impression and to beget an anxious anticipation of new obligations and acceptances.

Education. All types of social systems have established periods of organized education. However, the actual process of education always includes informal learning which begins in the first years of life. For many years youngsters learn techniques, customs, folklore, and all the many features of their cultural heritage without formal instruction by assigned pedagogues. Youngsters thus learn by listening to, watching, and accompanying the older people. Learning is by doing, with constant guidance, admonition, and encouragement from all the older people, and often with the especial interest or concern of an uncle, aunt, or grandparent. One of the most important factors in the learning process is motivation. Where every feature of the culture is in a sense immediately present rather than at a physical distance from the home, as in a downtown office, suburban factory, or library, and where adult participation is going to begin at puberty, the youngster is motivated to master techniques and learn as much as possible before he reaches puberty. Rewards for learning and achievement are derived from the approval or overt praise of respected adults.

A smaller segment of the cultural heritage may be imparted by formalized instruction, which usually occurs around the time of puberty and functions as part of the transition from childhood to adult participations. This transition has often been termed initiation. At this age, for example, youngsters among the Australian Blackfellows, East Africans, and Indians of the northwest United States are taken in hand, either as individuals or in groups, by specially assigned elders and are formally instructed for a period of months, in folklore, ceremonials, songs, and sometimes even in some ethical standards. The details of the content or manner of such formal teaching have not often been carefully noted by field ethnographers.

In some of the wealthier agricultural-pastoral societies formal instruction may be entrusted for longer periods to priests or to specialists of several kinds whose work is sometimes limited to the training of upper-class youngsters.

Lineage Relationships. Relationships found between relatives and in-laws vary from the extreme of extraordinary familiarity to the other extreme of avoidance. Familiarity customs may involve a joking relationship, employment of violently abusive language, the stealing or destruction of valuables or other personal effects, horseplay, and other comparable practices. Avoidance customs may take the form of speaking to an in-law only through an intermediary, the prohibition of bodily exposure in the presence of certain relatives, never looking directly into the face of such relatives, not using their personal names, and not eating in their presence. The avoidance may be between brother and sister following puberty, between in-laws, and between other members of the lineage.

In many culture areas there are extremes neither of familiarity nor of avoidance, but the frequency of occurrence of such extreme forms is striking. The fact that these customs are not universal indicates that they are not instinctive. Each instance of extreme or mild familiarity, or extreme or mild avoidance, can usually be accounted for in terms of the larger heritage of customs, beliefs, and basic social relationships of the area if and wherever enough is known of such matters. In all cases behavior of these types is a matter of correct etiquette, of doing a conventional, expected, and right thing so that the relative is not affronted, humiliated, or depreciated. It is an expression of due respect for the other person, manifested in a traditional manner.

These phenomena of familiarity and avoidance may be explained by the fact that in the social systems of primitive economies large numbers of relatives, or extended lineages, functioned as organized groups for mutual help. Insecurities and tensions arising out of living with extreme intimacy and permanence under technologically primitive conditions were such that in the course of time social behavior toward one or another relative tended to be patterned in ways which served to simplify or stylize social arrangements. Behavior towards one relative became stereotyped in one direction and towards another relative in another direction, as determined by the peculiar social features of each culture area. The stereotypes of social etiquette served efficiently where daily fumbling and readjustments might develop into emotionally unbearable or dangerous tensions. If a person acted automatically according to that etiquette stereotype which was customary for a particular relative, there would be no interpretation that there had been behavior of a suspicious, disapproving, or aggressive kind. Hatreds, passions, loves, frustrations, or aggressions would have become nonapparent because of the etiquette patterns, and everyone could manage his daily encounters without too much pulling, tugging, hauling, and emotional strain. In a society such as ours where social relationships with distant relatives approach a vanishing point, there is little that would be functional in etiquette stereotypes for such relatives, and in fact such etiquette is almost lacking. For close relatives such as parents-in-law a few vestigial etiquette forms are retained. But in our rapidly changing society such etiquette towards parents-in-law is now almost nonexistent so that tensions which frequently develop with such relatives now have to be adjusted anew, and often painfully, according to the special circumstances of each case.

Where male children have special obligations to the mother's brother and are singled out for special attention by him the relationship is termed the *avunculate*. Where female children have an analogous pattern of relationship to the father's sister, it is termed the *amitate*. Such ties, which have been found on every continent, sometimes seem to bind these relatives one to another to a degree as great as the tie between parent and child. Often the relationship is no more than a kind of corollary to a clan system (see p. 174). For example, the boy's maternal uncle is of his own clan, while his father is of another clan, or the girl's paternal aunt is of her own clan. It is to be expected therefore that such uncles or aunts would have special duties and responsibilities towards such nephews or nieces. In societies with features of this kind the parent-child relationship is thus significantly modified and supplemented. One reflection or symbol of such a social relationship may occur in the kinship terminology, for the uncle may be termed father, the aunt may be termed mother, and the children of such relatives may be called brother or sister rather than cousin.

CLAN AND TOTEMISM

Clans. On every continent some culture areas display clan groups within the communities, and other areas are clanless.

A clan, sometimes alternately termed a *sib,* is never a tribe as such. It is only a pattern of unilateral social relationship within a larger community pattern. It is composed of a number of actual and supposed relatives each of whom determines his membership in the clan by inheritance from one parent to the exclusion of the other parent for purposes of reckoning clan relationship. Some areas have matrilineal clans, and other areas have patrilineal clans, depending on whether membership is reckoned by inheritance from the mother or the father. Membership is a fact of birth and is therefore automatic. Almost all clans are exogamous—that is, a clan member does not seek a mate among the members of his own clan. For example, a member of the Bear clan would not marry another Bear because such a union would be regarded as incestuous.

Whereas the family unit is universally present and is always bilateral, the clan pattern which is found in many but not all communities is only supplementary to the family pattern. It constitutes a unilateral extended family or lineage group, some members of which are so remotely related as to be actually no closer biologically than are nonmembers. But from the clan members' point of view other clan members are considered relatives. Whereas a new family develops with a marriage and disappears with deaths, a clan goes on. In a sparsely populated district it may become extinct because the few children in it are of the sex other than that by which membership is transmitted.

Clans function in societies of meagre technology where persons are allied with one another as fictional relatives in order to carry out effectively obligations, services, and community assignments. In societies of most advanced economies, these functions are taken care of by other social groups. In simple food-gathering economies, however, groups are so small and function so well that few have clans or clanlike groupings except in Australia. On the Pacific Northwest Coast clans are found along the northerly third of the Coast but they are not found on much of Vancouver Island or further to the south. Clans appear in many if not most of the agricultural and pastoral areas. There seems to be a fuller role for a clan type of organization in social systems that are not on the most lowly level of technology, except in the case of Australians.

It is not known how early clans developed in human history but there seems every reason to presume that social relationship patterns as basic as the small family unit, the extended bilateral family, the work party of one or the other sex, and the encampment or small community were developed much earlier than was the clan. The very spottiness of the distribution of clans, their absence from some areas on every continent, and the universality of relationship patterns such as family, work party, and community indicate that in general the clan is a pattern of less importance and with fewer functions.

Clan functions or features almost always include exogamy (see p. 173); usually kinship terms of special kinds, for clan members of the same age call one another sibling and clan members of different ages are designated grandparent, parent, child, or grandchild; sometimes mutual aid of an economic sort; inheritance of property; sometimes responsibility for a member's misdeeds; and not least frequently, as among Australians and southwestern Pueblos, the performance of special rituals which are of outstanding importance to the whole community. Clans in a community or tribe may number from two to more than a dozen.

Where a community has only two clans, or two larger exogamous groupings each comprising several clans, these are called *moieties,* from the French word for half, *moitié.* Moieties may function as sides in competitive sports in the Eastern Woodlands, to fulfill obligations of a ritual kind, and as exogamous units.

Where two or three of the many clans in a community share functions of one or another kind, and two or three of the other clans also join for analogous services, they are referred to as linked clans or *phratries.* For example, a community could have two moieties, five or six phratries, and a dozen or more clans. But in spite of all these patterns of social relationship, none have as important a functional .ole in community life as the individual family.

The term *clan* covers a great variety of functions that may be assumed by unilateral pseudo-lineage aggregations. For example, Pacific Northwest Coast clans, which were matrilineal in southern Alaska and largely patrilineal on Vancouver Island, were few in number. Each clan functioned, in addition to the ways already indicated, as owner of a special myth heritage which validated crests and special privileges. But in the Southwest Pueblo area where there were many clans in each pueblo, the clans approximated hereditary committees upon which the community had conferred permanent assignments for the performance of special curing and rain-making ceremonials. Each of the many clans of a Southeastern Woodland village conducted ceremonies that honored clan animal ancestors.

Totemism. Mention of Southeastern Woodland and Australian clans brings up the anthropological concept of a totem, or of totemism. This is a concept which has been conceived in various ways. A serviceable though narrow definition would confine totems or totemism to certain phenomena of those special areas where there are clans each of which has an animal or bird name, and where the clan members believe themselves descended from their own clan animal or bird ancestor, refuse to eat its flesh or wear its fur, and also conduct magical rites of one or another kind that relate to such a creature. If this definition is used, then a great many but not all clans the world over are possessed of a totemistic facet.

It depends upon whether a narrow or broad definition of the term is used as to whether or not the Pacific Northwest Coast clans are to be judged totemistic in character. The members of these clans do not presume descent from a totem ancestor nor do they conduct magical ceremonials relative to such an ancestor or to his living animal descendants. The Southwest Pueblo clans are hardly totemistic, whereas the Eastern Woodland and Australian clans are.

Totemistic features actually comprise only a segregated group of features that may accrue to a clan heritage involving supposed relationship to animals. Totems and totemism are therefore only a curious facet of the larger fact of clan organization.

A popular and layman's use of the term *totem* is for any sort of supernatural being, such as an animal, plant, insect, or bird, which people of primitive economy accept as potent and capable of giving human assistance. There may be no objection to the broad use of the term *totem* for any sort of guardian spirit or other being with supernatural powers, but the tendency in anthropology has been to confine the concept to clan animal ancestors, and in some writers to include plants and natural forces which are identified with clans.

In layman's usage the term *totem pole* is well established as the term for a sculptured column placed in front of the cedar plank houses of southern Alaskan Indian villages. The sculpturings symbolize actors in lineage- or clan-owned myths. In a narrow definition of totems and totemism these carved posts are not representative of totems or of totemism, nor are they literally totem poles.

Clan and Totem Origins. It cannot be determined whether all clans and totemistic features found in clan systems had one origin. There may have been plural causation in terms of varied factors producing analogous social forms in different areas and times. A custom of patrilocal residence may have developed because of the need for men to continue residence in the hunting and fishing areas familiar to them or owned by them. This would constitute a situation favorable for patrilineal reckoning of membership and loyalty to unilateral lineage. It would be strengthened, as on the Pacific Northwest Coast, by private-property ownership by the lineage of such districts or sites. Where matrilocal residence had developed because of women's responsibility for garden work or private ownership by the lineage of tilled lands or of the house, favorable situations existed for the development of the clan. However, matrilineal clans are sometimes found in societies with patrilocal customs, and there are many other exceptions and complexities that suggest caution against an oversimplified theory of origins. The totemistic application of the names of fauna, as well as of flora or other natural phenomena, to co-operative groups of persons is probably associated with animistic ideology, which supposes that spiritual powers are present in the material world and can be secured for human purposes. The legitimate search for initial origins is, however, ordinarily less satisfying and less fruitful than the study of historic changes and proliferations of later forms and of the contemporary functioning of social life and culture.

Earlier writers were intensely interested in sib or clan origins and many believed that matrilineal clans constituted an earlier stage which tended to evolve into a higher stage of patrilineal clans or gens. If this process of change in sib customs actually occurred, one would expect to find matrilineal clans almost everywhere correlated with simpler economies and patrilineal clans or gens with advanced economies. But the wealthiest communities of the Pacific Northwest Coast, located in southern Alaska, exhibit matrilineal clans, and an adjacent area to the south in British Columbia which was not quite so wealthy was patrilineal; furthermore, patrilineal customs appear to have been in process of replacement by matrilineal customs possessed by the wealthier northerners. In Australia both matrilineal and patrilineal clans are found, without significant correlation with differences of economic level. In fact, the presence of both types of sib in food-gathering areas as in areas of more advanced economy suggests that matrilineal clans cannot be shown to have had temporal primacy or to have displayed any notable tendency to develop into patrilineal clans. Wherever changes of such a kind may be demonstrated for advanced agricultural-pastoral societies, the likelihood is that newly developed and valuable forms of property had gone into the hands of the masculine sex and such ownership constituted the decisive cause for the change to patrilineal reckoning of clan membership.

SELECTED READINGS

Barnouw, V. *Culture and Personality*. Homewood: Dorsey, 1963.

Cohen, Y. A. *Social Structure and Personality: A Casebook*. New York: Holt, Rinehart and Winston, 1961.

Goldenweiser, A. A. *Anthropology*. New York: Crofts, 1937. Pp. 296–374.

——. *History, Psychology, and Culture*. New York: Knopf, 1933. Pp. 213–356.

Haring, D. G., ed. *Personal Character and Cultural Milieu*. Syracuse: Syracuse Univ. Press, 1956.

Honigmann, J. J. *Culture and Personality*. New York: Harper, 1954.

Hsu, F. L. K. *Psychological Anthropology*. Homewood: Dorsey, 1961.

Kaplan, B. ed. *Studying Personality Cross-Culturally*. Evanston: Harper & Row, 1961.

Kluckhohn, C., H. A. Murray and D. M. Schneider, eds. *Personality in Nature, Society, and Culture*. New York: Knopf, 1953.

Kroeber, A. L., and T. T. Waterman. *Source Book in Anthropology*. New York: Harcourt, Brace, 1931 (rev. ed.). Pp. 267–338.

Linton, R. *The Study of Man*. New York: Appleton-Century, 1936. Pp. 152–230.

Lowie, R. H. *Primitive Society*. New York: Boni and Liveright, 1920. Pp. 1–185.

Malinowski, B. *Sex and Repression in Savage Society*. New York: Harcourt, Brace, 1927.

——. *The Sexual Life of Savages in North-Western Melanesia*. New York: Halcyon, 1929.

Mead, M. *Coming of Age in Samoa*. New York: Blue Ribbon, 1928.

——. *Growing Up in New Guinea*. New York: Morrow, 1930.

——. *Sex and Temperament*. New York: Morrow, 1935.

Murdock, G. P. *Social Structure*. New York: Macmillan, 1949.

Notes and Queries on Anthropology. London: Royal Anthrop. Inst., 1929 (5th ed.). Pp. 17–110, *passim*.

Piddington, R. *An Introduction to Social Anthropology*. Vol. 1. Edinburgh: Oliver and Boyd, 1950. Pp. 107–216.

Stern, B. J., ed. *The Family, Past and Present*. New York: Appleton-Century, 1938. Pp. 1–67, *passim*.

Whiting, J. M. W., and I. L. Child. *Child Training and Personality*. New Haven: Yale Univ. Press, 1953.

CHAPTER EIGHT

CLASSES, AGE GRADES, AND CLUBS

Introduction. The social relationship patterns designated community, family, extended family or lineage, and clan are either universal or widely found among the peoples of primitive economy. The present chapter treats of additional patterns of social relationship, some of which were not frequent features of social life in simple food-gathering economies. Age grades, clubs, and secret societies, which are found widely in advanced food-gathering, simple agricultural, and advanced agricultural-pastoral societies display great diversity of form and function. Class stratifications begin to develop in simple agricultural communities as well as in advanced food-gathering groups.

Rank. Whether a society has hereditary wealth and class differences as in advanced food-gathering and wealthy agricultural-pastoral societies, or lacks such status by birth and is thoroughly democratic, the individuals of each community are always ranked or evaluated in several ways. People, even twins, always vary to some degree in their general intelligence, character, bravery, reputation for ability to use supernatural power, skill in basketry, artistry, sense of humor, moods, and other attributes. Personal merits, demerits, skills, clumsiness, or disagreeableness are widely discussed and judgments are made accordingly. Moreover, in the most democratic and equalitarian societies there are age levels, if not formalized age grades, so that an ill-informed eight-year-old is ranked in one way and an oldster, who is rarely or never so ill-informed, in another way. However, it is of major importance not to confuse such rankings and evaluations, which are found in every society of all types, with class status, which is on another level of analysis and which appears in societies where economic inequalities exist.

Class. Because economically substantial surpluses were not pos-sible until the superior cutting tools of the Upper Paleolithic period were developed, it is likely that all societies until that time lacked inequalities in ownership of productive resources or significant forms of wealth. Hence all societies till the Upper Paleolithic period very likely lacked differences in class status. There were many differences in informal evaluations or rank, but not in actual class levels.

The concept of social class, like the concepts of clan, totem, or totemism, has been described or employed in different ways. A rea-sonable degree of agreement as to what ought to be meant by class may be obtained by borrowing or adapting the usage of economists, which defines class as a segment of the population whose pattern of social relationships is determined by its special ownership of the most productive resources, or by its special relationship to the owners of such resources.

Therefore in simple food-gathering and simple agricultural soci-eties of a relatively pure type there are no social classes, for they lack significant economic stratifications of any kind. The produc-tive resources are the property of all persons of the community; there are no differences in ownership of economically significant forms of wealth. For example, the fact that one Eskimo owns one sled, five dogs, three harpoons, and has one wife, and another Eskimo owns two sleds, twelve dogs, six harpoons, and has two wives, does not indicate a difference in economically significant wealth or in social class. Nor is it evidence of class status that the community has high regard for the energy, resourcefulness, courage, intelligence, and artistry in carving of the one man in contrast with the community disdain for the slovenliness, laziness, stupidity, and ineptitude of the other man. The Eskimo society where men differ markedly from one another in personal attributes and possessions is nonetheless equalitarian in a socio-economic sense because there is group ownership of major productive resources such as caribou herds and sealing areas. In a socio-economic sense the one Eskimo is not more powerful through his ownership of personal property than the other, although he is undoubtedly much more admired, envied, or valued. He is not a member of a superior class although he is a definitely superior man.

In spite of an absence of agriculture or economically important domesticated animals, the societies of the Pacific Northwest Coast had inequalities in one or more major productive resources such as slaves, fish-spearing sites, hunting areas, and shellfish beaches. The distribution of major products was also unequal because the upper class took larger portions. There was a class of hereditarily wealthy village headmen and their closer relatives, sometimes termed "good" persons; a class of poor or "pitiable" persons; and a class of raid-captives or purchased slaves.

Most peoples of primitive economy live in advanced agricultural-pastoral societies in which the major productive resources are the private property of individuals or lineages of upper class, and distribution of the products derived from these resources favors the members of that class. They have therefore a heritage of class stratifications. It is probable that all the communities of Africa except the Bushmen had classes. The Indians of the southern Mississippi Valley and of portions, if not all, of the southeastern United States had classes. Most of Mexico, Central America, and the Andean highland countries had class stratifications too. Except for Australia and Tasmania almost all volcanic or larger Oceanian islands south and east of Formosa were similarly stratified into classes.

The special features of these class patterns varied tremendously from area to area. For example, the upper class of the Anglo-Egyptian Sudan was composed of the cattle owners, who were numerically much larger than the lower classes, which included fisherfolk and iron workers; here the relatively few classes were also castes, in that each conducted its own specialized sort of productive work. In India there were many classes, which in each instance were also occupationally specialized and hence were castes. The classes of Latin American Indian and of most other areas have not yet been well described.

The existence of classes based on the unequal ownership of major productive resources does not mean that there are unbridgeable partitions between these classes, for the social process of movement of some persons from class to class is widespread.

Status of Sexes. Some writers have portrayed a halcyon era of the past when women were matriarchs, the carriers of the cultural heritage and the rulers of the community. Anthropological evidence regarding this or other claims concerning the history of woman's social status is fragmentary, but a few inferences can be made.

Until the later portions of the Paleolithic period, each sex had its assigned special occupations and skills and there was probably no more than a sexual division of labor. Nature had assigned woman the community obligation to bear infants and to nurse them. In simple food-gathering societies the men had no such obligation and enjoyed greater freedom of movement. They carried on certain tasks that were of great importance to the community and that would be ill-advisedly entrusted to those who must replenish the community, because such tasks involved long journeys, violent exertions, and immersions in chilly streams or seas. Hence the men hunted and fished, while women were assigned any productive work that could be done by persons who lacked much freedom of movement for long periods.

In such societies the productive work of the sexes was in general evaluated as equal. The occasionally greater dangers and glamor of men's work did not accord higher status to males. Men owned no productive property of a kind that women were forbidden to own. Women were not necessarily servile drudges. They merely did another kind of work that was of equal value to the community. Men were not chiefs or rulers. Bands or villages were run democratically, although those who had more mobility were often assigned the more responsible work. The important point is that during the long Paleolithic eras the sexes may well have enjoyed virtual equality of status. One finds no evidence that there ever could have been matriarchs—that is, women who prevailingly had economic or other dominance. Matrilineal clans or other forms of reckoning were consequences of residence or other customs, and were irrelevant to status.

Perhaps only towards the close of the Paleolithic period, and with the first development of advanced food-gathering societies, did men first capitalize on the biological fact of their permanent exclusion from childbearing and nursing and on their conventional assignments to work that demanded freedom of movement. Men were not necessarily so much more muscular that raiding and seizure of slaves became a new and proper sphere of activity for them, but they were freer than women for predatory ventures. At the same time they capitalized in still another way on their greater mobility. Some of the earliest developments of forms of private ownership of productive property and of large expropriations of surpluses were precisely in those resources in fishing and hunting that were men's traditional occupations. These must be among the main factors for men's rise in social status. Their acquisition of the most productive resources (the control of which had to go to those who were most mobile), their consequent assumption of governmental power, and their correlated acquisition of taxes and tribute-like revenues were the new features of social life which raised their status. In these advanced food-gathering societies all persons tended to become equated with monetary values and women were overtly purchased in marriage. Slaves were purchased too, and so every form of human property—that is, slaves and women—became a kind of marketable commodity. On the whole, woman's status on the Pacific Northwest Coast was not low, but it was definitely not on a parity with men as in simpler food-gathering societies.

The tendencies set in motion in advanced food-gathering societies were intensified in the much wealthier agricultural-pastoral societies. The status of woman appears to have reached all-time lows in Bronze Age and Iron Age societies such as those of the classical Mediterranean periods in Europe and in India, China, and Japan. In all these societies woman participated little in those activities which tied in with the major productive resources. In a few societies, as in parts of India, woman's status was that of another kind of slave. In societies such as these one also finds prostitutes and concubines, who were the publicly frank forms of purchasability of women.

With the disappearance of war-captive and chattel slavery following the dissolution of the Roman Empire, and with the development of guilds in the Middle Ages, a new process was set in motion. The status of woman began to improve and a few occupations were opened to her in addition to domestic chores. The factory system of recent years has speeded up the process. Woman's status has risen and occupations have opened up for her with almost spectacular rapidity, expanding the opportunities for the development of her personality. Where scientific medical care and nurseries have been made available in modern societies, the disabilities historically associated with her bearing and nursing of children have become a less decisive factor in determining her status. Women's rights have, moreover, been inextricably bound up with the broader problems of human rights, and improvements in the status of the people through other economic and social changes have invariably had favorable repercussions on the status of woman. Where the dominant ideas of a community become democratic and humanitarian and are geared to the enlargement of human freedom and the release of human potentialities, woman's status advances. On the other hand, in periods of cultural retrogression, as for example under fascism, when human rights are curtailed, the earlier customs which sanctioned and enforced the subordinate status of woman are revived.

Age Grades.   The abilities of people to do adult kinds of work vary in the same general way in every society. There are always children, who are only approaching competence at adult occupations; there are adults, who in societies of primitive economy are usually considered such from about puberty and until advanced years; and there are elderly people. Just as there is a natural sexual division of labor which segments all peoples of primitive economy into equal halves, so too there is everywhere a natural age grading into at least three levels—children, adults, and the aged. There are in some regions subdivisions of each of these three primary age gradings which are socially and historically and not biologically determined.

The passage from childhood to adult life occurs in most societies about the age of physiological puberty, because adequate mastery of adult techniques and occupations has been achieved by that time after some years of practice. In some of the advanced food-gathering and wealthy agricultural-pastoral societies where a woman becomes at puberty a kind of sexual commodity, the exact moment of puberty is the transition point from the age grade of childhood to that of adulthood. In some of these societies, because of her loss of her value as a potential bearer of children a woman becomes a member of the age grade of old women at menopause.

Highly formalized age grades occur in a few societies, mainly those of greater wealth. In parts of West Africa and East Africa each age level includes all persons who were born from four to seven years apart. The male members of an age grade constitute almost a club. They dress alike, change their garments together as they ascend to a higher age grade, are assigned special work, in East Africa enter the army together, are discharged from the army and then marry at about the same time, and so on throughout life. Another system of age classes has been found in parts of the Plains. Our own society also has many features of the order of formalized age grading in terms of schooling, occupations, dress, and the like.

Clubs. Few food-gathering communities ever developed clubs of any kind. Among the Plains Indians, however, there were a number of secular men's clubs, voluntarily joined, in which the members learned special songs and dances and feasted together. Such clubs served their members and the community in various ways. Some functioned as mutual help groups, like extended lineages and clans. Others served as a kind of special police during a crucially important buffalo hunt or for armed defense of the community. When these Plains Indians became horse pastoralists and considerable inequalities in wealth developed, entry into clubs was purchased.

No clubs of the kind usually termed secret societies are found among simple food-gathering peoples. Several such clubs developed in the wealthiest communities of the Pacific Northwest Coast where wealthier men performed special songs and dances or ceremonials. The so-called secret societies of the agricultural Southwest Pueblo Indians are actually ceremonial clubs, admission to which by both sexes occurs either by virtue of being cured by a club member or by birth. The main functions of Pueblo clubs are curing or rain making; in each instance incantation formulas were phrased in terms as if they were not for the sake of the members but rather for all the community. In advanced agricultural-pastoral areas, such as parts of Melanesia, a number of secret clubs are often found, membership in which is purchased and honorary advance in which depends upon the wealth of the individual or of his lineage. Usually in advanced agricultural-pastoral societies whenever there are women's clubs they are separate from men's clubs.

The functions and degree of secrecy of clubs vary widely in different areas and types of economy. Among the functions rendered by clubs are mutual help, military service, curing, rain making, and property acquisition by the pocketing of fees paid for entry. The special economic, cultural, religious, or other features of each area must be examined in order to determine the probable mode of development of the clubs and their functioning.

Etiquette. The customs followed in salutations, departures, sitting, eating, washing, love-making, trading, use of personal names and other titles, joking, mention of the deceased, and distinctive behavior towards persons of variant age level, sex, or class are legion, and knowledge regarding their origins, changes, and functions is slight or unavailable. Such etiquette among every people involves a long inventory of features of correct or preferred social behavior. It is impossible to say how people would behave socially were they without such acquired and stylized ways of doing things, for there is no natural or instinctive way of associating with others. Manners vary from the extreme of simplicity, directness, and unceremoniousness to an opposite extreme of elaborateness, indirection, and ceremoniousness. The advanced food-gathering and agricultural-pastoral societies tend to develop greater punctilio, indirection, and ceremoniousness than the societies where there is less tension in social relationships and certainly much less ill-will, snobbery, and hypocrisy. This is not to say that the people of simple food-gathering and agricultural societies lack good manners or elaborate etiquette.

Complexity in Social Organization. The evaluation of socioeconomic systems or culture areas as simple or complex has differed from writer to writer. The criterion of complexity has been variously accepted as defined in terms of the productivity of tools and food-producing procedures; in terms of the numbers of "associations," that is, the numbers of classes and clubs prevailing in addition to the primary social relationship patterns of small family, extended family, community, and clan; or in terms of the complexity of the kinship system and terminology. For example, it is often said that the Australian Blackfellows have a complex social organization. What has been meant is that customs relating to clan and kinship patterns are curiously proliferated among these technologically simplest of surviving peoples.

Judgments of the simplicity or complexity of the whole network of socio-economic features and patterns of a culture area seem to be subjective rather than objective or mathematical. At present the most justifiable procedure seems to be to avoid characterizations of simplicity and complexity in over-all social organization. One may, however, speak of a relatively simple or complex technological heritage, kinship terminology, clan system, or other segment of the heritage of a culture area.

SELECTED READINGS

Childe, V. G. *Social Evolution*. New York: Schuman, 1951.

Hsu, F. L. K. *Clan, Caste, and Club*. Princeton: Van Nostrand, 1963.

Kroeber, A. L., and T. T. Waterman. *Source Book in Anthropology*. New York: Harcourt, Brace, 1931 (rev. ed.). Pp. 317-338.

Lowie, R. H. *Primitive Society*. New York: Boni and Liveright, 1920. Pp. 257-357.

Mead, M. *Male and Female*. New York: Morrow, 1949.

Mishkin, B. *Rank and Warfare among the Plains Indians*. New York: Augustin, 1940 (Monograph 3, Amer. Ethnol. Soc.).

Piddington, R. *An Introduction to Social Anthropology*. Vol. 1. Edinburgh: Oliver and Boyd, 1950. Pp. 175-216.

Tozzer, A. M. *Social Origins and Continuities*. New York: Macmillan, 1925. Pp. 189-198.

CHAPTER NINE

LAW, JUSTICE, GOVERNMENT, AND WAR

LAW AND JUSTICE

Law. Law is the complex of remembered or recorded cases, precedents, procedures, and decisions, the people's customs and mythology, and the social or governmental machinery which resorts to such sanctioned sources for solutions of tension situations within the community. Every society possesses such a heritage of precedents, ideas, and customs, and a machinery of procedure which can be applied to new conflicts in social relationships. In this sense law is not a special and systematized kind of social control which is developed only in complexly organized societies, but is universal like the family, language, or art. However, the law operates in different ways in different social systems.

The simpler the technology and economic system, the less complex is the governmental machinery that is applied to tension situations. This is because the networks of kinship and other interpersonal obligations and ties are such as to constitute a kind of informal social machinery which functions in solutions of tension situations. Societies of lowest technological level are therefore not at all anarchic or lawless but their law operates in another way from ours. The small size of the community, its magico-religious sanctions, and its people's judgments hold each member of the community in line in a fashion that no densely populated region of advanced economy can effect. In an economically primitive society the potential lawbreaker does not often dare to commit disapproved acts because everyone knows what everyone else is doing, and the evaluation of one's behavior by the community determines one's success in life. In such a society public opinion is a major portion of the social machinery of the law, and it can usually operate more directly, rapidly, or crushingly than the impersonalized machinery of formal legal procedure, courts, and government in our complex society.

In many of the simple food-gathering societies the force of public opinion or the democratically-arrived-at decision of the majority is implemented, if need be, by organized action by an armed and voluntary committee which resorts to physical force or some sort of punitive measure. For example, a shaman who is accused of poisoning people through magic may be killed by such a committee, which operates something like a frontier posse in our society. In these societies the hundreds of remembered cases and the community decisions, the mythology, and the mores (see p. 193) constitute the body of precedents and laws. Faced by new trouble the community often democratically discusses its problem, applies sanctions from the mythology, precedents, and customs, and acts by according responsibility to those who indicate a willingness to accept the assignment for carrying out decisions. The simple agricultural societies are comparably democratic and act in trouble situations in much the same simple and direct way. Some simple food-gathering and agricultural societies limit the size of the group which discusses the trouble situation. A small number of the most respected older people who know the mythology, customs, and precedents most fully are informally delegated and they operate as a kind of tribal council or court which is ultimately democratically representative of the entire community.

Law in the undemocratic Pacific Northwest Coast societies is another matter. The government and the law were embodied in the person of the village wealthy headman. He was his own prosecuting attorney and judge, and his assistants carried out his decisions. Mythology, customs, and precedents probably always operated as limits upon these chieftains. Since they took a portion of every fine imposed, and had plenty of other opportunities for aggrandizement, they perhaps exhibited no frequent motivation to engage in extremely unconventional decisions which broke spectacularly with precedents. They had to live with their people and it would have done them little good to have acted cruelly and unconventionally. There is evidence that they often exercised power in a benign rather than an exploitative fashion.

The major formal difference between law in economically primitive societies on the one hand, and the more advanced food-gathering and agricultural-pastoral societies on the other, lies in general in the fact that one government is democratic, the other undemocratic, and governmental machinery is democratically delegated in the one case and autocratically assumed or appointed in the other to make decisions and to put the law into effect in a specific tension situation. The chief who broke the law or who transgressed custom could hardly be treated punitively in an advanced food-gathering or agricultural-pastoral society, except where he committed an offense against some other chief. He solved tension situations caused by his subjects by exacting fines or compensation money from offenders; he took a portion of each fine that he ordered paid to injured persons; he ordered executions and had his own assistants carry them out.

The law of advanced agricultural-pastoral societies is a further development, and in very wealthy societies an elaborate one, of the pattern of social relationships found in advanced food-gathering societies. Courts are set up by the chief or monarch and judges are appointed and supported by him. The governmental machinery of law thus tends to develop autocratically. Basic functions of this law and machinery are to secure revenue, obtain fines, expropriate offenders' property, and lessen the nuisance of trouble-makers who every so often disturb the position or comfort of the autocrat and his entourage, or who threaten their property and status.

Types of Offenses. A contrast may be made between crimes, which are offenses against and punished by the community, and torts, which are wrongs against and punished by individuals or their kin. The lower the technological level the relatively larger the percentage of torts, wherein the hurt individual and kin resolve the matter without action by the community. On the other hand, there are in societies of lowest economic level offenses which injure the entire community that are responded to by the community and that may be termed crimes; for example, the breaking of an Eskimo food taboo may be judged so calamitous that the entire community participates in punishing the offender, though he may be forgiven if he confesses his guilt.

Definition of crime as an offense against the community has to be qualified for advanced food-gathering and agricultural-pastoral societies, which are not democratic and in which certain offenders are handled by the self-perpetuating aristocracy and their legal and judicial arm, not necessarily with the well-being of the entire community in mind.

Evidence. Evidence of a concrete kind as well as witnesses are resorted to in all societies of primitive economy, when the case is of a kind that is not customarily solved by one or another type of special procedure such as oaths or ordeals, the latter a device found primarily in the Old World. The taking of an oath of innocence does not constitute evidence of innocence in our society but in a culture where belief in the vengeance of the supernatural is great, a guilty person is less likely to swear to being innocent. Nor would one feel today that the victor in a wrestling match or the survivor of a poisonous decoction in an ordeal had by such success exhibited evidence of innocence. But again in a society where few or none were skeptical regarding the supernatural, the guilty person would be expected to fail in the ordeal imposed. His capacity to withstand it would be impaired.

Motive. The weighing of intent to injure may be only a partial factor in the democratically conducted considerations of a simple food-gathering or agricultural society where the bare fact of injury or loss is of great moment to the harmed person and his kin. He and they must have that which was lost replaced. The swung axe which slipped out of one's hands and killed a bystander had, after all, killed a valued member of a family, and therefore no matter how innocent of evil intent the act was, the loss must be made good in some way. The extent of the loss is what has to be considered, and the case is resolved accordingly. On the other hand, a democratic society also lacks motive for cruel retribution when the perpetrator of an unintentional deed is one of the community, and in such a case the lack of intent is weighed. It may be enough to replace an accidentally killed person with someone who is unmarried. If the killer is an outsider, however, his motivation may be ignored.

Compensation. Trouble situations were handled in advanced food-gathering and wealthier agricultural-pastoral societies by monetary payments, with the amount in each situation determined by precedents and the decision of the autocrat varying of course according to the social status of those injured. Even murders or deaths thought to be caused by magic could be resolved by payments of money, as were any and all other offenses on the Pacific Northwest Coast. In the simpler economies gifts could be used to assuage some hurts, but tension situations were more often solved in other ways. Obviously compensation money would not appear in social systems that lacked money, that is, in simple food-gathering and simple agricultural societies.

Trials. Trials of accused persons no doubt occur in all types of social systems. The less advanced economic systems generally subjected some accused and witnesses to interrogation where the evidence was unclear before decision. The chieftains of the Pacific Northwest Coast sometimes interrogated the accused persons and witnesses, in a relatively informal trial.

Formally-set-up courts with appointed judges appear in the wealthier agricultural-pastoral societies as adjuncts of the state, possibly among the Aztecs of Mexico and the Incas of Peru, and definitely in the Guinea-Sudan countries. Among the latter there are courts, judges, prosecuting and defense attorneys, and other features of court procedure which, in general terms, are similar to European developments of recent centuries.

Justice. Little research has been conducted which would reveal the degree of humanitarianism, the extent of recourse to logic, and the premises or originality of the decisions made in tension situations in any types of social systems of primitive economy. An analysis of recordings of cases and decisions made by the Cheyenne Indian council claims a high level of jurisprudence in a Plains social system characterized by democratic features. In recent centuries, however, the Cheyennes have been in process of change to horse pastoralism and inequalities of wealth.

In general, imprisonment as a punitive solution appears only in the wealthiest economic systems. The peoples of primitive economy resorted to gifts, payments of fines, floggings, body mutilations, capital punishment, and other solutions.

The likelihood of just solutions would seem to be better in the societies of less advanced economy which are fundamentally democratic than in societies where inequality prevails and where a more or less autocratic hereditary personage made decisions about other people's lives, or assigned the work to judges appointed by him. The motivation of autocrats and their judges would be mixed at best, for frequently desires for profit or power rather than for justice would determine the decision.

Ethics, Mores, and Customs. Mores or folkways have long been familiar terms. They cover all those customary, relatively unconscious, unformulated, and largely unquestioned usages or forms of social behavior which the community approves. (The term *mores* is usually applied to those customs which have the force of law and ethical connotations that folkways lack, but the distinction between the two types of custom is by no means well defined.) When usages are formulated, they are given usually in the mythology or in the words of ancestors who sanction them as right and good.

Among people of primitive economies ethical behavior is almost always social behavior which is in line with the mores or folkways. A person is conceived as right or good not because what he does or is has received supernatural sanction or relates in any way to commandments pronounced by the supernatural. He is right or good simply because he has not contravened custom. In other words, ethics is a secular body of customs, folkways, or mores. Unlike our European heritage, ethics has little or nothing to do with religion or supernatural admonitions.

When an individual perpetrates some unethical, that is to say, uncustomary social behavior, a trouble situation may develop. It is usually solved in a secular way, without intervention of those who represent or interpret the supernatural.

GOVERNMENT AND STATE

Introduction. The topic of the government of peoples of primitive economy cannot be discussed as a unit except to contrast its simplicity with our own wealthy societies for the degree of complexity of structure and the development of specialized functionaries. As in the case of other highly varied patterns of social relationships among the peoples of primitive economy, a class ¬ication of existing intergrading forms may be made in terms of a few major contrasting types. The analysis of each of these will serve to point up the contrasted processes that have appeared in the different types of socio-economic systems.

Democratic Governments. Government in the simple food-gathering societies is fundamentally democratic. The term *gerontocracy,* rule by older men, often employed to characterize Australian government, demands qualification. Actually the people of a basically democratic and equalitarian small autonomous community such as an Australian encampment are likely to follow those who are most experienced and learned, and of either sex. No doubt all simple food-gathering societies are more or less guided by older people of both sexes. Important ceremonial and other functions assigned to men are led by the better informed men; ceremonials or other duties which are conventionally women's work are led by the better informed women. The basic feature of government in such societies is usually government by majority rule, with leaders often elected or replaced by those who have been assigned to one or another community responsibility. The Australian clans are kinds of hereditary organizations with permanent assignments to special magico-religious tasks. There are other and voluntary bodies, each with its leader selected by the members.

The essential functioning of government in simple agricultural societies is the same. Their small agricultural village often governs through universal adult participation as a kind of town meeting. There may be hereditary groups such as clans which serve the whole community. There may be voluntarily entered organizations, clubs, or so-called secret societies, each of which democratically selects its leaders.

Neither simple food-gathering nor simple agricultural societies have chiefs in the sense of autocratic functionaries. Powerful, self-perpetuating, or hereditary leaders who are not subject to a majority decision of the people are conspicuously absent. But the speakers, heads of groups, emissaries, or other types of leaders found are usually older people, because in a democratic group whose insecurities are many the older people are likely to be more resourceful, experienced, and safe to follow.

Undemocratic Governments. Government on the Pacific Northwest Coast was equivalent to the hereditary village wealthy headman. He was supported by his ownership of one or more productive resources such as slaves, fishing sites, hunting areas, or the like; by his acquirement of a larger share of proceeds of major fishing, hunting, or plant collecting; by portions of fines collected, and by gifts that were in effect a kind of tribute from the villagers; by the work done by his wives and the other persons who attached themselves to his household; or by the armed retainers who protected him or helped him raid distant villages for valuables and slaves. Well-to-do men were his relatives or allies, and they may have had influence upon his decisions, but in effect he was a kind of princeling on a very small scale. He may have had a speaker, and an emissary or two, in addition to his armed followers.

Government among most peoples of primitive economy—that is, in advanced agricultural-pastoral communities—is undemocratic and in the hands of the largest owners of lands, domesticated animals, and slaves. These chiefs, princes, potentates, monarchs, or whatever one may wish to term them are supported by soldiery or police groups of varying size, and by civil officials. The latter collect tribute, taxes, and fines and they constitute judgeships, courts, and even priesthoods in some instances. They may in some regions manage provinces. Other wealthy property owners may meet in feudal-like assemblies and exert some degree of influence upon the hereditary ruler.

Federations. The potential for complex governmental organization of one or another kind, such as federations, is present at every level of economy in time of special need. A number of democratic hunting peoples can become allies and each be represented in a temporary confederacy. So too peoples in agricultural societies of all kinds have engaged in temporary alliances. For example there were elaborate federations in the case of the Iroquois, Creek, Choctaw, and other groups of eastern North America.

FEUDS AND WARS

Feuds. A useful distinction may be made between small-scale fighting and feuding, and large-scale fighting or warfare. Fighting has probably always occurred, but fighting on any large scale, that is to say warfare, probably developed only in the Upper Paleolithic and later periods.

Information available regarding the motivations for and nature of fighting among simple food-gathering peoples can be employed as suggestive of the probably meagre extent of killing that occurred during the long Paleolithic eras. Societies of simple food-gathering type have murders because of jealousies, retaliatory murders or feuds in instances of deaths thought to be caused by magic, and murders of trespassers upon hunting or other food-productive areas which belong to the community. Occasionally an entire encampment may be wiped out because of its refusal to give satisfaction for the murder one of its members committed. In general, a single death is followed by only one or two deaths in retaliation. Such killings may, however, string along into a feud or vendetta and may be prolonged for generations.

Probably some advanced food-gathering and agricultural-pastoral societies witness a comparably small extent of killing and for motivations similar to those of simpler societies. This kind of social phenomenon may hardly be designated as warfare.

War. The earliest and most primitive beginnings of true warfare, in the sense of more extensive slaughterings, are best exemplified in some of the societies of the Pacific Northwest Coast. The phenomena there observed provide the only suggestions as to what may have occurred in some culture areas of the Upper Paleolithic period. The wealthier nobles of the Lower Columbia Valley and the coastal districts of British Columbia and southern Alaska engaged in raids on villages in order to secure money, other valuables, and slaves. A large percentage of the beleaguered villagers were sometimes killed in the attacks, which usually occurred before sunrise when the often unsuspecting victims were torpid and off guard.

Where more or less pacifistic simple food-gathering and simple agricultural communities found themselves contiguous to communities that had lately developed a predatory and wealthy agricultural-pastoral economy, a heritage of petty fighting that was no more than a sort of feuding and murdering was supplemented by plans for larger-scale fighting for purposes of defense or retaliation. In other words, warfare as practiced in the less economically advanced areas has been usually developed by groups that were geographically marginal in those areas, and contiguous to areas and populations in which predatory warfare had lately developed. For example, in pre-Columbian centuries marauding Athabaskan groups of the Southwest states had involved the relatively pacifistic Pueblo communities in occasional warfare.

Virtually all advanced agricultural-pastoral societies have developed social forms and heritages of warfare. Although the initial motivation for an onslaught on another community might sometimes have been magico-religious, the culmination of the conflict almost always witnessed the seizure of wealth and slaves.

Simple food-gathering and simple agricultural societies usually fought on a small scale so as to kill only a very few persons. Often their fighting was accompanied by torture and the death of those captured. But advanced food-gathering and agricultural-pastoral societies, whose leaders were sometimes less angry than predatory, tended to enslave rather than to torture their captives, as well as to seize other forms of property such as money, lands, and herds.

Although a fairly sharp dichotomy in motivations may be indicated, care should be taken to avoid too sharp a contrast in methods of fighting. Not all the petty fighting of the less economically advanced peoples has been characterized by torture and killing, nor has the wholesale capturing and massacring of the economically more advanced been invariably accompanied by the enslavement of those who were not killed. Oceanian peoples such as some Indonesians and Melanesians fought not in order to secure slaves but for heads in addition to valuables.

The capture of persons whose bodies or portions of anatomy are subsequently cooked and eaten is a feature of few if any simple food-gathering societies. Cannibalism has not been shown to be a frequent feature of societies on the most primitive economic levels, in spite of the *Sinanthropus* remains which give some suspicious indications of gnawing of human bones. There are suggestions of a slight development of magico-ceremonial bitings of human flesh in the wealthiest districts of the Pacific Northwest Coast.

Cannibalism in relation to captives appears to be limited to a few areas of rather advanced agricultural-pastoral economy. The motivations for such indulgence have not often been studied in a trustworthy manner by the excited or horrified reporters of such practices. In many instances one may assume, however, that acquirement of magical potency rather than the desire for food is the central motivation.

SELECTED READINGS

Barton, R. F. *Ifugao Law*. Berkeley: Univ. of California Press, 1919 (Univ. Cal. Pubs. Amer. Arch. and Ethnol., Vol. XV).

Childe, V. G. *Social Evolution*. New York: Schuman, 1951.

Fortes, M. and E. E. Evans-Pritchard. *African Political Systems*. Oxford: Oxford Univ. Press, 1940.

Goldenweiser, A. A. *Anthropology*. New York: Crofts, 1937. Chap. xxiv.

Hoebel, E. A. *The Political Organization and Law-ways of the Comanche Indians*. Menasha: Amer. Anthrop. Assoc., 1940 (Memoir 54).

——. *The Law of Primitive Man*. Cambridge: Harvard Univ. Press, 1955.

Kroeber, A. L., and T. T. Waterman. *Source Book in Anthropology*. New York: Harcourt, Brace, 1931 (rev. ed.). Pp. 346–373.

Leach, E. R. *Political Systems of Highland Burma: A Study of Kachin Social Structure*. Cambridge: Harvard Univ. Press, 1954.

Llewellyn, K. N., and E. A. Hoebel. *The Cheyenne Way*. Norman: Univ. of Oklahoma Press, 1941.

Mair, L. *Primitive Government*. Baltimore: Penguin Books, 1962.

Malinowski, B. *Crime and Custom in Savage Society*. London: Kegan Paul, 1926.

Notes and Queries on Anthropology. London: Royal Anthrop. Inst., 1929 (5th ed.). Pp. 142–167, *passim*.

Piddington, R. *An Introduction to Social Anthropology*. Vol. 1. Edinburgh: Oliver and Boyd, 1950. Pp. 319–355.

Radcliffe-Brown, A. R. "Primitive Law," in *Encyclopedia of the Social Sciences*, IX (1933), 202–206.

Radin, P. *Social Anthropology*. New York: McGraw-Hill, 1932. Pp. 27–131.

Rattray, R. S. *Ashanti Law and Constitution*. Oxford: Clarendon, 1929.

Richardson, J. *Law and Status among the Kiowa Indians*. New York: Augustin, 1940 (Monograph 1, Amer. Ethnol. Soc.).

Turney-High, H. H. *Primitive War*. Columbia, S. C.: Univ. of S. C., 1949.

CHAPTER TEN

SUPERNATURALISM: MAGIC AND RELIGION

Introduction. Magic and religion of one kind or another are undoubtedly present among all communities on primitive economic levels. Patterns of supernaturalism can best be discussed by segregating their ideological premises and content from the behavior involved.

The ethnocentric conceits of European observers, the frequently wretched rapport between them and their native informants, and the often hit-or-miss methods of observation have made the available printed data on the multifarious phenomena of supernaturalism uneven when they are not irresponsible and valueless. A great deal is known regarding supernaturalism in a small number of areas, but few if any individual communities have been exhaustively described. The variety and subtlety of religious conceptions, emotions, and nuances are such that only the most painstaking researches can reveal them. Descriptive field research on matters of the ideology of the supernatural, and on the correlated thinking and feeling of the people, therefore, demands verbatim dictation in the native language as well as summary formulations by the outside observer.

Animism. About seventy-five years ago Edward B. Tylor pointed out that all peoples in primitive economies believed in animism, that is, in the existence of intangible, nonmaterial, or spiritual beings which may be souls, ghosts, ancestor spirits, fauna, flora, ogres or monsters, or simply objects. The origins of beliefs in such spiritual beings are probably multiple, as Tylor suggested. The presence of vitality in a living person which is unquestionably absent from a corpse results in an animistic interpretation. The persons and things heard, seen, or felt in dreams, or in temporary hallucinatory experiences as in hot weather or when a person is exhausted, or when he is under the influence of drugs, yield the same result. Additional experiences which bring about or reinforce animistic beliefs are echoes, reflections in quiet pools, or other natural phenomena.

Tylor contended that once the basic premise of an animistic ideology—belief in the existence of many individual spiritual beings and souls—had been developed, the path was laid for eventual development to later stages of religious ideology. But before the second stage was reached the original belief in souls and spirit-beings had come to include beliefs in malevolent spirits or demons, and in the spirits of ancestors. Tylor presumed that the souls, ancestral spirits, and other supernatural beings of the first developmental stage tended to change as a second stage into other, higher, or more grandiose forms of supernatural beings such as nature gods. Neither proof nor disproof is available for such a sequence of stages because the peoples who are of the lowest economic level are not well enough known to indicate that they are largely or exclusively animistic. In fact, other forms of supernatural concepts, such as that of a single deity, also appear along with animistic concepts among such peoples.

No historical or developmental trend can therefore be portrayed in the ideology of the supernatural, from simple or pure animism to other types such as polytheism, the belief in plural gods, or to a kind of monotheism, which is the belief in one especially powerful or only one powerful god. Several simple food-gathering peoples, such as some Australians, appear to believe in a superior deity at the same time that they believe in many spiritual beings; that is, they are both animistic and monotheistic (see p. 201). In spite of the lack of evidence that animism is a dominant feature of the ideology of the supernatural among simple food-gathering peoples, it is nevertheless universally found among such peoples as well as all other peoples with primitive economies.

The special form of animism termed ancestor worship is on the whole meagrely developed wherever it appears among American Indians. It is not found everywhere among New World or Old World peoples. It is characteristic principally of some of the wealthy agricultural-pastoral societies such as those of some Sudanese and Bantu-speaking Negroids, and in socio-economic systems of more advanced levels as in ancient China.

Animatism and Mana. Another type of concept regarding the supernatural is termed *orenda* by the Iroquois, *manitu* by some Algonkins, *wakonda* by some Sioux, and *mana* by some Melanesians. This concept holds that a nonmaterial, impersonal, nonindividualized spiritual essence pervades all things, manifests itself in inanimate and animate things, can be employed or tapped as a source of great power, and is of miraculous efficacy.

Anthropology has not yet proved the universality of this notion of a supernatural or cosmic power which is diffuse and all-pervading rather than specific and individualized as in animism. But there can be no doubt that animatism or the *mana* concept was present on every continent. There is also no question that animatism could have developed under the conditions of living and thinking possible for peoples of simple food-gathering economies, and that it did so in some instances. It may be as ancient as, if not earlier than, animism. Moreover, animism and animatism are not necessarily mutually exclusive. Both may be present as in Melanesia.

Polytheism. Still another type of belief in the supernatural, the belief in more than one great spiritual being or in gods, is widely found and is possibly present at all socio-economic levels. It receives special elaboration in and is especially characteristic of some advanced agricultural-pastoral socio-economic systems and of cultures like those of ancient Egypt, Mesopotamia, Greece, and Rome. Anthropologists do not now accept, however, the evolutionary formulation of Tylor that an initial developmental level of animistic beliefs in a multitude of souls, ghosts, and other individualized spiritual beings tended to be succeeded by a higher developmental level of religious ideology termed polytheism, the belief in plural gods. There may have been such a trend, but proof depends on the establishment of the fact that polytheistic conceptions are rare among food-gathering peoples, and that such conceptions are predominant among the agricultural and pastoral peoples who not long before had had food-gathering economies. This has not yet been established.

Monotheism. The widely held idea that the belief in only one god, monotheism, is of recent development has not definitely been proved to be correct. However, no absolutely pure monotheism has ever developed among peoples in primitive economies and has never characterized any such society. This is known for societies of primitive economy because of available evidence regarding the universality of animistic ideologies among them. Yet the synchronous occurrence of such animistic ideologies along with a monotheistic-like belief in a high god is certain. Present knowledge of peoples in primitive economies suggests that there is no reason why a god concept should not have been present in Paleolithic and in modern food-gathering heritages at the same time that animistic beliefs were held. Where there are polytheistic beliefs there can also be, at the same time, beliefs in spirits, *mana,* and in one superior god, comparable to a monotheistic concept. There is nothing mutually exclusive about these four concepts of the supernatural, and sufficient evidence is lacking to enumerate their probable order of development. Furthermore, one cannot assert that a monotheistic concept tended to evolve often from an earlier stage of polytheism. It is possible that some polytheistic beliefs are historical combinations of several monotheistic concepts from each of several peoples whose ideologies have fused.

The absence of a monotheistic or polytheistic belief may be termed a kind of atheism, but all peoples in primitive economies, however atheistic, believed in animism or animatism or both. Pure atheism and concomitant absence of belief in any supernatural presence constitute a very late development as in India and Mediterranean or Western civilizations.

Magic. *Magic* is the term used to designate a special kind of behavior, not necessarily religious, which follows from the acceptance of beliefs in one or another type of supernaturalism. If people believe in animism they may act so as to get certain things done with the help of the spirit-beings whom they believe present. If people believe in *mana* or animatism, they may act in a somewhat different way in order to effect desired ends with the help of the impersonal sort of power they presume can be tapped. They may also assume that certain things will happen inevitably because the power has always operated in that way. If people believe in a pantheon of deities, one or another of those deities will be propitiated, sacrificed to, or wangled in some way in order to bring about other desired ends. However, the essential characteristic of magic is that its procedures tend to be mechanistic and to function automatically if one knows the proper formula. Religion and magic are thus alternative techniques, sometimes supplementary to each other and used by the same person, for the achievement of goals by means other than through natural processes.

Frazer contended that in certain general respects magical beliefs and behavior resemble scientific beliefs and behavior, for both magic and science assume that successive events are interconnected and that preceding events are the causes of consequent events. Magic is, however, an inventory of beliefs and forms of behavior which is not subject to criticism, recheck, and elimination if unsubstantiated; and contrary evidence is generally unrecognized, dismissed, or explained away. Science on the other hand requires validation and verification and yields to criticism and revision. Magic asserts and acts upon improbable causal interconnections and dynamic processes. It is very bad science indeed.

Malinowski suggested that the strength of conviction in presumed interconnections of a magical kind, that is to say of an unverifiable and improbable kind, lies in the insecurities in the way of life and the limitations or inadequacies of technology and resources of the peoples in primitive economies. Magic is thus wishful thinking and overhopeful behavior. It is given some of its special content and form by prevailing ideological premises regarding the potency and functioning of the supernatural powers the people suppose they can utilize. Magical procedures are utilized when people cannot proceed with other material techniques. Magic is the inventory of supplemental techniques of a special kind because nonmaterial power is assumed to render them operative and probably successful.

The Emotional Attitude or Response of Religion. Whether or not the assumed presence of the supernatural, or a ritual, ceremonial, prayer, or artistic form of expression in a religious context, stimulates a characteristic feeling or emotional response has been a subject of considerable controversy. Fear, love, wonder, awe, hope, self-abnegation, and other terms serve as rough characterizations of the kinds of emotional behavior which have been reported for religious experiences. These same responses occur in secular experiences. Such characterizations of emotional responses are not distinctive enough to provide a scientific definition of a specifically religious emotion.

No one doubts that magical and religious situations are accompanied by emotional concomitants on the part of some participants. The special qualities and degrees of uniqueness or distinctiveness of such responses have not been given and are not likely to be given scientific description, however, until the participants themselves vouchsafe detailed case analyses of their own lives. Terms such as *religious feeling, typical religious thrill,* or *religious emotion* represent phenomena varying greatly in kind, quality, and intensity, and something which is not a concomitant of every religious situation.

Immortality; Life after Death; Survival of the Soul. Probably few peoples of food-gathering economies and not many peoples of agricultural and pastoral economies believe in a long-standing or permanent survival of people in their spiritual form. Ghost souls of the recently deceased are believed in almost universally, but long survival of such ghost souls is not often assumed. In fact probably few peoples of primitive economies look forward with any pleasurable expectancy to a new and spirit way of life following the death of their mortal bodies. Many are more concerned about inducing the recently deceased's ghost to keep away than they are concerned or confident regarding the pleasantness of its nonmaterial way of life. They do not want people here to be bothered by dismal visitors, trouble-makers, or peepers from the land of the dead.

There are endless varieties of beliefs in the kinds of souls, journeys of the ghost to the other land, kinds of lands where ghost souls live, the manner of life there, and the duration of soul survival, but belief in a permanent immortality of souls is rarely found. Belief in a short, long, or everlasting survival of the soul is almost never an important feature of religions of peoples of primitive economies. It is always a facet of their cosmology, a facet to which they give especial attention in religious rites before or after a death. But religious observances occur in many other situations and seasons.

Cosmological Beliefs; Mythology and Theology. Portions of the folklore or mythology of every people describe and give sanction to their concepts of the material and the supernatural, their magic, rituals, or ceremonials, and their social organization. The structure of the universe is indicated in such oral literature. Where all the people learn and transmit it, there may be some inner inconsistencies in its portrayal of the universe and of the supernatural. This is true of all simple food-gathering and most advanced food-gathering peoples. It may be true of most of the simpler agricultural economies.

Where oral literature is handed on by word of mouth in an advanced agricultural-pastoral society within a restricted circle of specialists termed *priests,* the tendency is to eliminate all the inconsistencies, integrate the folk tales, expand previously inept, brief, or otherwise inadequate tales, and embroider much more elaborate patterns of cosmological theory.

In other words, many, if not most, of the simpler economies democratically transmitted series of myths, which appear in many alternative and sometimes contradictory versions (see p. 223). The picture of the cosmos varies to a degree from person to person within the community. In such societies cosmology is mythology which usually has not been reduced to order, patterning, or imaginative embellishment.

On the other hand, the priesthood specialists of advanced agricultural-pastoral societies sometimes become sole purveyors of the mythology and the cosmological premises cited in it. The priests tend to rework this mythology and add to it to such a degree that their more logical, consistent, and ornate product of cosmological portrayal may well be termed a theology. Among peoples of primitive economy theologies are thus usually products of social systems of unusual wealth and degree of specialization. The historical trend has therefore been for folklores and mythologies to change into theologies as socio-economic changes occurred under Neolithic conditions. The beginnings of such a process of development of an elaborate cosmology or theology can also be witnessed among a few of the wealthier food-gathering peoples, notably the Bella Coola Indians of the British Columbia coast.

The functional role of folk tales, myths, or orally transmitted cosmologies and theologies is to provide a kind of proof of the truth, necessity, and rightness as well as the origin of the supernatural, magical, and cosmological beliefs. and of all the magico-religious procedures such as rites, incantations, or ceremonials. The mythology

or theology is assumed to contain the ultimate proof and sanction
for the supplemental techniques, termed magico-religious, to which
the people customarily resort. The mythology or theology is designed
to answer every possible query or form of doubt. It tends to quell
uneasiness, still fears, comfort those who grieve, and offer certain
answers to the most portentous problems of life and death. Mythology or theology thus is utilized to make the people at home and
secure to a degree in their world. It is a well of potential reassurance
in times of hunger, need, sickness, or tragedy. No peoples in primitive economies lack such recourse for comfort, although it is an
escape into unreality.

Anthropologists have described the many kinds of world views or
cosmological portraits which peoples in primitive economies have
created. For example, there are universes on successive levels, several
heavens, and several nether worlds. Portrayals of the cosmos are
legion and constitute one of the especially fascinating aspects of the
study of the creative imagination of non-European peoples.

Medicine, Magic, and Religion. All peoples have had an inventory of teas, herbs, poultices, bandages, means of pulling teeth, and
other material remedies to which they have resorted for accidental
or minor ailments where they supposed that only a material sort of
causation was present. Many if not most peoples, including those in
food-gathering economies, also knew the use of splints. Premises for
the secular practice of medicine, unencumbered by supernaturalism,
are therefore found among all peoples. Such knowledge, which of
course was empirical and not analyzed in a scientific fashion, was
usually available to and utilized by all the people.

There were, however, innumerable afflictions which peoples in
primitive economies supposed were caused by factors of a nonmaterial kind. The treatment of such ailments required magical procedures, such as returning a lost soul-substance or extracting a
poisonous power injected by an evil shaman into his victim. Individuals who had acquired or who had inherited or purchased supernatural power and procedures based thereon were asked to help persons supposed to be ill from these nonmaterial causes. In the food-
gathering and simple agricultural societies such practitioners were
shamans. In several advanced food-gathering societies of north-

western California and southwestern Oregon shamans were of two distinct kinds, differentiated by the type and strength of supernatural power they possessed. Members of both types received fees for their services.

In all instances shamans were only part-time workers at curing and at some ceremonials for which their power also fitted them to act as functionaries. Special groups termed secret societies engaged in magical curing in the simple agricultural economies of the south western United States, but most other simple agricultural districts probably had true shamans. Frequently shamans both cured by extraction and rendered ill by insertion, since they were the individuals who had power to handle the postulated poisonous substances of a nonmaterial kind.

In the advanced agricultural-pastoral societies shamans had largely or wholly divested themselves of poisoning and curing functions and they had become merely priestly specialists in theology and ceremonial and other less mundane uses of supernatural power. Their former potency in curing and poisoning fell into the hands of lowlier herb doctors and witch doctors.

The practice of medicine among the peoples in primitive economies is thus everywhere characterized by a few actually useful devices and drugs, by incorrect theories as to causation of more deadly ailments, and by resort to the supernatural for treatment of the latter.

Shamanism and Priesthoods. In simple food-gathering societies there are of course no full-time religious specialists. Individuals, male or female, who are alleged to have acquired unusual control over or assistance from supernatural beings conduct special rites for purposes of curing and in crisis situations, seasonal ceremonials, or other special occasions. Otherwise indistinguishable from their fellows and not necessarily the expert transmitters of ritual, persons such as these may be termed *shamans*. In a single encampment there may be three, four, or more of them. They vary considerably in their powers and in the services they render to their little community or to neighboring communities. The people give them gifts for their overtime curing or other magico-religious work, or merely accord them community approval for the contribution they make.

On the Pacific Northwest Coast women shamans were relatively few in the wealthier districts. Special groups, clubs, or so-called secret societies of the more well-to-do men were in process of taking control of special ceremonials. These groups, which were the primitive beginnings of organizations of magico-religious or ceremonial specialists, may be designated *inchoate priesthoods*.

The same sort of beginning of magico-religious specialization appears in some primitive agricultural societies such as those of the Pueblo Southwest, where so-called priesthoods have long been a familiar subject of anthropological research. But as on the Northwest Coast there is not yet a true priesthood in the sense of full-time theological and magico-religious functionaries. The Pueblos actually lack shamans and have only religious organizations of one or another kind. Priesthoods composed of full-time specialists developed only in advanced agricultural-pastoral or more complex socio-economic systems.

Shamans usually claim to have the most direct kinds of contact with supernatural beings. Priesthoods tend to have remoter ties with the supernatural but develop mythologies into theologies, devise rituals, and carry on educational and artistic work. Abnormal mental and emotional states, sometimes only temporary and sometimes a permanent feature of personality, characterize most shamans.

Religion and Ethics. An adhesion of rules of right and wrong social behavior to the supernatural is a distinctive feature of the Mediterranean European heritage. Among most peoples of primitive economy the premises of social ethics may receive sanction in the folklore or mythology, but the supernatural beings themselves are rarely concerned with people's misdeeds. The intermediaries with the supernatural, the shamans and priesthoods, have interests and contributions to make other than that of advising people regarding right and wrong in the arena of social relationships. Non-European religions interest themselves primarily in supernatural power and in rites which help to secure such power. Ethics or good and bad social behavior are by and large dissociated from supernatural threats, punishments, praise, or rewards. Religion and ethics tend to be only remotely connected if at all. Every community has, however, its sanctioned rules of conduct, its secular ethical code.

Ceremonial. All peoples conduct more or less stereotyped magico-religious rites at intervals during the year. Ceremonials are the traditional, formalized, and organized procedures of a magical sort, the rites or rituals, that constitute an overt behavioral aspect of religions. Rituals or ceremonials are participated in by all the people in simple food-gathering societies, or by assigned segments such as men or women or clan members. In wealthier parts of the Pacific Northwest Coast the men's clubs have developed some special ceremonials. In simple agricultural societies of the Southwest the clans are assigned special ceremonials. In the advanced agricultural-pastoral societies there is a progressive restriction of participation and its assumption by priesthoods or other specialist groups.

There is general agreement that the development and function of ceremonials, as of religions of peoples in primitive economies, has to do with crises, insecurities, and other situations that are threatening, dangerous, or economically important. The people lack techniques for meeting these recurrent situations with absolute certainty and in realistic fashion. The things they can do with their technological resources are therefore supplemented by procedures based upon their belief in supernatural resources, namely by ceremonials. The ceremonials are supported by wishful thinking when they are performed. The people therefore feel more assured of recovery from illness, more certain of long life, of the availability of game, of the success of the harvest, and of victory in battle. The length and beauty of the ceremonial, and the support given in economically primitive but democratic societies by the united participation of all the people, often intensify feelings of security and lessen fear of misfortune. On the other hand, in some societies, ceremonials underscore tension situations by institutionalizing them and, far from minimizing stress, they may be a source of anxieties and neuroses.

Religion and Art. The tie between religion and art is so powerful in societies with primitive economies that some scholars have considered the origins of art in the larger area of religion and magic. This thought once seemed plausible because the Upper Paleolithic pictures of animals supposedly served magical purposes. Upper Paleolithic figurines of the female body were also supposed to be magically potent or fetish objects of some kind. Moreover, a variety of objects of art obtained from modern peoples have primarily served religious purposes. Although arts do not always originate in religion, for they are also associated in primitive economies with secular objects and pursuits, religions always have one or more forms of aesthetic expression.

The facets of religion which are treated artistically are many. Mythology is told not just as history but as literature and poetry. Prayers, incantations, chants, and formulae are not simply recited in the accents of everyday speech but receive poetic treatment. Magicoreligious dances and ceremonials are not merely performed mechanically. They become dramatic and beautiful performances. Songs which are addressed to the supernatural are not sung casually but according to the canons of an art style. Ceremonial regalia such as masks are often crude representations or symbolizations of supernatural beings but they are sometimes exquisitely designed and fashioned. The more beautiful the myth, music, dance, ceremonial, regalia, prayer, or other religious expression, the truer the people's beliefs appear to them, and the more secure they are in their conviction that the objectives they are seeking by supernatural pro cedures will be achieved.

How Cults Developed. While a scientist describes and categorizes religious phenomena, and reports on their functioning and interrelationships, his task is also to determine if possible how and why such phenomena developed and changed. A study of the dynamic processes of cults among peoples with primitive economies may reveal by cautious analogy the nature of the processes which may have been operative in religions whose origins and earlier changes can no longer be observed directly.

Several modern or contemporary cults may be used for illustrative purposes. In the 1870's in California the surviving Indians of the central and northern parts of the state participated in so-called Ghost Dance cults. During the previous twenty years a number of simple food-gathering socio-economic systems that were already debilitated by diseases, and that were in process of transformation because of newly acquired artifacts, had been enveloped by frontier whites seeking gold. Brawling, murders, venereal infections, polluted streams, destruction of reserves of game animals, and fenced-in lands left the Indians without meaningful occupations and ruined their younger people. The natives whiled away their time wretchedly, hopelessly, and in bewilderment in unfamiliar and unhealthful cabins. Before 1860 the defense of their homelands and persons by military action against the whites had failed. Appeals to the government for aid also failed. No technique of a material or organized kind produced results. Realism or matter-of-fact procedures availed nothing.

Following years of such a hopeless way of life, several Indians sought guardian-spirit visions as they had done in their older regional faith, and learned new power songs and dances. They reported that the spirits assured them that if the people danced and sang sufficiently the recently deceased would come back to life, game would return to be hunted, fish would come up the now polluted streams, plant foods would be available, the hated whites would vanish magically, and all would be well and as it had been in earlier times. The Indians therefore organized themselves, built dance houses, and spread the ideology and its ceremonial accompaniments from community to community. Emissaries carried the cult messages, songs, and dances almost to the state of Washington in the north. But the whites never did vanish, the foods did not return, the departed never reappeared. After a while the ceremonial weakened and fell into disuse.

Another and related Ghost Dance religion, brought to a final form by a Nevada Indian named Wovoka about 1890, spread fanwise over an enormous area from Nevada almost to the Mississippi. The buffalo herds, the major economic resource of the Plains Indians, had been progressively decimated and shortly after 1880 vanished entirely, leaving the Indians destitute and starving. The whites had long been pouring across the Plains and towards the close of the 1880's they had homesteaded in most districts. Almost a decade of final envelopment, together with bedevilment of the kind characteristic of frontiers developed by the expanding whites, led to shattering of the Indian cultures. Pleas for help were unavailing and many of the Indians gave up hope of utilizing worldly means of doing anything about their fate. They turned to a magico-ceremonial means of achieving what they wished: that is, the disappearance of the whites, the return of the buffalo and other features of their former life, and the return of recently and prematurely deceased Indians. Emissaries and organizers spread the religion far and wide, and creative additions to the cult appeared in various districts.

The visit of a Winnebago Sioux named Rave to an Oklahoma group in 1893–94 was followed by the development of several new religious sects among the Nebraskan Winnebagos. This happened at the same time or followed directly upon the Ghost Dance religion in this region. Rave learned in Oklahoma about eating the dried top taken from a *peyote,* a cactus plant, whose alkaloids produce varied visions and emotional effects. His visions induced by peyote resulted in the development of a Winnebago peyote-eating cult. Later a Christianized Winnebago named Hensley added Christian ideological, ethical, and ceremonial features to the practice of eating peyote for visions, and still later Hensley seceded from the cult with some followers. A third Winnebago peyote sect developed when a Winnebago named Clay introduced a largely Christian ritual from the Arapahos.

Another religion developed in western Washington during the 1880's, in a district also progressively enveloped by frontier whites. Here the illness of an Indian named Slocum was interpreted by numbers of other Indians as a visit to heaven. Enthusiasts taught their people to erect churches, use certain dance-songs, cure the sick, engage in semi-Christianized ceremonial features, and avoid swearing, smoking, and alcohol. Organizing and missionary-minded members of this so-called Shaker Indian religion spread the faith from California into Canada during the next fifty years. Except for several peyote sects among the Winnebagos, the Shaker religion has a larger component of borrowed Christian content than the other religions mentioned.

These examples of new religions agree in the following dynamic processes and features: (1) There were preceding and accompanying them socio-economic and cultural crises which could not be met or solved by realistic procedures. (2) Abnormal or pathological mental experiences were manifested by way of fasting, trance states, hallucinations, or drugs; these experiences, which may be merely ideological and ceremonial or ethical as among some peyote-eaters and all Shakers, were then reported by the initiators, prophets, or seers of the new faith. (3) Some features of the people's older religion were retained and were creatively fused with new features either gotten in hallucinatory experiences or borrowed from the religion of the enveloping culture or both. (4) Organizational work was undertaken by the seer himself or by his early followers and there was missionary work or enthusiastic diffusion and further organization of the faith.

The new religions functioned to give their converts new security, confidence, or hope. If nothing else was achieved the people were given work to do such as building new religious edifices and they were rewarded by receiving social approbation for their efforts. The members channeled grief, anger, and frustrated energies by doing something which they believed would produce efficacious results, because they wished for them so intensely. The people were sure they had an ideology and a magico-ceremonial technique which would solve their troubles. Faithful acceptance of the new cult accorded them an at-homeness in the strange new world into which their people were so suddenly plunged. No doubt many Ghost Dance, peyote, and Shaker Indians did get a degree of solace, self-assurance, and ego-bolstering which permitted them to live on as relatively sane members of a tortured minority in a callous white world. Yet their fundamental wishes could never be fulfilled and they lived in an illusory and unreal world of faith.

The points listed are characteristic historical and social processes of the early decades of many new religions among people of primitive economies. Whether or not these points will be found in comparative study of most new cults remains to be seen.

Summary. From the evidence presented in this chapter, it is clear that a person can be intensely religious and at the same time lack a strong religious thrill, a belief in immortality, in God, and in the sanctity of decent behavior or the sinfulness of antisocial behavior. For the religions of peoples in primitive economies involve behavior and concepts different from those of the religions of the wealthiest civilizations, and function somewhat differently.

Religions therefore cannot be simply defined. It is incorrect to single out one, two, or three features as most basic to all religions

Every religion is an elaborate complex, a many-faceted part of the culture within which it has developed and functioned.

All religions of peoples in primitive economies involve animism and an inventory of supposedly effective magical interconnections. All such religions include at least some individuals who have special kinds of emotional responses or religious thrills in a religious situation. All display a variety of forms of social and artistic behavior. All have an inventory of myths, and a few have, in addition, a theology; all conduct rites or ceremonies; all dance, sing, or chant in poetic fashion in such ceremonies; all express religious beliefs of one or another sort in artistic symbolism—that is, through sculpture, architecture, and paintings; all have either shamans or priesthoods. Any definition of religions of peoples in primitive economies should there fore include reference to these universal characteristics.

On the other hand, there are features which are definitely not always associated with religion, that are found only in some regions. These are polytheism, pure monotheism, ethics, and a belief in permanent immortality. Widely found, but not yet proved to have a universal distribution, are beliefs in a deity who is outstanding among other forms of the supernatural, and animatism or *mana*.

Many writers have claimed that religion has necessarily always been among the most conservative aspects of culture in its rate of change. Assertions that this has been so may appear to be supported by the history of some of the religions of the wealthiest Eurasian cultures of the past two thousand years. But proof that religions have been always less subject to change than other features of culture has not been given. The rapid succession of new religions among the American Indians and the proliferation of faiths and rituals among white Americans during the past 150 years is one among many indications that religions may not always have been more conservative than other traditional features of a cultural heritage.

A possibly useful approach to the problem may be to indicate that no simple food-gathering societies had religious vested-interest groups. Some advanced food-gathering communities of the Pacific Northwest Coast, however, where secret societies or clubs of men conducted special magico-religious ceremonials, were beginning to develop vested interests in religion. The members of these clubs of specialists also made innovations in religious mythology as well as in ceremonials. They lacked any vested interest in an unchanged cult, for it was more to their interest to introduce changes in the religion. In advanced agricultural-pastoral societies priesthoods may sometimes also have served their own interests by changes in mythology and ceremonials rather than by maintenance of them in their rigidly traditional content and form.

In other words, religion as such bears witness to no general tendency to remain unchanged or to resist change. Everything depends on the kind of culture and the circumstances of the time, which affect the interests of those who transmit religion. Where it has been transmitted by all the people as in the simple food-gathering and simple agricultural societies, religion has changed at about the pace that every other aspect in the culture has changed. In the advanced food-gathering and wealthier agricultural-pastoral societies, the specialists who carried and transmitted religion either conservatively maintained its contents and forms or changed it according to their interests. The scientist's problem is to ascertain the role and functions played by each religion in its given situation or cultural context, and to generalize by showing the types of situations or cultures that make for religious stability or orthodoxy, and the other types that make for change or unorthodoxy.

SELECTED READINGS

Calverton, V. F., ed. *The Making of Man*. New York: Modern Library, 1931. Sect. 5.

Du Bois, C. *The 1870 Ghost Dance*. Berkeley: Anthropological Records, Vol. III (1939), i.

Goldenweiser, A. A. *Anthropology*. New York: Crofts, 1937. Pt. II, Sect. 3.

——. *Early Civilization*. New York: Knopf, 1922. Pp. 184–234.

——. *History, Psychology, and Culture*. New York: Knopf, 1933. Pt. IV.

Howells, W. W. *The Heathens*. New York: Doubleday, 1948.

Kroeber, A. L., and T. T. Waterman. *Source Book in Anthropology*. New York: Harcourt, Brace, 1931 (rev. ed.). Pp. 412–463.

Leslie, C., ed. *Anthropology of Folk Religion*. New York: Vintage, 1960.

Lessa, W. A. and E. Z. Vogt, eds. *Reader in Comparative Religion: An Anthropological Approach*. Evanston: Row Peterson, 1958.

Lowie, R. H. *Primitive Religion*. New York: Boni and Liveright, 1924.

Malinowski, B. "Magic, Science, and Religion," in J. Needham, ed., *Science, Religion, and Reality*. New York: Macmillan, 1925.

Marett, R. R. *Faith, Hope, and Charity in Primitive Religion.* New York: Macmillan, 1932.

——. *The Threshold of Religion.* London: Methuen, 1914 (2nd ed.).

Mooney, J. *The Ghost Dance Religion and the Sioux Outbreak of 1890.* Washington: Bur. Amer. Ethnol., 1896 (14th Annual Report).

Norbeck, E. *Religion in Primitive Society.* New York: Harper, 1961.

Notes and Queries on Anthropology. London: Royal Anthrop. Inst., 1929 (5th ed.). Pp. 174–186.

Piddington, R. *An Introduction to Social Anthropology.* Vol. 1. Edinburgh: Oliver and Boyd, 1950. Pp. 356–391.

Radin, P. *Primitive Religion.* New York: Viking, 1937.

——. *Social Anthropology.* New York: McGraw-Hill, 1932. Pp. 243–338.

Spier, L. *The Prophet Dance of the Northwest and Its Derivatives: The Source of the Ghost Dance.* Menasha: General Series in Anthrop., 1935, No. 1.

Tozzer, A. M. *Social Origins and Continuities.* New York: Macmillan, 1925. Pp. 109–125, *passim;* 221–224.

Wallis, W. D. *Religion in Primitive Society.* New York: Crofts, 1939.

Yinger, J. M. *Religion, Society and the Individual.* New York: Macmillan, 1957.

CHAPTER ELEVEN

ART: INTRODUCTION

The Scientific Study of Art. The arts of peoples with primitive economies are of at least four kinds: oral literature, music, dance, and the plastic and graphic arts. Probably no society lacks examples of artistry in each of these four media. But the techniques of expression, patterned forms, social functioning, and qualities of these arts differ so notably from area to area, and each is itself so unique in technique, content, and style, that they require separate treatment.

Cultural anthropology approaches the study of these arts in a scientific spirit. It attempts to determine their origins and changes in time, their content or themes, their stylized forms, their social role or functioning, and other topics which will explain them. It tends to make few qualitative judgments, if it does not entirely renounce them, on the presupposition that only those who are fully acquainted with the themes, styles, and techniques available for artistic expression can provide trustworthy evaluations of aesthetic achievement.

Many writers on primitive art have discussed plastic and graphic arts exclusively. In spite of great differences in techniques, themes, and styles, all arts have important features in common and therefore the term *primitive art* should include oral literature, music, and dance with the plastic and graphic arts. The features shared by the arts are these: (1) There are instruments or resources employed for stylistic expression such as language, stories, the voice, the body, knives, chisels, awls, paints, fibers, and clay. (2) The people have a heritage of technical ways of employing such instruments. (3) They practice for years to master such learned techniques and at length attain technical competence of a very high order. (4) A few who have attained such a degree of skill go beyond it because they are free to play with the technique. They utilize the transmitted techniques, themes, and stylized forms in original or creative ways. This is what is meant by artistry and every subarea has some artists and some works of art.

Evolution and Change in Art. Archeological and other types of evidence indicate that no modern art is exactly like its predecessor of centuries ago. Like religions and other features of cultural and social life, all arts are in constant process of change. There is reason to believe that some of the themes of the plastic and graphic arts tend to change with special rapidity. It is improbable that a continuity of Magdelenian bone and ivory carving style could have led to contemporary Eskimo carving, or that Capsian painting could have resulted in modern Bushman painting, because no art style has ever been shown to have had continuity through so many thousands of years without profound changes.

Many writers have suggested that the earliest stage of art was realistic or representative in expression and that art subsequently tended to become geometric, symbolic, and decorative in expression—that the tendency to change was in a direction of progressive simplification and conventionalization. Evidences in favor of such a direction of change can be found, but only in a few of the plastic and graphic arts and only in a few areas as in western Europe, where Paleolithic cave paintings of a relatively realistic kind are the earliest paintings known, and in the cases of carvings from New Guinea and pottery from Central America. Another series of changes in art has been conceived for a number of the wealthiest societies, for which the sequence is the formative, the archaic or initially known phase, the mature, the flamboyant, and the decadent. Examples of this series among peoples studied by anthropology are Mayan sculpture and Nasca pottery of Peru.

Each series of stages is relevant for only one among the many art styles of the area in question; the stages claimed are so generalized as to reveal nothing of the details of the art; the diffusion of the art is not indicated, nor are the borrowings which also affected its themes and style; the many special historical, magico-religious, or cultural factors which affected the style are not shown; the materials and tools employed, and the consequent technical or manipulative problems and their influence upon the style, are also not revealed. The main defect in evolutionary theories of art change is therefore that they leave too much to be explained. The changes over time of each art style must be accounted for not in terms of any inner dynamic tendency towards conventionalization, maturity, flamboyancy, or decadence, but rather in terms of the historical and cultural setting in which the art has functioned and the factors of that setting which have influenced it, and also in terms of the factors which arose from the materials and technical manipulations involved in its production.

Consideration of the latter, and a check-up on specific plastic or graphic arts, indicate that the earlier phases of art styles in textile or basketry materials necessarily allow only geometric and symbolic decoration. The manipulations themselves limit the possibilities in design. Only when techniques of weaving are mastered to a very high degree are the possibilities for design so increased that there can be a choice of realistic representation. Similarly the earliest-fashioned pottery cannot be given as smooth a surface as is possible in later periods when the technique is more fully mastered. That is why realistic portrayals appear if at all only after a long period of increasing technical control of the possibilities in the utilization of clay. Soft woods can, however, be sculptured with realistic portrayals by peoples who have only stone tools.

In short, food-gathering peoples can have several plastic and graphic arts, some of which may be representative or realistic, others decorative, symbolic, or geometric. The degree of technical mastery of given materials is often the major factor, and not any over-all trend for representative art to precede decorative art. In fact, in textiles the trend has been the opposite, for it has developed from crudely decorative or symbolic art towards representative or realistic art. These considerations have little or no relevance for those arts whose instruments for expression are language, the voice, and the body.

All arts can be shown, however, to be affected by invention, diffusion, and patterning or integration. The circumstances within which creative or inventive work appears depend on the occupations of the people, their heritage of technical processes, the available materials that can be worked with their tools and technical processes, the degree of specialization of labor, the degree and kinds of participation allowed the people, the social rewards accorded excellence, the magico-religious and ideological heritage, and the stimuli from adjacent peoples. These conditions are best discussed separately for each type of art, but in general it can be shown that invention or creativity occurs in terms of a number of factors localized in the heritage of a culture area or in a specific time and place.

The process of diffusion is also affected by these factors. In general the history of every art style has been influenced by the diffusions of styles from adjacent areas. Several students of art have shown that borrowed designs or folkloristic motifs have been given different treatments and interpretations or have acquired different symbolic meanings in terms of the cultures in which they have been utilized. For example, in the western states one and the same design on a moccasin is interpreted as the morning star by Arapaho, feathers by Sioux, and the sun and its rays and also the thunderbird by Shoshonean Indians. The design had clearly first diffused among these tribes and subsequently different interpretations and symbolic meanings had been associated with it. There are also localized styles or patterns of the interpretation of designs that have diffused over a considerable region. The Siouan type of interpretation, for example, is martial whereas the Arapaho is religious, although these peoples share the same designs.

Genius in Art. If genius in art is defined simply by a high degree of originality and creativity, no scientific data are available to show the amounts of inherent potentiality for genius or the numbers of individuals who have such potentialities in any group or population. No one social system or community can offer evidence regarding the ceiling of aesthetic creativity possible for a population, because no one knows all the factors that assist in fulfilling latent potentialities or that throw obstacles in the path of such fulfillment. The fact that geniuses of the stature of Beethoven, Leonardo da Vinci, Phidias, Goethe, or Tolstoy have been extremely infrequent in European civilizations tells nothing regarding the possible frequency of genius in the same European population if it had had other kinds of social systems. There is not the slightest evidence that there are specific genes that are inherited, or that appear in mutations, which predispose to genius for culturally determined activities such as composition for stringed instruments, painting on canvases, or oratory. The causes for outstanding aesthetic creativity must therefore be sought in features of a social and cultural heritage which offer opportunities to individuals to participate in and master an already present art style. Genius in art cannot be explained exclusively in biological terms. It can be accounted for largely in terms of participations, opportunities, and rewards. Some social systems probably produce many times as many geniuses as do other systems. The opportunities available in different kinds of social systems are best discussed for each type of art.

SELECTED READINGS

Boas, F. *Primitive Art*. Irvington-on-Hudson: Capital Hill, 1951.
Goldenweiser, A. A. *Anthropology*. New York: Crofts, 1937. Pt. II, Sect. 2.
——. *Early Civilization*. New York: Knopf, 1922. Pp. 165–183.

CHAPTER TWELVE

ORAL LITERATURE

Introduction. All peoples who possess a primitive level of technology tell stories of at least two kinds. One of these consists of matter-of-fact narrations of experiences and of recent events, which are described in conversational styles and whose patterns need to be studied but generally lack aesthetic interest. The other consists of narrations of a special kind, whose contents and artistic styles of rendition have long been studied by the science of folklore. The role played by the second type, which constitutes a complex literary art form, is important in social systems that lack both techniques of writing and specialists or other public performers who give professional entertainment.

Since all peoples have comparably high intelligence as well as languages of equal developmental levels, all possess comparably complex instruments for literary expression. Nevertheless, contemporary society has long erroneously assumed that translated editions of the folk literatures of other peoples are more suitable for children than for the serious attention of adults. Although there is every justification for making selected examples from oral literatures available to youth, it must not be supposed that such literatures have only puerile content, simple style. and aesthetically meagre interest. They are true literatures although they are created, transmitted, and expressed in ways different from written literatures. The social insight, poetry, philosophy, humor, and artistry exhibited in some oral literatures are such that they deserve attention as serious as that accorded other forms of artistic expression created in any kind of social system.

Folkloristic Research. Scientific procedures in the collection and recording of the oral literature of peoples with primitive economies began to be standardized in the 1880's. Prior to that time stories had usually been dictated by natives in European languages, an adequate control of which the informants rarely possessed; the translation of their words was often not rechecked properly. Informants sometimes censored out and failed to tell portions of stories that they thought would offend European ears, or omitted items which they suspected would be considered boresome or repetitious. European collectors did not get a fair sampling of the variety of oral literature available, for they often asked specifically for origin tales and sacred stories and not for other types. They also inquired ill-advisedly for the "right version," and for the services of only the very best raconteur. They did not comprehend the importance of noting many alternate versions given by the same informant or versions of a variety of raconteurs. Often they published stories pieced together arbitrarily in clusters which they termed cycles or epics, or they recombined variant versions, when no such arrangements characterized the native literature. Sometimes they published translations that they had embellished with stylistic features, taken from European literature, which were not present in the native literature. Early workers were satisfied with a sample handful of stories and thus they rarely obtained more than a small segment of the entire literature. For these reasons, knowledge of folklore before 1890 was based largely upon fragmentary and untrustworthy source material. Most of the artistic aspects of the original literatures were hopelessly distorted or lost in the published translations.

The canons of scientific accuracy in the collection of oral literature now demand that stories be recorded wherever possible not in a European language known to the informant, but in a phonetic transcription of the native language and later in a full and careful translation. Such transcriptions and translations are termed texts. As a check upon the accuracy of the texts a few stories are redictated and recorded electrically. These are minimal requirements for preservation of the theme and plot content of folklore and also most of its features as an art style. Furthermore, every effort is made to establish excellent rapport with the informants so that they will not permit themselves to omit or distort. It is hoped that they will attempt to narrate as fully and artistically as possible in spite of the artificial conditions of dictation. The entire inventory of stories in the literature is sought, together with many alternate versions. The whole literature is at least sampled in a random way and the special interests of the outsider are ignored during the process of recording.

Oral literature is rarely or never absolutely standardized as is a novel or book of poems printed by a commercial publishing house today. Oral literature is not in fixed editions but is created and endlessly recreated by many persons. Each person's version may differ considerably with each of his renditions. Only in the few regions where an oral literature, or a portion of it, is memorized is a single dictation adequate.

Origins of Oral Literature.　Since languages may have been in process of development before the Paleolithic period, it is not unreasonable to suppose that Early Paleolithic near-humans described past events. Whether or not any degree of formalization or stylization developed in such early narrations can never be learned. In fact little more can be said regarding the remote origins of folklore than of the origins of language (see p. 279). It is impossible to assume a single origin for languages since there must have been many independent developments of linguistic features. These linguistic innovations diffused to such a degree that every language is a composite of diffused and locally developed features. Features of a folkloristic kind were also invented by every population and diffused much more readily, rapidly, and distantly than did most features of language. Therefore all folklores are composites of elements derived from more sources than are any languages.

The questions of the origins of features of folklore can only be handled by treating in succession each of the major aspects of folk tales, the motifs or minimal units of plot, larger plots, points of stories, actors, and formal literary style or structural features.

The origins of motifs and plots have been widely discussed. Very few writers have supposed and none can now suppose that some one or several great centers such as Mesopotamia and India were largely or exclusively creative of the world's oral literatures, and that folklores everywhere received their plot content by diffusion from these curiously prolific sources. There are too many different plots found in various parts of the world, and not at all in Mesopotamia or

India, to give credence to such a theory of diffusion from single important centers.

A number of scholars have believed that phenomena of nature such as the seasons, the phases of the moon, the daily path of the sun, comets, shooting stars, tides, storms, lightning and thunder, floods, forest fires, and fogs were handled allegorically by reading zoomorphic and anthropomorphic characters into them, and that in a sense all motifs and plots of folk tales have their origin in allegorical or nature symbolism. Whether this kind of creative imagination operates cannot be proved or disproved in the case of most stories, since their actual origin occurred in the distant past under circumstances which cannot be examined. The authors of most stories that are told in the modern period have long been dead and forgotten. Moreover, even if a given plot is told in several hundred contiguous communities, its imaginative creator could nevertheless have been a native of only one of the communities. The presence of the plot in all the other communities would have to be explained on the basis of its diffusion. Hence a theory of cosmogonic origin of all tales would have to be supplemented by a theory of diffusion which would account for the spread of the tales. The many changes made in the course of the diffusion of a tale would also have to be explained in terms of processes of integration and patterning.

Another theory of allegorical origin is derived from psychoanalysis, according to which folkloristic characters, plots, and stylistic features originated in symbolization and distortion not of cosmic phenomena but of sex drives and other subconscious patterns found by psychiatrists in the study of dreams, neuroses, or other mental phenomena. Proof or disproof of the actual operation of such dynamic processes of myth creation is not possible except where the inventor is still alive and can be interviewed at length.

Another theory of folkloristic origins suggests that myths are narrative explanations of natural and cultural phenomena in terms of zoomorphic and anthropomorphic beings. According to this theory, myths are essentially explanatory or etiological tales. Evidence shows, however, that the explanatory "that's why" endings of tales about, for example, the teeth, claws, fur, or habits of animals have often been tagged on to plots of stories already in circulation.

The purport of another origin theory is that stories evolved at different stages of cultural development, and that when similar stories are found in disparate areas, it is evidence of identical developmental level, not of diffusion. The evidence of rapid diffusion of stories is now overwhelmingly great so that a simple evolutionary theory of this kind is not valid.

Still another theory of the origin of folk tales assumes that among nonliterate peoples actual events and situations are repeatedly discussed or are recounted as tall tales, and that these narratives become progressively embellished, further distorted, exaggerated, or changed according to the kinds of humor and creative imagination made possible by the basic ideological and cultural heritage. It is not claimed that this is the process of origin of all folklore themes or plots, but it may account for many. Furthermore, narratives which originated in this way, for all their initial rooting in facts or light fancies told of in daily life, become less and less like their originals as they become integrated into the already present body of highly stylized folk tales. The type of actors utilized, motivation, plot type, and purely literary stylistic features change in time. In other words during many tens of thousands of years, the more every new narrative was told, the more it became only a typical folk tale narrative with successive renditions and distortions or changes of a creative kind. The old tales that were stylized influenced the new tales and gave them their essential emphases and form at the same time that the whole body of the literature slowly changed. This process of integration or patterning also applies to tales that diffused to other communities, as most tales have done. No tales ever long remained entirely unique in content or in formal features.

The search for ultimate origins of motifs and plots, as of features of style, is of slight value compared with the search for processes of change, spread, and patterns of acceptance and of remolding of tales, and the processes by which features of style change. Cultures themselves contain the dynamic determinants of the changes in tales and literary patterns, and of the manner of and reasons for their spread. The proper inquiry into folkloristic processes is a search not so much for origins as for the causes of folkloristic changes. This type of study can be effectively carried on today, because vast numbers of people in primitive economies are still constantly creating and changing all features of their folkloristic heritage.

Types of Plots. Areas that have characteristic types of plots do not fully coincide with socio-economic or culture areas. A goodly percentage of the themes, motifs, and plots which earlier diffused into the former areas have been so recombined and handled as to be told in terms of a very limited number of plot types emphasized in those areas. For example, California-Oregon Indians utilize many themes or motifs as components of plots wherein two antagonistic beings argue and then decide what will happen in the future. Among the Plateau and Plains Indians the same motifs, which diffused into these areas long ago, have been woven into plots that are simply narrations of the discussion of a council of animals. In the northwestern states some of these motifs are found again but here they have been strung along in a plot type which deals with the travel upstream of a culture hero and trickster capable of transforming persons, animals, and objects. Southwestern Pueblos have a plot type which portrays successive occurrences in the people's ancient migration, their arrival in the world above, and the journey there to the people's present Pueblo home. In each of these examples a common ancient heritage of motifs, many of them borrowed, as well as a group of locally developed motifs that are not so old, has been fitted into a plot type emphasized in that local area.

Not one but several plot types appear and in a sense compete within each area. For example, Oregon Indians have plot patterns of a trickster culture hero's travels, of two antagonistic beings, of dangerous animals and ogres that attack people, of women who marry nonhuman beings, of the conferring of spirit-power, and several others. The frequency with which stories of one plot type are told in an area undoubtedly reflects basic cultural features and interests of that area.

Elaborate types of plots termed cycles and epics seem to have developed to a greater degree of complexity in Eurasia than in other areas. A possible explanation for this may lie in the long duration of the Neolithic and Metal Age socio-economic systems in the central portions of Eurasia, and hence the opportunity afforded professional or specialist storytellers to introduce further structural complexities in oral literature, much as sacred myths became the basis for a consistent theological scheme in the hands of Neolithic priesthoods.

The Diffusion of Folk Tales. Each culture area has themes, plots, and stories which are not found in any other part of the world but are widespread within the area. Smaller portions of culture areas also have themes or tales which are narrowly localized and have obviously not diffused far from their point of origin. In all probability every small district the world over can give evidence of local creativity in folklore, and of the failure of such locally recounted tales to diffuse. However, a great many minimal units of folklore such as themes, motifs, or incidents are found continuously over enormous areas. So too are some larger plots.

In fact, a number of plots are found more or less continuously in three or more contiguous continents. A classic example of almost world-wide diffusion of a plot which does not seem likely to have been developed more than once is the magic-flight plot, in which the fleeing hero successively casts small things over his shoulder and magically creates formidable obstacles which are only slowly surmounted by a pursuing ogre. Other plots which are also found widely in both the Old World and the New World and which were transmitted from community to community and into America by way of Bering Strait, are the plots of the swan maidens, of the killing of the ogre whose head lice are frogs, and of the bringing up of the earth by an animal who dives beneath the world flood waters. Each of these complex plots, which have been popular in many areas, is continuously distributed from community to community in such a fashion that a single ancient origin rather than a multiple origin is probable.

A few well-known themes, as for example the chain of linked arrows extending up to the sky country, are not continuously distributed in this manner. The arrow-chain motif appears in one area of Oceania and in a limited area of North America. In such instances the possibility of dual origin must be considered. Scientific folklorists have sought to work out the single or multiple origin of folkloristic themes by means of spot maps that indicate continuities and discontinuities in distribution.

Neither geographical nor linguistic barriers have held up the spread of a majority of a people's folkloristic heritage for long. In fact, the scores or hundreds of stories possessed by any small tribe or comparable community usually include only a small fraction of stories that are exclusively their own and unknown to neighboring groups.

When Europeans and their Negroid slaves arrived in the Americas, they rapidly shared Old World tales with the American Indians. As a result there are striking additions of French, Spanish, Nigerian, and other folk tales to American Indian inventories. These added stories have usually been quickly refurbished and told according to almost purely native American Indian stylistic canons. The same sort of folkloristic diffusion and rapid integration into an alien style pattern occurred wherever immigrants brought their folklore.

Types of Actors. The many themes, motifs, and larger plots which have diffused over wide areas have been ascribed to different actors during the course of their spread. For example, stories told of Raven on the northern Pacific Coast of North America are told of Mink, Bluejay, Coyote, or other actors in coastal districts to the south, with concomitant changes of character delineation and motivation that in each instance suit the special traits of the actor. In some parts of the world the regional folklores utilize a number of giant, monstrous, or ogre-like creatures, and in other regions humanlike actors are featured. An insect, the mantis, is a well-known figure of Bushman mythology, and many stories are told of the rabbit in the southern United States. These are only a few illustrations of the variety in *dramatis personae* of the world's folklores.

The Function of Folk Tales. Oral literatures function in different ways from area to area. Among the Indians of the coast of British Columbia a principal point or source of motivation of the raconteur is to authenticate the privileges and other perquisites of his lineage or clan. In the Columbia River areas the motivations are entertainment and the portrayal of a portion of the region's ancient mythological history so that the people will know why customs and geographical features have taken their present form. Some Oregon coastal tales are told in order to inculcate minor moral lessons. European folk tales stressed moral training to a much greater degree.

Everywhere stories are told as excellently, artistically, and entertainingly as possible in spite of the fact that pure entertainment on an artistic level is rarely the sole motivation. There is usually at least some minor educational function and purposeful pointing up of the story.

Folklore and Its Cultural Setting. European folklore is almost unique among folklores the world over because the European story plots and actors reflect a way of life of many centuries past. Everywhere among peoples with primitive economies the stories describe social relationships, religions, incidents, and scenes of daily living that are not the least different from the peoples' culture immediately preceding the advent of Europeans. Folklore that functions as the peoples' only literature is by and large a mirror reflection of much of their culture.

Literary Style. Only limitations of human language and memory, whatever these may be, determine the absolute limits of the complexity and subtlety of form or style in oral literature. Every oral literature is told within the framework of an elaborate set of rules, of many of which both the raconteur and the mature members of his audience may be conscious. These rules of literary form are a kind of grammar of literature, much of which is clearly recognized as such in contrast with language patterns that are for the most part not so identified.

The rules of literary style vary from region to region, but mention of a few rules or canons according to which stories must be told will exemplify what is meant by literary style. In some regions, as in European folklore, everything has to be done in terms of three brothers, or three bears, or with three arrows; in other regions it must be four persons, things, acts, or incidents; or five, or seven. These sacred, mystic, or pattern numbers feature the style of every oral literature. If there are five bears or five brothers they may act invariably in order of age, with the youngest able to solve that which his older brothers had failed to do. Everywhere there are patterns of rhythmic repetitions and repetitions leading to a climax.

Everywhere also there are introductory and closing formulae such as "Once upon a time" and "They lived happily ever after," which are peculiar to European folklore. Everywhere sub-dialect features of pitch, nasality, and consonant changes are used for special actors such as a lion, bear, rabbit, meadowlark, or skunk. In many areas a number of archaic words and forms or special grammatical features are found, such as a past tense which is used only in myth narratives. A characteristically simplified sentence structure may be found which lacks features of grammatical subordination. The numbers of stylized and required features such as these are legion, and every literature can be shown to possess them in large numbers.

In addition, however, an oral literary style must also be understood to function in a certain stylized social setting, very much as our theatre must function with an audience and a stage. The raconteur sits or stands and recounts the myth, in a dramatic style as well as with features of verbal or literary style. The audience may have to sit or lie in a stylized posture. It may have to repeat the raconteur's sentences following him, or respond in other ways.

Few oral literatures and their settings have thus far been described or analyzed for their stylistic features with any completeness. Nor have such features been correlated with other aspects of the social setting and culture of peoples so that the manner and reason why one developed within the framework of the other might be known. The enormous quantities of research in the collection of folk tales and in the analysis of theme and plot contents of folklores may be contrasted regretfully with the little that has been done to indicate stylistic traits and patterns. This unevenness in the work of folkloristic science is unfortunate because folklore as an art has at least two important interconnected facets, content and style. The enjoyment of the art as well as its effectiveness and social function depend upon both.

Dramatic oral presentation and type of audience participation each also operate to give shape to folkloristic styles. The styles characteristic of written literatures are as complex as folklore styles, but are necessarily different because of the different medium of written expression. It is incorrect to underestimate, as many writers have done, the degree of or potentialities for stylistic complexity and ornateness in oral literature.

Folklore as Art; Literary Artists. Each raconteur has heard a folk tale many times in many versions. The older he is the more often he has also told the tale. After many renditions his command of the tale approaches a degree of technical mastery which permits him greater freedom from mechanical matters such as memorization. He has an increasing inner assurance that he will be able to give expression to every needed word, motif, gesture, facial expression, and tone of voice. He will not err on the sequence of episodes or in building up towards the climax. The person who has achieved such technical mastery is free to "play with the technique." This he does most often when he is in just the right setting and with the right audience. The technical master now is free to become a virtuoso or artist for the occasion. In an artistic performance he adds, subtracts, embellishes, and changes creatively without sacrifice of demanded stylistic items, and he does so to his own and his audience's delight.

A technically perfect, errorless, and also imaginatively and stylistically creative rendition of a folk tale is not likely to occur in a setting artificially imposed by an alien anthropologist seated at a table, writing furiously in a notebook, and interrupting constantly in order to request repetition of a missed word. In completely correct settings and in healthily functioning cultures, however, artistic performances may be notable.

The artistry of many raconteurs in economically simple and advanced food-gathering and in simple agricultural societies, and of specialist storytellers in advanced agricultural-pastoral societies, cannot be doubted in spite of the meagreness of transcribed testimony of the quality and originality of their aesthetic and dramatic achievements. There is every reason for assuming a high frequency of literary artistry in such societies, for each culture has scores or hundreds of tales, a flexible and rich language, audience stimulation and community approbation for work well done, years of opportunity accorded every person for hearing fine performances, and years for practicing at the technique of telling stories. A noteworthy rendition of a folk tale influences many auditors who in their turn carry on in the artistic ways created by their artist predecessors. There is no permanent edition or script to restrain or place absolute limits upon creative changes they may make later. Their literature is not fixed in form but is constantly changing.

Oral literatures as well as music and dance products among peoples in primitive economies are joint creations of successive artists, not permanent individual productions. One finds no individuals who create like Dante, Goethe, Tolstoy, Zola, Thackeray, or Dreiser. The literary products of literate societies are not strictly comparable as creative achievements with the literary products of series of raconteurs. The conditions within which literate specialists create are not comparable to those which influence the creators of oral literature. The latter succeed in creating artistic products of another and hardly comparable kind.

Translations of oral literature inevitably result in the loss of much of their stylistic and artistic quality, so that a full appreciation of these matters can be acquired only by mastery of native languages and by examination of literary performances recorded electrically or in sound on film reels.

Prose and Poetry. Prose and poetry are terms used to characterize contrasting types of literary expression which have developed in the economically most advanced social systems. Folklore and mythology may often be so rendered by nonliterate artists as to approach in a general way the distinctive features of style, such as allegorical expression, imagery, and rhythm, which characterize the heritage of European poetry. In this sense it is correct to assert that poetic and prose expression occur among all peoples in primitive economies. Other types of poetry-like expression found among nonliterate peoples are exemplified in their rituals, incantations, ceremonial recitatives, or the words of their songs. Rhyme is perhaps never found except in written literary products. However, much oral literature has the quality of blank verse. The dissociation of a literary form termed poetry from either folklore or song possibly did not occur until the advent of a technique of writing.

Drama. Dramatic renderings of folk tales and myths probably are found in every society with a primitive economy. Every oral literature functions as a kind of drama, although its cast of one hardly justifies the technical use of that term.

Drama of the kind known in European society performed by a troupe of specialist actors is not found in food-gathering societies unless some of the mimetic dances found in many regions, and the elaborate ceremonials found, for example, among the Australian

Blackfellows and the Pacific Northwest Coast "secret societies," are termed drama.

Drama which is more closely reminiscent of the forms developed in Periclean Athens and continued with changing characteristics down to the present period appears in many of the advanced agricultural and pastoral civilizations. Dramas performed by specialized actors are reported, for example, from Inca Peru and from the wealthier parts of Negroid Africa. Full-length films, complete texts, scientific descriptions, or other carefully documented reports of such art forms are not yet available for anthropological study.

Oratory. Closely related to oral literature is oratory. Unfortunately few if any accurate recordings of oratory are available. There are many approximate versions in European languages, but they suggest only stylistic ornateness, sententious and imaginative content, and emotion-stirring appeals. Much scientific field collecting remains to be done, preferably with electrical recordings that are later transcribed and translated, before this facet of art can be adequately examined.

However, it may be anticipated that oratory of outstanding aesthetic quality will be found among peoples of the lowest economic level simply because they possess the necessary instruments for expression, that is, language and the voice, and as much motivation for oratorical expression as is present in our society. Occasions for oratory may also be especially frequent in social systems such as those of the simpler food-gathering and agricultural peoples.

Other Folkloristic Arts. Proverbs, riddles, magical formulas, sayings, and other types of verbal art have also been found among many peoples of primitive economy. True proverbs are lacking in the Americas. It is suggested that they spread throughout most of the Old World, since or not long before the end of the Pleistocene era, from some unknown region of development. Riddles also appear to be absent in the Americas, except for Alaskan and Eskimo districts, and so a similar recency of development somewhere in the Old World has been inferred. The study of the origin and the dissemination, of the content and style, of these additional forms of verbal artistry is intensely interesting and important due to the noteworthy role these expressions play in cultures where they exist. However, phonetic transcriptions and trustworthy translations of such forms, as well as variants, have been obtained in only a few areas. Investigation has hardly touched the changes in these and other verbal arts and their relations to both cultural and psychological phenomena. Specialists in the collection of folklore have devoted themselves, more often than cultural anthropologists and psychologists, to researches on the verbal arts. Perhaps this is because only a few social scientists have considered themselves competent to record phenomena of language. As a result, dynamic, functional, or psychological explanations of the cultural role of these expressions are still undeveloped.

SELECTED READINGS

Benedict, R. "Folklore," in *Encyclopedia of the Social Sciences,* VI (1931), 288–293.

Boas, F. *Primitive Art.* Irvington-on-Hudson: Capital Hill, 1951.

——. *Race, Language, and Culture.* New York: Macmillan, 1940. Pp. 397–406, 451–502.

Herskovits, M. J., and F. S. Herskovits. *Dahomean Narrative.* Evanston: Northwestern Univ. Press, 1958. Pp. 1–122.

Jacobs, M. *The Content and Style of an Oral Literature.* New York: Viking Fund Pubs. in Anthropology, No. 26; Chicago: Univ. of Chicago Press, 1959.

Lessa, W. A. *Tales from Ulithi Atoll.* Berkeley and Los Angeles: Univ. of California Press, 1961.

Malinowski, B. *Myth in Primitive Psychology.* New York: Norton, 1926.

Notes and Queries on Anthropology. London: Royal Anthrop. Inst., 1929 (5th ed.). Pp. 327–330.

Radin, P. *Primitive Man as Philosopher.* New York: Appleton, 1927.

——. *Social Anthropology.* New York: McGraw-Hill, 1932. Pp. 341–410.

Thomas, W. I. *Primitive Behavior.* New York: McGraw-Hill, 1937. Pp. 650–664.

Thompson, S. *The Folktale.* New York: Dryden Press, 1947.

CHAPTER THIRTEEN

MUSIC AND THE DANCE

MUSIC

Introduction. All peoples have songs and styles according to which those songs are sung. Many Old World peoples also have forms of musical expression the musical style of which has been determined to a degree by musical instruments rather than by the voice.

The origins of musical expression were probably in song rather than in devised instruments. The time of origin is of course beyond determination, but there is no reason to doubt that it may have been in extremely remote times.

It cannot be said definitely, with Karl Bücher, that songs originated as accompaniments or stimulants to rhythmical labor. Songs may well have preceded many forms of rhythmical work, such as basketry and weaving, which developed only along with later technological achievements. Perhaps early forms of rhythmical activity which were accompanied by singing were the rocking of infants or walking, but there is no proof that the rhythms of the earliest sung music were determined by the tempo of rocking or walking, or by repeated acts of labor.

Sung music may have preceded any instrumental music by long epochs of time. There must have been little instrumental music until the Neolithic period and after, when improved cutting tools, specialization of labor, and other unprecedented features of wealthy agricultural and pastoral societies led to the manufacture of ever more richly expressive mechanical musical instruments. The *evolution* of music thus had two stages. The first was the music of the long Paleolithic and earlier Neolithic eras, much of which may have been sung and the stylistic features of which could have ranged through all the possibilities offered by the human voice. The second was the music of the later Neolithic and more recent eras of the Old World, wherein an increasing percentage of musical expression was rendered by fashioned instruments, and its stylistic features were affected by the possibilities offered by those instruments.

Musical Instruments. Musical instruments with taut strings over a sounding board probably never appeared during the Paleolithic eras. Carved and hollowed flageolet-, flute-, or piccolo-like instruments made of wood, bamboo, or bone were, however, very likely to be found in most regions. There may have been some percussion instruments such as rattles, tambourines, and various drums. Perhaps xylophone-like instruments of wood or bamboo were also developed. Some peoples may have had bull-roarers. Not many of these instruments, with their few tones and their meagre range of effects, are likely to be discovered archeologically, nor were they likely to offer other than minor features of musical styles.

Not until the later Neolithic or Metal Age periods of the Old World continents did advances in technology and specialization of labor succeed in developing complex instruments capable of effects so varied as to influence many musical styles. Stringed instruments, notably the multistringed lyre and cithara, probably then spread from the Near East to most parts of the Old World, and became ever more complex and rich in their musical effects. They were brought to America by the Spaniards, for the American Indians had never developed a true string instrument.

There are three major factors in the history of modern European music—the writing, symbolic representation, and analysis of music; the cumulative advances in the technology of string instruments; and the development of harmony.

Musicological Research. The patterns of musical expression among the peoples in primitive economies are complex and very different from European musical forms. It is therefore impossible to describe non-European music through field recording techniques utilizing pencil and paper. In the field-work situation the musicologist cannot write fast enough, or make note of every feature of musical style. Moreover, his ear must become attuned to subtle features of intonation and rhythm which are new to his experience. He begins to perceive these only after prolonged familiarity and repeated careful listening. For these reasons all scientific study of non-European music has had to be made on a basis of mechanical recordings, whether on the older type of wax cylinders, or on the more recent disk, film, tape, or wire recordings that are made electrically. Such recordings can be replayed until every stylistic feature and nuance of expression is analyzed. For the study of more exacting problems, such as the variation and the flexibility of intonation, electrical recordings can be analyzed by the use of refined acoustical apparatus, exact measurements, and statistical methods.

As in the case of oral literature, it is difficult to find standardized or ideal renderings of songs in societies where each singer may omit, add, or embellish creatively as he wishes. Since every rendering of a song influences all auditors, the history of such a musical style is affected by all the renderings. Therefore, it is necessary to make a sampling of songs. It is preferable to request and secure a number of performances of a single song from several good singers as well as a number of renditions of the same piece from average singers, for one version may be insufficient for scientific purposes.

The problem is somewhat different where professionalization, specialization, and standardization have developed to a noteworthy degree, as in the songs of some "secret societies" of the Northwest Coast, or the songs of comparable clubs in the communities of the Southwest, or the songs or other art forms of musical specialists in the wealthier and more stratified societies. Here single versions by individuals who are recognized as outstanding may be sufficient. In general, however, it has been found best to record many alternative forms of each composition. In all cases a musical style, like all else in human affairs, manifests changes with time, and so samples at successive periods are required.

Since every community has a variety of musical forms of expression such as lullabies, magico-ceremonial songs of different kinds, work songs, play songs, mourning music, and other special kinds, a large sample of each type must be secured. All societies have many hundreds of songs or other musical compositions. At the time that each composition is recorded the scientific collector makes careful note of any words or nonsense syllables that accompany the musical notes, and of every aspect of the correlated ceremonial, religion, work, or other social features of the culture. Judgments of listening natives regarding the worth of each performance are also noted.

There are millions of songs or pieces played by instrument among the peoples of low economic level the world over. Musicology now has recordings of only a few tens of thousands of these. Only rarely has a tribe or community had a large sampling of its music made available on records for purposes of scientific study. Each of hundreds of groups is represented by a few score songs or other compositions. This is a wretched sort of sampling and indicates how young the science of descriptive and comparative musicology really is. Large areas have barely been touched for purposes of recording. Characterizations of the major stylistic features of most areas are not even possible with present fragmentary record collections and in the absence of scientific analysis of most of the small collections already obtained.

The musicologist whose historical and scientific training has been based on European musical literatures, supplemented perhaps by some training and experience in Far Eastern musical literatures, is not sufficiently equipped to analyze the music of American Indians, Melanesians, or Africans. Special training and a certain length of experience in the scientific analysis of music of these other areas is a prerequisite for trustworthy inquiry, just as special training in the phonetics and grammatical features of American Indian languages is demanded of Indo-European linguists who venture into native America and beyond their familiar territory of scientific research.

Participation in Music. The progressive narrowing of participation in music parallels what has already been indicated for the history of oral literature. In simple food-gathering societies every adolescent tends to have learned all the music of his or her sex, and in some areas as in western North America every adolescent has heard every song and can have learned to sing it. But in northerly and wealthier districts of the economically advanced food-gathering

Pacific Northwest Coast several inventories of songs have become the property of clans, lineages, secret societies, or other special groups, and nonmembers of these groups do not sing such songs. At the same time one is likely to find an especially large total of songs in a society where specialist groups develop songs for their own purposes. So too in the simple agricultural societies of the Southwest the ceremonial clubs or so-called secret societies each have their special songs in large numbers.

The degree of specialization becomes so great in advanced agricultural-pastoral and economically more advanced societies that only a segment of the music may be known to any nonspecialist. In such wealthy societies one of the specialist groups may be composed of professional or semiprofessional musicians and musical composers.

In a simple food-gathering society musical composers constituted a considerable percentage of the people. In the western parts of the United States the songs heard by seekers of guardian spirits were stylistically much the same as other songs except for minor innovations in theme, melodic line, scale, rhythm, and vocal mannerisms. In societies where the sexes were of equal status musical composers were not usually better represented by one than by the other sex. In such societies musical composers were not as infrequent as in our social system.

The relative number of musical composers probably decreased notably when musical creativity was customarily assigned to specialist composers. For this reason the rarity of great composers in modern European society must be attributed much more to the nature of the social system than to any genetic rarity of potentiality for originality in musical composition. Only those who have been accorded opportunity to receive musical training, and who afterwards also have opportunity to compose, are able to create in musical terms. Many persons may have the same creative potentialities but may fail to receive either the necessary musical training or subsequent opportunities for musical composition. No such barriers existed in the simple food-gathering societies. In them most persons could learn the entire musical heritage of the culture, and the belief that there was equal opportunity to create and to perform new musical products is generally evidenced.

Rhythm. When people sing or play instruments they frame the melody in terms of one or another rhythm pattern. Since all peoples have the same central nervous system and also possess two hands and two feet for purposes of rhythmic punctuation and percussion accompaniment, they all can contribute to the complexities of rhythm or percussion and there are no known limits to their variety.

The rhythm patterns of recent centuries of European music are relatively simple compared to the complex and frequently changing rhythms of some areas of non-European music such as African. The absence or simplicity of musical instruments does not necessarily bring about a simplicity of rhythm patterns or a meager development of percussion devices. In fact some non-European rhythms recently heard by European composers have opened up broader possibilities of rhythmic expression than were previously known for the history of European music.

Percussion devices, besides the use of hands, body, or thighs, can be simple sticks, house walls, complexly carved and hollowed-out rattles, and hollowed out wooden logs. *Idiophone* is a generic term used to characterize such percussion instruments. Hide-covered drums are called *membranophones*. Percussion instruments are sometimes tuned carefully for tone color or pitch.

In a few regions the rhythm of the music may be accompanied by one or more additional rhythm patterns of body movement or percussion instrument. A striking feature, for example, of some of the music in the northwestern United States is the lack of consonance between the music rhythm and the rhythm of the stick or skin drum employed as a percussion instrument.

There is no reason to suppose that any one people is innately more addicted to rhythms of a certain kind than is another. Although all peoples are capable of rhythmic responses, specific rhythm patterns are entirely learned. Their presence in any period and area can be accounted for only in terms of historical processes and circumstances of that period and area.

Two of the varying ideas on the creation of musical rhythms are Bücher's theory maintaining that they originated in repetitive body movements in work, and Wundt's theory of origin in dance movements. Neither account for the facts of complexity and change of rhythms in modern music styles nor for the changes in such rhythms that occurred during many thousands of years. These theories may, however, partially account for such phenomena.

Tonal Patterns and Scales. Where peoples lack complex musical instruments with fixed pitches and the principal instruments are their own voices, there are no mechanical factors that limit severely the variety, complexity, or range of tonal patterns. Quarter tones or intervals other than half and whole tones are likely to be found in every area that has no complex mechanical instruments.

Possible tonal patterns are many. Our octave is divided into twelve equidistant tone intervals, the Javanese into five, the Siamese into seven. There are undoubtedly many other patterns of intervals in different musical areas. The appearance and increase in the use of mechanical musical instruments, which spread from the Near East during the past 4000 or more years, may have lessened the varieties and complexities of intonational patterns, while stimulating new ones.

Scales are only the recorded representations and schematized portrayals of tonal patterns. Such analytic writing began little if at all earlier than classical Greece. Once scales were noted on paper, however, they also served to restrict free play with patterns of intonation. Subsequent musical expression was often framed within the confines noted by the recorded patterns or scales. On the other hand, any written analysis also serves as a tool by which new kinds of scales or other features of music can be devised.

Claims by musicologists that the tonal patterns found in some culture areas are extremely simple and primitive are in some cases based on study of only a small number of recorded songs, and thus have left an erroneous general impression as to the style of the music of people in primitive economies. If the report of extreme simplicity in tone patterns be verified by extensive sampling for all kinds of music of a people, the inference does not follow that the musical style as a whole is simple. Similarly, European styles of music are characterized by a very small range of possible rhythms, each quite simple, yet this does not mean that our music is a simple and primitive heritage. It is necessary to examine each and every facet of a musical style, not to characterize a whole style by one or two of its simplest components.

Melodic Patterns. The human voice, which is innervated by the central nervous system, is capable of so many tones and of such a long series of tones in so many melodic patterns that the absolute limits in number and variety of such patterns are for practical purposes infinite. That is why many extremely different melodic patterns, including complex ones, are found among food-gathering peoples, whose major or sole instrument for musical expression is the voice. The only limitations are the melodic patterns learned in childhood from older people. The number of possible patterns is reduced somewhat only when the people acquire fixed-pitch or fixed-interval instruments and choose to express themselves musically only within the rigidly fixed tonal range permitted by those instruments. This may have been especially true when the instruments were simple and permitted a relatively small range of tones as seems to be true of the Near Eastern string and wind instruments that have been described as pre-Christian Bronze Age and Iron Age.

When the technological level and the specialization of labor of later Neolithic periods and of the Bronze Age and Iron Age permitted fabrication of ever more complex wind and string instruments, their possessors experimented with the kinds of musical expression possible with such instruments. The composers, performers, and auditors were so intrigued with the special effects made possible by the instruments that everywhere the trend seems to have been for vocal mannerisms, tonal range, and tonal patterns which were characteristic of older singing styles to change, and at times to be simplified in the direction of an imitation of and limitation to the new range of expression of the musical instruments. In our own musical heritage this is illustrated by the coloratura vocal style, as well as by melodic patterns characteristic of the flute or the piccolo.

A woven fabric of several melodic patterns, or true choral and polyphonic singing, has not been found among the Indians of any part of the Americas but for a few extremely simple exceptions. However, beginnings of part singing may have been present in very wealthy communities such as among the Aztecs of Mexico. True part or choral singing developed in some African areas as well as in Eurasian countries; an interweaving of several simultaneous tones must have occurred in the latter considerably earlier than classical Greek times.

Melodies are specific variants which in outline still follow the sequence imposed by the established melodic patterns. Words and vocables or nonsense syllables (like *tra la la*) are tacked on or secondary to such melodies, though as a rule melody and song text are conceived as formations which grew simultaneously and held each other in balance. However, there are prayer, chant, or recitative forms, especially in ceremonials, where the words are primary and the melody is only an adaptation to and a secondary attachment to the words.

Vocal Technique or Manner of Singing. The varieties of vocal techniques and mannerisms possible are as many as the varieties of sounds possible in phonetics (see p. 286). Each musical area, however, has its stylized and conventional ways of using the voice, and fails to utilize other possible ways. As noted previously, when complex wind and string instruments came to be used, vocal technique and mannerisms sometimes tended to approximate the sounds produced by the mechanical instruments.

One of the most important factors in the formal style of songs, as in the style of oral literature, is the manner of employment of the voice. Analysis of a song style which has not been long affected by instruments is especially difficult because the voice may be employed in more varied and complex ways for which transcriptional indicators are lacking.

Primitive Music as Art. The range of expression possible with an instrument as flexible as the voice has led many complex styles of musical expression to develop. Percussion and rhythm were also not confined by lack of mechanical resources. In every community of later Paleolithic and Neolithic times many individuals could have mastered their culture's heritage of musical expression, attained technical competence, achieved a release from technical problems, and "played with the technique" so imaginatively as to have created works of art. Such individuals may readily be termed artists and composers.

The achievement of an individual European composer such as Bach, Haydn, Beethoven, or Mozart may not strictly be compared, however, with the comparable but always joint achievement of groups of musical artists and composers in societies of primitive economies. The two contrasted kinds of musical creativity are on levels too remote for just comparison and evaluation. There is, furthermore, insufficient knowledge of the history of a primitive musical style to judge the quality and extent of creative achievement at any one point in its course. However, students of primitive societies are in agreement that the performers of music, as well as those who transmit the art heritages of folklore, dance, and plastic and graphic forms, display continuous creative activity. These native artists reshape traditional compositions and styles by imperceptible degrees and sometimes so slowly that cumulative effects of their creativity may not become perceptible until generations have passed.

Non-European musical artists perform very well before the microphones of portable field recorders. The motivations for omissions, garbled versions, and the like are much weaker in musical symbolism than in words of folk tales and myths which phrase beliefs that Europeans have flouted. Therefore electrical recordings of primitive music may be expected to include samples of artistry more often than do transcriptions of folk tales.

The problem arises as to who is to identify and judge works of musical art. For all their comparative knowledge and analytic skill, musicologists cannot quickly perceive the stylistically demanded and stylistically original components of the music they have recorded or analyzed. Their word as to what compositions are artistic (in the sense of creatively original) always requires corroboration from native musical critics, that is, from those who comprehend what is essential for technical competence and virtuosity. In most instances judgments regarding the artistic achievements of native musicians and composers must be withheld until full field information has been acquired.

Even though critical evaluations are uncertain, the compositions in a non-European musical style may be enjoyed to the degree to which one becomes familiar with that style. Any initial reaction of strangeness or dislike is comparable to and as meaningful as the giggling reaction of an English-speaking adolescent when he first hears Chinese or Siouan speech. This does not mean that an affection must be developed for every non-European musical style when one has become sufficiently acquainted with it. There is no more justification in demanding that all people become enamored of an exotic musical style than there is justification in demanding that everyone become enamored of Bach organ fugues or Beethoven quartets. One may hope all may acquire a liking for them, but if they fail to develop such appreciation, it is only a matter of their missing the aesthetic experience.

The question may be posed as to whether European music of the last two centuries is of higher aesthetic developmental level than, for example, Navajo ceremonial singing. There can be no quarrel with aesthetic preferences that are unaffected by ethnocentric conceits, but on a rational level European and Navajo music may only be considered extraordinarily different in kind, not superior or inferior to each other. They are poles apart in stylistic features. They come from entirely different heritages. They symbolize entirely different aspects of life. Their levels of expression are not equatable; hence comparisons as well as evaluations are improper. It is the obligation of science to preserve and describe, as well as to account for, the creative achievements that have been produced by both art styles, and to encourage people to acquaint themselves with, to understand, and to enjoy the best in each.

DANCE

Introduction. Dancing is a universal feature of human society. Religious or magico-ceremonial dancing, play dancing, and other specific types of dancing are all probably found in every society of primitive economy.

Dramatic and symbolic dances are potentially available to all peoples no matter what their type of social system may be, because the human body which is utilized for dance expression has the same nervous system and muscle equipment among all peoples. For this reason dance styles can be as complex and beautiful among peoples of the lowest technological level as among any others. Peoples in primitive economic systems suffer from no handicap whatever in this one of all the arts, and in fact there is general agreement that their dances often display superb aesthetic quality.

Research in the Dance. No minutely accurate and serviceable transcription of themes, body movements, and group dance behavior has been devised for most non-European styles of dance. Scientific research therefore requires the employment of sound on film. The musical background which is almost always inextricable from the dance style must also be recorded. Only films give repetitions sufficient to permit painstaking analysis of every unit trait of a style. The science of dance analysis is poorly developed in contrast with the analysis of non-European music.

In scientific research on the dance a number of dances, if not all the dances, of each type must be filmed to assure adequate sampling. Moreover, the performances of a variety of individuals must be obtained, in order to determine variability. The films must be supplemented not merely by careful notations regarding the cultural meaning and role of each dance, but also by a critical analysis and comments from the best informed natives regarding the quality of each performance. Analysis of non-European dances cannot be accepted with full confidence until considerable experience in the scientific study of such dance styles has been acquired. Few if any research workers of this kind have been developed.

Dance Origins and History. The ultimate beginnings of the dance cannot be dated but may have been far back in Paleolithic times. But no dance style of today can be considered representative of Paleolithic dances in any specific way. Dance themes or motifs, body movements and symbolisms, and choreography have diffused from community to community just like other traits of culture. As a result all dances of today include borrowed content and patterns. Most social systems in primitive economies are now of Neolithic or later patterning, and very few of the food-gathering systems are even in their technological features like their Paleolithic predecessors. Dance expression symbolizes current cultural features of a relatively specific kind. Consequently no dance styles are exactly like those of Paleolithic times except in a few very general traits.

Although ultimate origins are beyond reconstruction, the **kinds** of changes that tend to occur in dance forms, as well as the social or other circumstances responsible to a degree for those changes, can nevertheless be ascertained. The social and cultural functions of the dance can also be determined. Systematic researches have rarely if ever been pursued toward these ends.

Ethnographic reports indicate that among contemporary peoples of most primitive economies, the dancer's body has not often been supplemented by elaborate or confining dance accoutrements. He may be painted, be ornamented with feathers, use rattles, and the like, but the human body which is his natural equipment for the dance can be and usually is employed with few or no garments or ornaments that limit the possible forms of expression. On the other hand, in societies which have a higher level of technology, the use of cutting tools and the wealth, leisure, and specialization allow the manufacture of dance regalia such as masks and special dance garments. In general the higher the economic level, the more progressively intriguing the dance regalia become and the more often they are utilized. Hence the history of the dance may show a rather late trend towards much greater employment of dance regalia and therefore more circumscribed possibilities for bodily expression.

Curt Sachs assumes that the dances of modern peoples have features of a specific kind which indicate ancient features of the dance. He supposes, for example, that Lower Paleolithic dancers performed as individuals within a loose circle of dancers, and that the dances of some modern food-gathering peoples indicate that Mousterian dances were very complex, both extrovert and introvert, both solo and in a loose circle, and that soloist Mousterians must have danced imitations of war practices and of animal behavior. He contends too that the dances of some other modern preagriculturalists indicate that Upper Paleolithic dances were also complex and variable. Correlations and historical perspectives such as Sachs's are beyond proof or disproof. One can only be sure that the later Paleolithic peoples could have danced as great a variety of themes, movements, and choreographic forms as have any modern peoples.

When, in recent millennia, dance specialists had at length become the main creators and carriers of dance styles, the themes they expressed tended to be less often expressive of religion, ceremonial, and broad interests common to all the people, and more often expressive of the interests of the nobility or others who paid for the services of the best dancers. Thus in the most recent periods of history, dance themes more often became entertainingly sexual or caricature in nature, rather than associated with magic or religion.

Participation in Dance. Since the human body is the instrument for dance expression and since the social patterns of the societies of the simplest economies both permitted and encouraged everyone to participate, all persons may have practiced all their people's dance patterns, or the patterns of their own sex or clan, during very ancient epochs. Some of the people may have been excluded in Upper Paleolithic and later times with the development of social systems in which specialist groups, clubs, or secret societies appeared. In wealthy Neolithic and later agricultural and pastoral systems, in which specialist dance troupes or religious organizations developed, dances are found in which only a few persons participated and all others were excluded except as observers. The history of the dance as in the case of literature and music has perhaps been marked by a progressive decline in the percentage of the people who were accorded opportunity to master techniques and to become virtuosos.

In most of the technologically lower societies everybody was in a position to learn from the better dancers. At the other extreme, in a society like our own, the most artistic dance heritages can be learned by only a very few pupils from a few teachers. With its long heritage of an ideology of sinfulness attached to dance symbolism, our society is also a special instance of broad discouragement of participation in dancing.

In all societies individuals engage in a long period of practice from childhood on, before they approach or attain technical competence, for everywhere the dance styles are complex. Artistry is achieved following release from the effort to dance competently. Artistry, creativity, or originality may be achieved by large numbers of persons in those societies where social approval is accorded participants for their efforts to master the techniques.

A change in the dance style in a society where there are many artists is probably more often a cumulative achievement of these artists than a spectacular innovation of only one artist. That is why geniuses in the dance seem to be peculiar not to one or another race but rather to that kind of social system which allows few to attain technical competence and artistry and where those few are specialists. Especially when artists are rare, geniuses are said to be present. When artists are many, the creative changes that occur follow one upon another more rapidly, but these changes are participated in jointly by all the artists, and so one is less likely to assume that only a genius can be responsible for a major change.

Dance Patterns and Features of Style. Sachs has supplied a number of designations for contrasting forms of dance expression. Body positions and movements vary from convulsive or inharmonious to exalted, rhythmic, and harmonious. Expanded-movement dances with leaping, skipping, lunging, lifting on toes, and so on as in southeastern Africa contrast with close-movement dances with swaying and calm, restrained gesturings as in parts of Oceania.

Dance themes vary between extremes which are termed mimetic as contrasted with abstract or symbolic. Dance forms or choreography vary between extremes which are termed individual as contrasted with group or choral. The latter are round, linear, or columnar in form. Each may be continuous in one direction or relatively static.

All themes, movements, or forms may appear in any type of society, although especially complex choral developments are found in parts of Oceania and Africa, sometimes in consequence of the formation of specialized religious organizations in such cultures. Few dance styles allow for dance movements where the bodies of the dancers are in very close contact.

The many symbols used to represent animals and objects in a decorative art style are paralleled in each dance style by a considerable inventory of gestures, mimic representations, and symbolic or succinctly descriptive body movements which constitute the minimal units of meaning. Masks and other regalia constitute additions to such inventories. Comparisons of each dance area's inventory of symbolic movements have not yet been undertaken.

Primitive Dance as Art. An evolution from simple to complex and higher types of dance styles cannot be said to have occurred during the later Paleolithic or modern periods. Many new movements, choral patterns, and themes, however, were accorded much more opportunity to develop during the Upper Paleolithic and Neolithic periods and in later social systems, largely because of the new specialization, the new dance regalia that could be made, and the new features of social and religious organization and ideology. These made notable additions to the already long list of possible forms of dance expression. The new social features cannot, however, be said to have permitted aesthetically superior forms of art. Assertions that the ballet, for example, is superior to the best in the primitive dance are to be regarded as based on ethnocentric limitations.

The arbiters of aesthetic achievement in the primitive dance are those who know the details of themes, movements, and forms, and who can judge the degree of technical perfection and of originality. Few or no outsiders can become rapidly familiar with intricacies of the themes and symbolism which the native participants in a dance heritage take years to master.

When peoples in societies on a low economic level become modernized as well as educated like Europeans, the magico-religious or other motivations and social functions of their dances change. The dance styles, however, can be retained for a period with new motivations that involve more purely aesthetic appreciation.

SELECTED READINGS

Boas, F. *Primitive Art*. Irvington-on-Hudson: Capital Hill, 1951.

Boas, Franziska. *The Function of Dance in Human Society*. New York: Franziska Boas, 323 W. 21 St., 1944.

Evans, B. and M. G. *American Indian Dance Steps*. New York: A. S. Barnes, 1931.

Herzog, G. *Research in Primitive and Folk Music in the United States*. Washington: Amer. Counc. Learned Societies, 1936 (Bulletin No. 24).

Notes and Queries on Anthropology. London: Royal Anthrop. Inst., 1929 (5th ed.). Pp. 295–320.

Nettl, B. *Music in Primitive Culture*. Cambridge: Harvard Univ. Press, 1956.

Roberts, H. H. "Primitive Music," in *Encyclopedia of the Social Sciences*, XI, (1933), 150–152.

Sachs, C. *World History of the Dance*. New York: Norton, 1937.

CHAPTER FOURTEEN

THE PLASTIC AND GRAPHIC ARTS

Introduction. To most people the art of peoples on primitive economic levels is primarily their sculpture, basketry, pottery, beaded moccasins or garments, and other forms of plastic or graphic expression rather than the art forms discussed in the foregoing sections. Even some recent encyclopedia treatments of primitive art have omitted mention of nonmaterial forms of art, in spite of the fact that the most elaborate as well as socially important arts of the peoples of primitive economy are their literature, their music, and their dance. There are obvious reasons why both anthropologists and non-anthropologists have failed to think of literature, music, and dance as the most important and aesthetically original art forms created by and functioning in the daily lives of non-European peoples. These nonmaterial art forms have not often been made available or intelligible to Europeans, whereas the plastic and graphic art products have had direct appeal and intelligibility. Their translation was not technical or beyond comprehension. Plastic and graphic forms of art can be brought to museums and art galleries, illustrated in magazines and books, and even displayed in homes. On the other hand, transcriptions of oral literature, music, and dance either have been inaccurate and have not done justice to the art, or if accurate are often alien or incomprehensible in content and form. One of the sad features of the present period of transformation in the lives of hundreds of millions of people living in primitive economies is the fact that the art forms for which they had technical resources about as advanced as those possessed by modern European cultures were peculiarly perishable, ephemeral, or too difficult to comprehend for most people.

The peoples in primitive economies contrast sharply with more advanced economies in the poverty of their cutting tools, their meagre technical knowledge, and the paucity of their materials for aesthetic expression in plastic and graphic forms. Nevertheless some of these forms were well developed even among the peoples on the lowest economic levels.

Among the tasks of anthropology is to determine the social or other processes which operated in the development of individual plastic and graphic art forms, the role such arts played in the cultures in which they appeared, the causes for the stylistic features and for changes in such features, the causes for the themes expressed, and the reasons why such themes changed.

Origins and History of Artistry in Plastic and Graphic Forms. Earlier writers on primitive art often attempted an over-all sketch of the evolution of the plastic and graphic arts, by the utilization for example of Aurignacian and Magdalenian polychrome paintings inside French and Spanish caves. Several errors were committed in such thinking. There is no chance whatever that the earliest art forms developed in and were expressed on interior surfaces of caves, or that they were at once as extraordinarily mature in conception and execution as the Paleolithic drawings. However, abstract representations of the female figure modeled with mastery in stone and ivory figurines were also Aurignacian and equally represent an early development of art work in such materials.

The earliest forms of artistic expression in solid materials are lost forever because they were made with decayable materials. The aesthetic achievements of surviving food-gathering peoples in wood, bark, and fibers can be examined but these arts throw as little light on the earliest Paleolithic aesthetic work as modern religions, languages, music, or dance forms are suggestive of the earliest Paleolithic developments in such forms of expression. Paleolithic archeology offers no help because until the Upper Paleolithic it reveals only the imperishable materials which were virtually intractable for aesthetic purposes.

The art work of children has often been considered in conjunction with primitive art, as if there were much in common between them. However, if primitive art is correctly defined as that which is made possible and appears only following long practice with a complex heritage of techniques, themes, and patterns, the art of children is assuredly on another and different level. When the untaught child paints, draws, or models he abstracts and symbolizes only what he perceives or what to him is essential, significant, and real, and he may add nonvisible details which he believes are present. But he omits everything else. He rarely decorates. Above all, he follows few stylized conventions. Primitive arts, on the other hand, are always the products of a long heritage of themes and styles. Their only primitiveness lies in the socio-economic system in which the carriers of the art traditions lived, in the crudity of the cutting or other tools employed, and in the limitations in materials which could be worked. It is therefore quite incorrect to equate them with the processes operative in the art of untutored children.

In the discussion of the improbability of a historical connection between Upper Paleolithic art and Eskimo art, and between Capsian and Bushman art, the point was made that no art is stable for long periods (see p. 218). Factors in rapid aesthetic change are the borrowing of techniques, themes, and units of design, the masterly play with technique, and original changes. Superimposed strata revealed by archeology in the southwest United States display rapid changes in pottery styles. Each style endured only through a few human generations.

Research in Plastic and Graphic Arts. The value of the finds and collections of art made by archeologists should not be underestimated. Examples of prehistoric art that can sometimes be dated make it possible to determine the area of initial development of designs and the extent of their later diffusion. Historical changes in arts can thus be indicated by archeological research. But the value of such arts for other scientific purposes can also be overestimated. The interpretation of designs, for example, is no longer possible when the persons who lived in the culture are gone, and when their culture is substantially changed. Nor can the religious or social functioning of a prehistoric art be indicated in any detail.

Research in contemporary plastic and graphic forms is more revealing because both the artists themselves and competent native critics of their work can be interviewed at length. The collection of samples of art for scientific purposes always has to be carried on as part of a larger ethnographic project, which means the securing of full information regarding the culture, and as much material as possible regarding the individual artists whose work has been collected. For scientific purposes it is usually unnecessary to purchase and take away specimen pieces if excellent photographs of them can be obtained and each is fully discussed, interpreted, and criticized by a sufficient number of the best informed natives. Historical changes that preceded an existing art form can usually be revealed only by a combination of archeological work and of spot maps of each technical and stylistic feature of the art, obtained from researches conducted in all adjacent and, if necessary, distant districts.

Participation in Plastic and Graphic Arts.   Some forms of decorative art that were the earliest to develop must have been largely women's work. Until the complex socio-economic levels of later Neolithic times were attained, women probably did most of the weaving and pottery, and basketry was almost always women's work. Carving, incising, and sculpturing in general were almost invariably men's work, probably because men made and repaired the equipment they used for hunting and fishing and therefore were skilled in woodcraft. No special sexual significance need be attached to these observations. One sex has not been shown to have any inherited traits for aesthetic creativity that are absent in the other sex. The fact that some particular art is associated with the one sex rather than the other is to be explained in terms of the circumstances of the division of labor in the cultural heritage, not of biological aptitude.

The meagre degree of participation in plastic and graphic arts and the rarity of artists in our society is in striking contrast to the extent of popular participation and the high percentages of the people who are artists in most societies of low economic level. For example, almost every girl in the food-gathering societies of western North America practiced at basketry work before she reached puberty; she continued making baskets during the rest of her life. Her teachers were her own female relatives or covillagers, many of whom were technically competent or were artists. Her community included exemplary critics and was also characterized by the greatest general respect for and approval of artistry. Baskets made for everyday use were embellished with taste more often than not. Many additional basketry pieces were turned out as aesthetic *tours de force,* with no especial utility intended. In the Pueblo Southwest, pottery was produced under much the same conditions.

Specialists in wood carving on the Northwest Coast of America were supported by the nobility and received intense approbation from the entire community. Sometimes a number of artists co-operated in the fashioning of a single carved pole.

The village specialization in pot, hat, and other manufactures which featured many advanced agricultural-pastoral societies, or those in process of change from simple agricultural to advanced agricultural-pastoral societies, was characterized by more or less general participation of the population of each village in the one or two handicrafts whose product was sold in the region's market center.

Wherever many members of a community lived in an environment characterized by the presence of several older persons who were critics, artists, or both, and by general handicraft participation by the members of one or both sexes, the results were likely to be affected by spirited competitiveness. The products were often of a high order of technical excellence at the very least. In the case of handicrafts even in the simple food-gathering and simple agricultural societies, covillagers vied with one another for community applause. In the advanced agricultural-pastoral societies as in West Africa such applause was supplemented by the lure of market profits, which in the absence of a system of mass production resulted in little or no cheapening, commercialization, or other sort of aesthetic degeneration.

The degree of callousness of modern Europeans to art forms produced by non-Europeans has so far been such that the latter have lost interest in artistic work when their cultures have been shattered and their people have been enveloped by European immigrants and brought into the maelstrom of a European type of economy. There is then no longer respect or reward for aesthetic achievement. Participation lessens, and in a short time the last artists die. Hundreds of art forms have thus vanished during the four and a half centuries of European expansion.

Principles of Design. As has already been mentioned (see p. 218) some students of primitive art have approached the study of art with an evolutionary theory that the development of decorative design proceeded from realistic to geometric or other conventionalized design. It has been indicated that the opposite course of development was as likely to have occurred where early and crude technical manipulations prevented realistic representation until later periods when much greater mastery of the technique was acquired. It has been shown also that many interpretations that were given to decorative motifs that have diffused were only secondary associations, often consequent upon a style of interpretation of design motifs already present.

No simple trend from realistic to conventionalized design can be admitted for any Late Pleistocene or modern era, because there has always been a style of decoration already established, whether it be realistic, conventionalized, or intermediate, that has been applied to similar materials. The styles already present have influenced any new kind of art expression in a new artifact or material.

Nor can the influence of the tools or the shape and texture of the materials employed, that is to say, the technical manipulations, be shown to have determined entirely the kinds of designs. At least the small details of design have been rarely so influenced. Even where technical factors are almost equatable, designs differ markedly, as in mat-work and pottery styles in a number of historically unconnected areas.

Given a mastery of technical manipulation and a sufficiently wide range of possibilities of decoration, the play of creative imagination results in a variety of forms of decoration. Only the most careful study of the special historical circumstances and cultural setting within each group or subarea can suggest why such play with technique tended to result in one or another specific design.

The tendency to play within the limits of the possibilities of the technique leads, for example, to the use of rhythmic, symmetrical, or balanced arrangements, groupings, bandings, and the like. Sometimes few or no observers will even perceive these arrangements, which were created by the artists largely as a matter of enjoyment of technical mastery and of play with the resources and skills available. Rhythmical decorative arrangement in basketry, textiles, pottery, sculpture, and architecture does not merely flow from play with technique. It seems to be associated with the fundamental pleasure in rhythm that also finds expression in oral literature, music, and dance.

In design, a very few parts may be sketchily or symbolically indicated as representative of all the anatomical complexity of an animal or of the structural complexity of a plant, artifact, or other object. A certain few features are accented, and all others are disregarded. Thus a diamond may symbolize a lake; the symbol of a dorsal fin may represent a killer whale; a cross may stand for a star; or a zigzag line may portray a snake or lightning. This is conventional or abstract art design in extreme form.

No art ever achieves microscopically exact realism. The artist omits one aspect and stresses another. A few parts suggest the whole. Some peoples have suggested reality by the X-ray-like representation of that which is known to be present but is not visible. Thus the heart, lungs, or stomach have been drawn within the outline of an animal by various American Indian groups, North Australians, and Melanesians. Capsian, Bushman, Eskimo, and other artists followed silhouette principles of representation. Few art areas utilized perspective until the European Renaissance. Pictograph or cartoon-like representative styles appeared in several areas as in the hide garments and tipi (or tepee) covers of the Plains Indians.

Many details are derived from anatomical reality in the relatively realistic sculpturing of Guinea-Sudan Africa, Melanesia, Central America, Peru, and other areas. In Peru masterpieces of portraiture were achieved in pottery; in Nigeria, in wood, bronze, and stone; in other areas, more often in wood.

Realism or naturalism in graphic art rather than in sculpture has to do with the optical impression received in a precise moment in time; or it implies the representation of details known to be present but not necessarily perceptible.

Some Freudian-minded critics of arts of peoples of primitive economies have supposed that sexual drives and processes in the unconscious have been a major factor in representations, symbolic motifs, and patterns of design. It is true that sexual representation or symbolization appears frequently in non-European art styles. Such motifs, however, are on a par with any other important design elements that are integral components of the style. The reasons for recourse to such elements lie embedded in the ethnography and art history of each subarea. Unless that background is known in some detail one remains hopelessly at a loss to account for any of the components of the style.

Just as each oral literature has its many component features of themes, plots, formal or stylistic elements, and the like, so too each plastic or graphic art style could be analyzed into its component design motifs, themes, or decorative units, and its rhythmic features, kinds of banding, symmetry, contrasted masses, balance, texture, and luster. It is the challenge to play with all these resources in decorative units, materials, and features of style that stimulates the artist to produce a masterpiece. He is challenged to succeed without transgressing a single rule of conventionally used content or style, and at the same time to do it perfectly and as originally as possible.

Painting. The earliest painting could very well have developed in Paleolithic eras so remote that there would be no possibility of survival of examples. The technique of polychrome painting was simple because of the availability of grease, wax, marrow, and other substances with which pigments such as red ochre could be mixed. Finger painting could long have preceded brushes, although the latter could easily have been made in earlier Pleistocene times. The oldest paintings known, which may be over twenty thousand years of age, survived only because of their location inside caves. Artists agree that the Aurignacian and later Upper Paleolithic painters achieved masterpieces. Since these painters lived in the types of food-gathering socio-economic systems that in modern times have also produced beautiful oral literature, music, dance, basketry, and sculpture in bone and wood, it is not surprising that painting of the finest quality also occurred here and there in such systems in Paleolithic times. The social conditions as well as the material equipment that made such achievement possible were present. The specific circumstances that brought about Upper Paleolithic painting are not known, nor is it possible to ascertain the precise magico-ceremonial or other motivations for the portrayal of game animals in that period.

Capsian rock paintings and chippings, masterful in their rendering of movement and excitement, may be from 5000 to 10,000 years old. In style they are similar to modern Bushman rock paintings in South Africa. Bushman art at its best is polychrome. It represents humans and animals and in some districts the representations are chipped rather than painted. Some paintings display foreshortening which gives the effect of perspective.

Painting on pottery is widely found but rarely approaches realistic representation until there has been a long period of development of technical skill with clays and paints on clay.

Painting of landscapes or other scenes is a late development which appeared earlier in Asia than in Europe. It rarely occurs in any culture area among peoples with primitive economies. A few styles that may be regarded as illustrated maps or diagrams appear on bark among some Australians and on hides among the Indians, and some Bushman rock paintings are of the same general type.

Sand Painting.　Australian Blackfellows, Navajos, Pueblos, Plains Indians, and some other peoples, notably several who live in desert or sub-desert regions, prepare intricate and sometimes aesthetically remarkable polychrome designs in the sand, usually during special rituals. Colored reproductions and photographs of this type of art are available. It may have developed a number of times in remote Paleolithic eras but no archeological evidence of this is possible.

Tattooing.　Body tattooing as an art form may seem almost like a contradiction in terms, for most regional examples of tattooing are not illustrative of anything that can be termed aesthetic. In rare instances, however, particularly among the Maori of New Zealand, and the Marquesans, the designs are so successfully conceived in relation to available surface areas that many individuals can be said to wear artistic masterpieces for life. Polynesian specialists, who were well remunerated for their labors in tattooing persons, applied designs borrowed from wood carving and painting. Populations of very dark pigmentation either do not resort to tattooing or have employed it only slightly.

Body Ornamentation.　Scarification of the body is widely found among the very dark pigmented peoples, probably because tattooing is not sufficiently visible among them. The beauty of ornamental scars is open to question although the attempt to produce aesthetically attractive results cannot be doubted. The same applies to perforated ear lobes, filed teeth, ear and lip plugs, head deformation, and other mutilations practiced here and there as means of becoming more attractive or of being properly garbed for life.

Body and face painting, like tattooing, may attain an aesthetic level comparable to the best known Maori or Marquesan tattooing. Temporary painting of the body, which is perhaps found among all peoples, probably developed at a very early time. Aurignacian skeletons give testimony to the use of red ochre 20,000 years ago.

Hairdressing is often especially painstaking and amounts to a kind of sculpturing in some regions. The woolly hair of some African Negroid and Melanesian peoples is built up into artistic masses. Some Mongoloid peoples, including American Indians, also succeeded in arranging their hair in aesthetic forms.

Art in Feathers. Paleolithic peoples probably had technical resources for snaring, netting, and trapping birds, and must have used colored feathers for decorative purposes. Feathers can be glued on to the body in various designs, as is done by modern Australian Blackfellows. They can be woven into cloaks or sewed onto garments as modern Hawaiians have done. Feathers are inserted as a cover over richly decorated coiled baskets made by the Pomo Indians in north-central California. Multicolored feather designs thus appear in various areas and at every level of economy. This is to be expected since peoples of the lowest economic level are not handicapped in technical resources for this kind of artistic work.

Dress. The degree of bodily exposure is not at all correlated with beauty in dress. Some tropic dwellers who have few or no garments, like the Nilotic peoples and the Australian Blackfellows, decorated their bodies with feathers that were glued on and with paints and other materials, especially on ceremonial occasions, so that body ornamentation verged on a kind of artistic dress. Artistically carved combs are worn in several regions.

Superbly tailored skin, gut, and fur garments of various kinds, with varicolored pieces for decorative trims and other effects, were developed by some northerly peoples such as the Eskimos.

Embroidery with shells and beads, and with various materials

such as dyed porcupine quills, was highly developed on hide garments made by North American Indians. Garments worn on ceremonial occasions were usually more artistic than garments for everyday use.

Art in Bark. The possibility of the use of beaten bark for cloth,
of shredded bark for skirts, and of larger strips of bark for utensils
may be presumed to have long antedated the Upper Paleolithic. The
tapa or beaten bark cloths of Polynesian and Melanesian islanders
display a wide range of artistically painted designs. Geometric designs were painted or incised on a great variety of bark utensils and
other artifacts, especially in the vast bark-using area of northern
North America.

Basketry. The finest basketry arts are found among modern food-
gathering peoples. Bulky and fragile pottery containers are not efficient for peoples who have to be seasonally mobile and for this
reason the making of baskets received special attention. Some excellent basketry also appears among horticultural and pastoral peoples. There is no reason to doubt that basketry could have been
made in the earlier Paleolithic epochs and was among the works
of art that have long since decayed.

Interlacings of warp and woof strands derived from split roots,
grasses, or other fibers are of various forms such as wicker weave,
checker weave, twilling, and twining. Finely twined baskets allow
an especially great range of decorative possibilities and some magnificent arts based on this technique have appeared, as for example
in California and districts to the north. Another type of basketry is
essentially a kind of sewing with an awl upon a grass, splint, or rod
foundation which coils up from its start at the bottom of the basket.
Coiled baskets are firm and hard and they allow both a wide range
of decorative opportunities and a possibility of a number of beautifully sculptured shapes. Many western American groups have both
soft twined or woven and hard coiled basketry. Some have thirty or
more distinctive techniques and styles of decorative treatment, for
each of which the native language has a name. A few groups which
are on extremely low economic levels as in California, and some
others as in Mexico, play so freely with their mastered techniques
that they turn out many exquisitely designed pieces that either are

too diminutive for use or are employed solely for special dress or ceremonial occasions.

Matting has been found in many regions and is highly developed, for example, in Middle America and Polynesia.

Sculpture and Carving in Wood. A few Late Paleolithic peoples may have sculptured in the softer woods, but no samples of so remote an epoch can have survived. Even for recent centuries only a few samples of arts in wood are available except in the case of desert regions.

Among the food-gathering peoples, the wealthiest Northwest Coast natives, who were relatively sedentary, achieved one of the most remarkable art styles of any modern areas. Specialists who were attached to noblemen's households carved ladles, boxes, rattles, masks and other ceremonial objects, canoes, house posts, and lately totem poles (see p. 134). A few pieces approached realism, but the art in general was highly abstract and conventionalized. The Haida Indians of the Queen Charlotte Islands off southern Alaska transferred this Northwest Coast style with superb effect to the difficult medium of black slate and turned out beautiful platters, sculptured figurines, and other pieces in this stone. The Chilkats of southern Alaska carried box designs over into blankets.

All other modern peoples who have achieved noteworthy styles in wood work are basically agricultural. Examples are the Maoris with their remarkably ornate house ornamentation, the Africans with their beautiful sculptures in various districts south of the Sahara, and some Indonesian and Melanesian peoples. Somewhat related art styles occur on gourds and calabashes in a number of regions.

African wood, bronze, and stone sculpturing from the Guinea-Sudan countries during the past thousand years has influenced modern European art decisively. European artists and critics have marveled both at the technical mastery and at the achievement of a style which they have characterized as possessed of extraordinary vitality, emphasis on the essential, complete plastic freedom and conception of form in three dimensions, and almost architectural sequences of structural planes and masses. The shapes of the wooden materials employed—that is, the round cylindrical or cubic blocks—seem to have been a major factor in the development of the distinctively geometric style of expression. The round block style of the Guinea-Sudan countries also varied progressively in the direction of realistic representation which is freed from the original shape of the materials employed. The carving specialists of the wealthy Guinea-Sudan countries produced objects for practical and magico-ceremonial purposes, and also statuettes, miniatures, and other pieces which probably served no function other than to delight their makers and art lovers.

An important technical factor in wood sculpture was the cutting tool, which was a stone adze in Melanesia and on the Pacific Northwest Coast, and was made of steel in Negroid Africa. Pieces were chopped rather than carved and so the finished surface frequently exhibited the unplaned marks of the tool.

Each of these areas also utilized effective polychrome painting, which further heightened the designs and surfaces of the sculptured product.

The intimate relationship between religion and art is exhibited by the use of symbols to represent supernatural beings in sculptured pieces, masks, and other magico-ceremonial regalia. Especially notable art styles in masks are found among the Iroquois and Pacific Northwest Coast Indians, in West Africa, Melanesia, and a number of wealthier areas of Asia. Mythological, sacred, or ancestral beings are also sculptured in the same and many additional districts. Closely related to or identical with such sculpturings are sculptured fetishes, objects infused with *mana*-like power, which are found in West Africa and other regions, and which are treated in a variety of ways depending on the regional religion.

Art Work in Precious Metals. Although some hammering of softer metals into bracelets or other ornaments may have occurred in Paleolithic eras, the period of extensive artistic work in the precious metals apparently began in the Neolithic period when there were fairly advanced agriculture and intense specialization of labor. Superb designing and sculpturing in gold are known to have occurred in some Andean and Central American countries not long before the Spanish Conquest, in spite of the paucity of pieces that escaped melting at the hands of the Spanish conquerors. During the past twenty years archeological researches in Mexico and Central

America have revealed quantities of aesthetically magnificent work in gold. Other aesthetically sculptured products in gold can be noted from comparably wealthy regions such as West Africa. India, Malaysia, ancient Egypt, and Middle America each employed the "lost wax" (*cire perdue*) method for sculpturing in precious metals.

Art in Bronze. The artistic work in bronze in the Near East following 3000 B.C., and in middle Europe and Scandinavia over a thousand years later, reached a magnificent climax on the Gulf of Guinea Coast of Africa during the Middle Ages, especially in the unsurpassed bronze sculpturings of Benin Nigeria, discovered after 1897. The bronzes of Benin certainly rank among the greatest art forms ever created. However, the symbolism and function of this art can never be known because so many centuries have passed since the days of its creators. It is significant that the technologically and socially most complex part of Negroid Africa should also have been the district of outstanding aesthetic creativity. Benin bronzes were models of animals, human beings, human heads, and also reliefs of animals, humans, myth symbols, or scenes. These bronzes were made by the "lost wax" method also used for sculptures in precious metals.

Bone, Ivory, and Horn Work. Artistic carving and incising in bone, ivory, and horn is available in Aurignacian and especially Magdalenian finds, in styles not very remote from those of modern Eskimo artistry in the same materials. With cutting tools of stone that are used upon substances of identical texture and shapes, the possibilities of stylistic expression are relatively limited and therefore, as already noted (see p. 218), the similarities are probably parallel developments, not historically connected forms. Wherever wood was hard to obtain, Upper Paleolithic peoples apparently often resorted to aesthetic expression in the more difficult media of bone and ivory. Harpoon points and other artifacts were often beautifully embellished.

In the Pacific Northwest the wood-carving style was carried over to art work on ladle handles made of mountain goat horn and also to many sculptured pendants and other pieces of bone and ivory. Specialist carvers produced such luxury articles for the wealthy. Wood-carving styles of other parts of the world, such as Africa south of the Sahara, were also carried over to elephant tusk ivory or similar hard materials.

Art in Stone. The earliest art work in stone is probably that on the blades produced by Mousterian craftsmen. Progressively superior work in stone occurred during the Upper Paleolithic period, with increasing possibilities due to pressure flaking.

A very few people in food-gathering technologies have mastered incising or carving in stone to the point of achieving aesthetically important results. For example in the Northwest United States there are many carved figures, now badly worn, which were made in pre-Columbian eras, but their aesthetic value seems poor. Slate dishes, figurines, and other pieces were carved by the Haidas, in the style of wood carving current among them.

Apart from these and a few other developments, artistic work in stone has apparently almost always followed the introduction of agriculture and the development of specialized craftsmen. In many or most instances it followed upon and stylistically resembled or copied earlier work done in wood or clay. The regions which have produced art styles in stone are numerous.

The earliest Neolithic socio-economic level to witness outstanding aesthetic achievement in stone sculpture was probably that of the Mayas. Comparable stone work in the Old World was always facilitated by bronze or superior metal tools. But the Mayas worked only with cutting tools of stone. They and the Aztecs to the North also cut fine small sculptures in crystal, jade, obsidian, and alabaster.

Architecture. The painted tipi of the Plains Indians is an example of architectural form which was possible under Paleolithic conditions. Another is the long cedar plank house of the Northwest Coast, which is technically complex but whose aesthetic interest resides not so much in its form as in its sculptured posts, carved doors, and painted façade. A variety of pole, mat, and thatch dwellings could have been constructed by Paleolithic peoples but unfortunately no remains can be found. The beehive-shaped house of snow blocks produced by Eskimos east of the Mackenzie is of aesthetic interest.

Several culture areas produced one or another new kind of architecture, of aesthetic worth, following the development of agriculture.

Examples are the elaborately carved houses of the Maori Polynesians, and the ornate structures of many Indonesian islands which were much influenced by India. Masonry and brick structures are usually severely simple but were tastefully constructed in many parts of the world.

Massive architecture of several kinds may well have preceded the Bronze Age of kings, priesthoods, palaces, temples, and tombs. The enormous gabled wooden structures built by men's clubs in Melanesia, and large community dwelling houses in Indonesia and the Amazon, are all in primitive agricultural areas. For this reason it cannot be assumed that great structures appeared in history only after about 4000 B.C.

It is true, however, that Neolithic western Europe was more or less contemporaneous with the Copper and Bronze Ages of Egypt and that at that time it cut its first monoliths for graves and temples, when the Egyptians and some other Near Eastern cultures were already producing stupendous and beautiful structures.

Quarrying, cutting, transporting, and fitting of great blocks of stone into larger structures has never been done by a preagricultural people. Such labors began in history only in slave-owning Neolithic or economically more advanced civilizations as in Central and Andean American regions, in western Europe in Neolithic times, and in the Near East.

Clay and Pottery. It has already been noted that clay was modeled into a few figures in Upper Paleolithic times in western Europe, and that fired clay pots that are only crudely decorated have been found among a very few modern food-gathering peoples.

Artistry in fired clay vessels, as far as is known, is limited to Neolithic or later agricultural and a very few pastoral peoples (see pp. 100 ff.). The technique is apparently too intricate to have been independently invented often.

All peoples molded and turned vessels of soft clay by hand until the Egyptian invention of the potter's wheel about 3000 B.C. The wheel-turned technique spread slowly and never reached the American Indians. In different regions many technical devices have been added to the original techniques of molding a lump of clay or of building up a pot with ribbon spirals of clay, and of firing. During the Bronze Age, Egypt invented glass and the glassy coating termed glazing. Various regions invented a painted surface coat or slip of fine clay which then allowed multicolored painting. China invented true porcelain just before 700 A.D., eleven hundred years before its manufacture in Europe.

Many possibilities of sculpturing as well as of realistic or symbolic decorative treatment are latent in pottery, especially in the finer forms that are glazed or of porcelain. Some of the most successful exploitation of the aesthetic possibilities in pottery appears, however, in Incan Andean and Central American districts which lacked the wheel-turned, glass, glazing, and porcelain techniques of the Old World. Some West Africans did sculpturing in clay similar to the superb sculptures in bronze and stone. But the portrait sculpturing in clay of pre-Columbian Peruvians is perhaps without a peer in wood or any other medium.

Pottery vessels are either embellished plastically in the course of fashioning, by corrugations, indentations, incising, or sheer sculpturing, or embellishment is applied in a pictorial way following the shaping—that is, by painting. Paints may also be used together with plastic embellishment.

Textiles. Paleolithic societies very likely wove few fine textiles, and those that they did weave may have been smaller pieces such as belts, arm bands, or head bands. Wools obtained from wild animals were probably rarely made into artistic pieces. The nonagricultural Indians of the Northwest Coast spun only into thick and coarse threads which were woven into coarse, heavy blankets that were artistically unsatisfactory except for those produced by the Chilkats. Finely spun threads and woven stuffs appeared in many regions following the domestication of plants and animals with consequent quantity production of fibers.

Extremely exact control of the technique and perfect visualization of the planned pattern are indispensable for aesthetic success in textile art. The loss or unnecessary addition of a single stitch can ruin the aesthetic effect.

Only the finest spinning and weaving will permit curved lines. Therefore most textile arts limit patterns to combinations of linear, angular, and geometric elements and color contrasts. Just as the pre-Columbian Peruvians displayed the greatest technical skill and imaginative creativity in sculpture in clay, so too the textile compositions of these Indians surpassed all other peoples. Patterns developed in Peruvian weaving were probably transferred to some of their pottery.

In both hemispheres textile workers in agricultural communities made many technical advances in the loom, which permitted ever superior textile arts.

Hide and Leather Work. Skin garments, moccasins, belts, bags, and the like were doubtless made by Paleolithic peoples, and they were probably given sea shell, seed, painted, fringe, or other ornamentation. The Indians of the northern United States offer many examples of arts of this kind.

The Old World domestication of animals was no doubt followed by quantity production of hides, and specialist production of artistically embellished hide garments and other hide products. These Neolithic arts have left no surviving pieces and therefore no generalizations can be made about them.

The Level of Primitive Plastic and Graphic Arts. Attempts at comparisons of art styles that have developed under very different conditions of technology and living are gratuitous. The scientist's manner of approach to the arts of each people in primitive economies must remain a matter of accurate reporting, and determination of the role of the arts in the culture, of the social relationships of the artistic participants, and of the responses of the best informed natives regarding the art work of their people.

The ways of perceiving and of aesthetic representation of reality, as well as of decorating, are many. Each art style emphasizes certain features for representation or symbolization, and suppresses or omits all other features. The worth of these canons of expression cannot easily or justly be evaluated although careful field research will allow trustworthy reporting on the extent of the mastery of the technique, of the fulfillment of other aesthetic principles of the art style, and of the degree of originality. The fashion in which the native artist has perceived, emphasized. or decorated can be appreciated in spite of the fact that no analogous art heritage of our own has enabled our artists to perceive or embellish in the same way. Above all, due sus-

picion must be developed of ethnocentric evaluations of our own
arts as superior achievements and as examples of a greater degree of
genius than that present among other peoples.

SELECTED READINGS

Adam, L. *Primitive Art*. Revised and enlarged edition. Harmondsworth:
Penguin, 1949.

Boas, F. *Primitive Art*. Irvington-on-Hudson: Capital Hill, 1951.

——. *Race, Language, and Culture*. New York: Macmillan, 1940. Pp. 535–540,
546–592.

Davis, R. T. *Native Arts of the Pacific Northwest*. Stanford, California: Stanford University Press, 1949.

Douglas, F. H., and R. D'Harnoncourt. *Indian Art of the United States*.
New York: Museum of Modern Art, 1941.

Kelemen, P. *Medieval American Art*. New York: Macmillan, 1943 (2 vols.)
Rev. ed. in 1 vol., 1957.

Kroeber, A. L., and T. T. Waterman. *Source Book in Anthropology*. New
York: Harcourt, Brace, 1931 (rev. ed.). Pp. 374–388.

Linton, R., and P. S. Wingert. *Art of the South Seas*. New York: Simon and
Schuster, 1946.

Notes and Queries on Anthropology. London: Royal Anthrop. Inst., 1929
(5th ed.). Pp. 187–276 *passim*, 288–294.

Wingert, P. S. *African Negro Sculpture*. San Francisco: M. H. DeYoung
Memorial Museum, 1948.

——. *The Sculpture of Negro Africa*. New York: Columbia Univ. Press, 1950.

Weltfish, G. *The Origins of Art*. New York: Bobbs-Merrill, 1953.

Wingert, P. S. *African Negro Sculpture*. San Francisco: M. H. DeYoung
Memorial Museum, 1948.

——. *The Sculpture of Negro Africa*. New York: Columbia Univ. Press, 1950.

CHAPTER FIFTEEN

KNOWLEDGE

Introduction. It is desirable to distinguish between science and common-sense knowledge. Science involves not common-sense knowledge but special kinds of knowledge and techniques of prediction that are obtained by uniquely rigorous and rational procedures which may be designated as scientific methods. Science is characterized by the use of well-reasoned anticipatory ideas, the initiation of inquiries designed to check up on these ideas or on any other preconceived ideas, the anticipatory and tentative arrangement and classification of facts, the accurate determination and exact measurement of the facts, a constant readiness to discard ideas or hypotheses that do not square with the facts, and a public availability of all hypotheses and results. Science in this strict sense was not developed until about the 5th century B.C. or shortly following in Greece. Until the 16th or 17th centuries in Europe it had a precarious continuity in the hands of few persons, whose occupations, or whose leisure through wealth, permitted them to function as specialists in scientific work. An ever increasing number of specialists have made important contributions to the development of science since that time. In spite of its revolutionary effects on human behavior, the permanence of science is as yet by no means absolutely assured. The numbers and influence of those who are antiscientific in the United States, for example, are still very great, and the recent wanton uprooting of the scientific study of social and historical phenomena in the Nazi countries indicates what can be done by determined antiscientific groups.

Common-sense knowledge and common-sense methods of acquiring knowledge, more or less independent of supernatural premises, must have been present among all peoples for many thousands of years. Such knowledge is gained by observation of factual successions, of uniform sequences, or of seemingly interconnected events. For example, the Eskimos know that seals gnaw holes through ice in order to breathe. All peoples are aware of the fact that plants grow from seeds. A great many peoples know that certain fish swim upstream at special seasons. Almost all peoples realize that friction produces heat, and that dry tinder can be set afire with ease.

All peoples in societies with primitive technologies thus possess a body of rules and concepts based on experience and derived from it by logical inference. But they do not all know or attempt to verify why their generalizations may be correct because they do not inquire regarding the relationship between antecedent and consequent phenomena. They do not compare alternative explanations of sequences in order to select the formulation that is simpler or is characterized by greater appropriateness.

There is little doubt, however, that some peoples in relatively primitive economies have explicit theoretical laws of knowledge open to control by experiment and critique by reason. As Malinowski has pointed out, the native shipwright, for example, knows of buoyancy, leverage, and equilibrium not only in a practical sense. He must not only obey the laws while on water, but he must also have the principles in mind while he is making the canoe. He must instruct his helpers by giving them the traditional rules and in a crude or simple manner, with a limited technical vocabulary, he must also explain some general laws of hydrodynamics and equilibrium. Science here is as yet not detached from craftsmanship, but this is the matrix of science.

Common-sense knowledge and science are similar in that their explanations of sequences are not formulated in supernatural terms. Science, however, differs from common sense because of the special explicitness and systematization of its procedures and formulations, and in its other ways of surmounting the many defects of common sense.

Technological Knowledge. Peoples with primitive economies have an enormous amount of knowledge of woods, grasses, fibers, roots, hides, and the physical or chemical processes that permit manufacture of artifacts. There are a number of especially striking examples of technological knowledge such as the Eskimo beehive-shaped ice-block house, tailored fur clothing, dog-team harness and sled; the South African Bushman sucking-tube for drawing water from beneath the desert floor; the outrigger canoe of Oceania; fire and bow drills; the preservation of foods by sun-drying and smoking; various elaborate frameworks for houses; the tropical South American hammock; the blowgun; the needle; the bow and arrow; the return boomerang of Australia; felting; Alaskan gut raincoats; bark canoes and other artifacts; and fishing by drugging the water. The list could be extended to include tens of thousands of items of technological knowledge.

The possessors of such common-sense information usually acquire and use it without inquiry regarding the underlying mechanical or chemical principles or the formulation of such principles. If people are curious as to why such achievements are possible they are usually referred to mythological explanations.

Yet empirical knowledge of mechanical principles among peoples with primitive economies was well defined. They knew and used the principle of the lever and inclined plane in the construction of traps and deadfalls, and to obtain a strong pull for many purposes. They also knew the principles of centrifugal force, torsion, elasticity, air pressure, suction, buoyancy, and friction. Eskimos, whose mechanical knowledge was exceptionally well developed, even knew the principle of pulleys, which they applied in the task of hauling heavy sea mammals ashore.

Chemical processes were also known and applied extensively, especially in the preparation and preservation of foods and the manufacture of paints and dyes. Leaching was used to separate soluble substances from pastes. The preparation of drinks involved the principle of fermentation. Poisons were extracted, as in the preparation of cassava in Brazil, or in the fashioning of poison-tipped darts or arrows in many regions. In Africa iron ores were reduced in order to obtain metallic iron. Limonite was burned to produce red ochre. Gypsum was dehydrated to yield whitening, and salt was obtained by evaporating sea water or saline spring water.

Knowledge of Materials. The selection of materials by peoples in primitive economies required discrimination and an often intimate knowledge of their properties. Tough stones were chosen for thrusting instruments, brittle stones for flaking, and soft stones for carvings. They acquired knowledge of the texture, hardness, and mineralogic make-up of stones used for gems and ornamental stones. Among the woods ash, yew, and betel palm were chosen for their elasticity in the making of bows. They selected easily splitting wood for planks, insect-resisting woods for building, and fine-grained wood for carvings. Appropriate twigs, barks, and fiber were employed for tying and rope making. The knowledge of flora and fauna utilized for food was vast.

Knowledge of Crafts. The making of baskets and pottery are crafts as well as arts (see pp. 262, 267) and involve technological knowledge and skills of the first order. Basket weaving utilized knowledge of wicker work, twining, twilling, and the making of knots in an infinite variety of forms, many of which required mastery of complex techniques. Pottery required knowledge of practical chemistry, physics, and geology. The choice of raw materials was crucial to the success of pottery, and it was important to know when the clay had the correct amount of plasticity. The tempering of clay by the use of sand, pounded shells or stones, or pulverized pottery was widespread. The molding and firing of pottery also required an exact knowledge of technical processes.

Other crafts demanded comparable knowledge of materials and processes. The preparation of weirs and nets to obtain fish and of devices for trapping animals, for example, were occupations requiring complex skills.

Mathematical Knowledge. Numerical abstractions such as one, two, and three are universal. All mathematics of peoples in primitive economies deals with mere substitute words, that is to say, with numerals for objects or actions. Mathematics does not in most of these societies involve an analysis of logical or formal relationships but only a simple counting of subject matter. The highest numeral used by some Fuegians has been said to be five, and three or four is the highest numeral used by a few peoples who also have slight occasion to count beyond these small figures. For more than four or five the word for *many* or combinations of the simple numerals may be used. The Pacific Northwest Indians counted fluently into the tens of thousands, but in their culture they had constant occasion for counting, for fines were imposed, commodities were bought and sold, and money beads were calculated. Most mathematics among the peoples of low technological levels was simple counting and even simpler addition. Other facets of mathematics were barely if at all developed.

However, the specialists of some advanced agricultural-pastoral societies, above all the Mayan priesthood astronomers of pre-Christian times, developed mathematics to such a remarkable degree that they invented the concept of zero and the position system in notation even before it was utilized in the Old World.

The standards of linear measurement are generally taken from parts of the body, such as on the coast of British Columbia where a long span was from the thumb to the tip of the fourth finger, a short span from the thumb to the tip of the first finger, and a cubit from the elbow to the tip of the second finger. The Peruvians invented beam scales with an original method of determining equilibrium. Among some advanced food-gathering peoples as on the Northwest Coast of America geometric principles were applied in the laying out of lines for a house and in the making of square boxes.

Astronomical Knowledge. Many preagricultural peoples accumulated an extensive terminology for the heavenly bodies, and also a rough knowledge of months, seasons, and the length of the year, designated largely according to the changing nature of the vegetation. Observations on the tides are widely found. Accurate mathematical formulations regarding the length of the lunar month and the year did not appear, however, until a specialized priesthood of the Neolithic Age had the leisure and motivation to study such matters. The Mayan Indians alone in America developed such astronomical knowledge, with the help of their zero concept in the pre-Christian Era, although their socio-economic system was not as advanced as that of the Mesopotamian astrologers or astronomers of the third millennium B.C. The practical astronomical knowledge of the Polynesians of five to ten centuries ago facilitated their extraordinary migrations across uncharted seas. The Micronesians not only used the constellations as guides in navigation but also observed the direction of the swell of the sea. On the basis of these observations they made sailing charts consisting of frames of thin rods tied together in such a manner as to serve effectively as guides.

Philosophical and Psychological Knowledge. Individual anthropologists have often commented on the philosophical curiosity and reflectiveness found among the peoples with primitive economies that they have visited, and others have been impressed by the sharpness of insight into human nature possessed by some non-European peoples. Careful field studies of these matters have not yet been ventured. Intensive research is needed to document such reports, and to supplement the already available evidence of a special but relevant kind which is to be found in folklore.

Medical Knowledge. Food-gathering peoples have had a tremendous amount of common-sense knowledge regarding the fauna and flora of their environment, especially of materials which they obtained for their own use. In almost every region the people knew the botanical resources which were of genuine worth medicinally and as poisons, intoxicants, and narcotics. Andean Indians trephined successfully. They used coca leaves to lessen sensitivity to pain and it was from them that Europeans learned about cocaine and quinine. Many peoples treated skin infections successfully and used splints for broken bones. They knew the practice of massage and of cauterization and used emetics. Sweat baths were found on several continents and their value for therapeutical purposes was often considerable. Every community knew terms for and the characteristics of hundreds of plants and animals, and had a long inventory of medical or therapeutic techniques which were entirely dissociated from the supernatural.

Knowledge of History. Before writing was known, whatever knowledge of the past peoples possessed was derived from oral tradition (see p. 222). Usually at least two levels of time were referred to. The one level was that of the myths and folk tales; the other was that of stories involving known persons and events of a few generations preceding. The level of mythology and folklore, whose stories refer to bygone ages when, it is thought, things were different from what they are now, is sometimes further subdivided into successive epochs of time.

There has been considerable discussion regarding the trustworthiness of the descriptions of the past by nonliterate peoples. Each culture area has to be judged separately in this regard. The Polynesians' prolific citations of names, genealogies, and migration accounts may be of unexampled accuracy among nonliterate peoples. Such details go back, however, hardly more than 700 or 800 years and portray only a few features of the life and events of earlier centuries. Literary stylization had proceeded to such a degree that very little of the history of the last millennium is known by the Polynesians.

Most mythologies or folklores serve as only minor sources of ancient history by suggesting that migrations or catastrophes may have occurred. The task of the prehistorian is to check the validity of myth by the use of archeological, cultural anthropological, and linguistic techniques. Folklores are so highly stylized, and have been transmitted by so many persons, that they serve merely as a body of cues and feeble corroborations of the historical perspectives revealed through other anthropological techniques.

The folkloristic stories which people tell of recent events must also be treated with great caution as historical sources. The literary stylization which is imposed results in omissions, distortions, and other changes in anything which is recounted. Everywhere, however, peoples believe that they know their own history, and the history of the most important parts of the world, through the mythology and folklore which they treasure. Actually their accurate knowledge of the past hardly precedes the lives of those elders to whom they have listened.

Summary. The amount and quality of knowledge possessed by most people of primitive economy are impressive. Theirs is, however, only common-sense knowledge, not scientific knowledge. Their knowledge of history is often a voluminous mythology, which is almost always extremely inaccurate. Their knowledge of practical psychology is often detailed and sensitive and permits accurate prediction of human behavior. The philosophical-mindedness of some peoples with primitive economies is notable.

The important difference between educated persons in our society and members of nonliterate societies lies in our possession of writing, books, and the accumulated heritage of technology, science, logic, and scientific method, which offer the means by which a person can acquire more and accurate knowledge, and check on the accuracy of his thinking. The absence of a knowledge of writing, the poverty of the technological base, the few objects produced for purposes of trade, the relatively scant margin of wealth which permitted few risks, the conformity demanded within closely related groups, the meagre division and specialization of labor, which diminished the possibilities of experimentation, and the isolation which limited horizons and experience and allowed for a negligible number of contacts with novel concepts from outside the community, all contributed to the delay in the development of science in societies with primitive economies.

SELECTED READINGS

Childe, V. G. *Man Makes Himself*. New York: Penguin, 1951.

——. *Social Evolution*. New York: Schuman, 1951.

Kroeber, A. L., and T. T. Waterman. *Source Book in Anthropology*. New York: Harcourt, 1931 (rev. ed.). Pp. 489–505.

Lowie, R. H. *An Introduction to Cultural Anthropology*. New York: Farrar and Rinehart, 1940 (rev. ed.). Pp. 329–341.

Notes and Queries on Anthropology. London: Royal Anthrop. Inst., 1929 (5th ed.). Pp. 334–350, *et passim*.

Radin, P. *Primitive Man as Philosopher*. New York: Appleton, 1927.

Rickard, T. A. *Man and Metals*. New York: McGraw-Hill, 1932. *Passim*.

CHAPTER SIXTEEN

LANGUAGE

The Primitive Beginnings of Languages. The theory has been suggested that prehumans of possibly Late Pliocene dating developed artifacts and acquired historically transmitted patterns of social relationships in the place of patterns based on instinctual behavior. The primitive beginnings of words, true sound units, and formalized word sequences were therefore probably present in all the regions then inhabited. These primitive beginnings of language assumed varying forms, qualities, and meanings in different regions and no one region can be supposed to have been notably more creative in language than any other region. All present-day languages are products of language developments and changes that stem ultimately, and with innumerable unknown details from beginnings of possibly more than a million years ago.

Since all Pleistocene populations were sparse and had a low level of technology until the advent and spread of Upper Paleolithic pressure-flaked cutting tools, there must have been many thousands of mutually unintelligible idioms or languages. Each was the vehicle of expression of some hundreds or very few thousands of persons in rather isolated districts. When entry into the Americas occurred during or after the last glaciation, another thousand or more languages evolved from the small number of languages initially brought from Siberia into western Alaska.

Throughout a million or more years populations have been constantly dropping items from or adding to their linguistic heritage. All languages have changed so profoundly, and at such a pace, that no known languages offer the slightest clue as to the kinds of languages spoken in Early Pleistocene, let alone Pliocene, eras. The specific earliest origins of language cannot therefore be reconstructed. Claims that the earliest words were sound-imitative (ono-matopoetic) or emotion-determined—namely, the well-known "ding-dong," "bow-wow," or similar theories of the origin of language—cannot be substantiated. The dynamic processes of change in languages are much more important to ascertain than are the crude initial ventures, which in any case cannot ever be ascertained.

The Principal Language Stocks. The world's mutually unintelligible languages now number less than 3000. Hundreds are spoken by handfuls of persons, and many of these languages will soon be superseded by the European or Asiatic language of peoples who have lately enveloped them. By a similar process hundreds of other languages have vanished during the past four hundred years. The acquisition of agricultural and pastoral techniques favored the expansion of the languages of those peoples who dwelt in districts where the economy was first transformed and who increased in numbers, wealth, and power by the possession of these superior food-producing techniques. A small number of languages of the Upper Paleolithic period thus spread over enormous regions. These expanding languages displaced, during the Neolithic period and on into the twentieth century, the languages of peoples dwelling in less productive economies and of subjugated peoples. Linguistic stocks of a few food-gathering groups, such as the Uto-Aztekans and Athabaskans of western North America, were enabled to spread over a vast domain, possibly because of the extreme sparsity of population in intramontane and subdesert districts.

Languages now mutually unintelligible, for example Irish Gaelic and Bengali of India, or German and Greek, probably diverged from a common ancient language group of Upper Paleolithic or Mesolithic times. These four languages are only distant linguistic cousins. Grammatical differences and other evidences indicate that the nearly 3000 existing languages actually fall into forty or fifty relatively unrelated linguistic stocks or families.

In Europe these stocks are (1) the Basque or Iberian (southwestern France and northern Spain), (2) the North Caucasus, (3) the South Caucasus (which includes Georgian), (4) the Indo-European, and (5) the Ural-Altaic; the latter group may in fact constitute several stocks.

The Indo-European probably came from an area east of the Caspian in western central Asia. Speakers of Indo-European by chance lived in the districts first enriched by the major Neolithic advances of cereal grass agriculture and of the pastoralism of cattle, sheep, goats, and swine. From such districts they spread to the Atlantic in the west and to India and Sinkiang in the east. Indo-European language subdivisions that survive include (a) Celtic (Scotch Gaelic, Irish Gaelic, Manx, Welsh, Breton, and the recently extinct Cornish language); (b) Italic or Latin or Romance (Latin, Portuguese, Spanish, French, Italian, Catalan-Provençal, Rhaeto-Romanic in southern Switzerland, and Romanian); (c) Germanic (Swedish, Danish, Dano-Norwegian, Norwegian Landsmaal, Icelandic, Frisian, English, Dutch-Flemish, Low German, High German, and Yiddish); (d) Baltic (Latvian and Lithuanian); (e) Slavic (Great Russian, White Russian, Ukrainian, Polish, Czech, Slovak, Slovene, Croat, Serb, and Bulgarian); (f) Albanian; (g) Greek; (h) Armenian; (i) Iranian or Persian (spoken in many languages and large numbers of dialects); and (j) Indic (also spoken in many languages and by three hundred million East Indians). English descends from the Frisian subdivision of Germanic.

Ural-Altaic languages of Europe are probably Asiatic in origin. The supposed stock includes (a) the Finno-Ugrian subdivision composed of Lappish, Finnish, Carelian, Mordvine, Esthonian. Hungarian or Magyar, and a number of languages in the Soviet Union; (b) the even larger Turkic or Turco-Tartar or Altaic subdivision (Turkish, Azerbaijani, Kirgiz, Uzbeg, Bashkir, Chuvash, Kashgar, and many others); (c) the Mongol languages; and (d) the Tungus-Manchu group. In pre-Christian times, some of the groups of speakers of Ural-Altaic happened to dwell in districts where the newly domesticated horse and the cart had rendered their central Asiatic possessors numerous, wealthy, militarily potent, and predatory. The result was the spectacular spread of Ural-Altaic to Hungary in the west, and into Manchu China in the east.

More linguistic stocks are found in Asia than in Europe. Besides large numbers of Indo-European and Ural-Altaic languages, Asia has (6) Semitic languages, in Arabia (Semitic languages are also found across North Africa); (7) Dravidian, in a number of East

Indian languages, most of which are in the south; (8) Burushaski, in India; (9) Munda or Kolarian, also in India; (10) Andamanese, the languages of two or more thousand inhabitants of the Andaman Islands in the Indian Ocean; (11) Mon-Khmer, which possibly includes languages of the inhabitants of the Nicobar Islands in the Indian Ocean and of the Annamites of French Indo-China, and definitely comprises other groups of southeastern Asia, especially Cambodia and southern Burma. In central eastern Asia, there are a half billion speakers of (12) Sinitic (or Tibeto-Chinese, Sino-Tibetan, Indo-Chinese), in subdivisions of (a) many Chinese languages, (b) Tai or Siamese, and (c) Tibeto-Burman. The latter two groups have also been considered by authorities to be independent stocks (13). The extensive dispersion of Sinitic languages may be ascribed to the fact that districts of eastern Asia where ancestral forms of Sinitic languages were spoken were the first regions to be made populous and wealthy in eastern Asia by the acquisition or development of Neolithic techniques of production. Other linguistic stocks of Asia are (14) Korean, (15) Japanese, (16) Ainu, (17) Eskimo, (18) Yukaghir, (19) Koryak, (20) Chukchee, (21) Kamchadal, and (22) Gilyak. Some authorities contend that the last four named are subdivisions of a larger stock.

In addition there is (23) the Austronesian or Malayo-Polynesian language group, which comprises hundreds of languages and extends from the Malay Peninsula out into the easternmost island of Oceania, Easter Island. Its four main subdivisions are (a) the Indonesian languages, (b) the Melanesian languages, (c) the Micronesian, and (d) Polynesian languages. The (24) Papuan language stock in New Guinea has not yet been substantiated with certainty and there may be more than two stocks in Australia, where at present the many indigenous languages are classified as (25) North Australian and (26) South Australian. The now extinct languages of Tasmania appear to have been of South Australian affinity. The sweep of Austronesian languages across much of Oceania indicates that 7000 or 8000 years ago or more recently the ancestral Austronesian languages were located in Indonesian or in adjacent mainland districts to which Neolithic agriculture first diffused.

Several linguistic stocks have spread widely in Africa. Indo-Europeans speaking Greek, Latin, and more recently French, Italian, and Spanish have populated North Africa. Speakers of English and Dutch have colonized in South Africa. The (27) Hamito-Semitic or Afroasiatic stock may once have occupied a smaller district in Arabia and about the Red Sea. It now extends across North Africa in a crescent of many languages. Its subdivisions include: (a) ancient Egyptian and later Coptic. (b) Semitic, which includes Arabic, ancient Hebrew, Aramaic, and various languages of Mesopotamia. Arabic spread rapidly to the west across northern Africa during the seventh and eighth centuries A.D., and now is found in all African Mediterranean coastal countries as well as in Egypt. Other Semitic languages which spread earlier predominate in Ethiopia. (c) Berber, across North Africa. (d) Cushite, in Northeast Africa. (e) Chad. The enormous (28) Niger-Congo group of languages extends from Senegal across the Gulf of Guinea Coast through the Congo and East Africa to the Cape of Good Hope. Additional language stocks of Africa include the relatively large groups termed (29) Songhai, (30) Central Sudanic, (31) Central Saharan, (32) Eastern Sudanic, and the group of (33) Bushman, Hottentot, and other Click languages which constitute the most southerly of African language stocks. There may be as many as nine additional stocks in Africa, each occupying comparatively small areas. The terms for them (34 to 42) are Maban, Mimi, Fur, Temainian, Kordofanian, Koman, Berta, Kunama, and Nyangiya. This total of sixteen stocks that are native to Africa is only a tentative estimate which almost certainly will be revised because intensive and comparative research on the languages of the continent is in its infancy. Austronesian is spoken by most of the two or three million natives of Madagascar and is traceable to a Sumatran conquest and colonization during the era of the Roman Empire. The earlier spread of Niger-Congo appears to be a consequence of the entry of peoples utilizing Neolithic agricultural and pastoral techniques into districts where other linguistic forms were spoken a few thousand years ago.

Many stocks, as well as hundreds or even thousands of languages, may have vanished during the expansions of the Indo-European, Finno-Ugrian, Turkic, Dravidian, Mon-Khmer, Sinitic, Austronesian, Hamito-Semitic and Niger-Congo groups. The survival and spread of groups such as these is not because they were fitter but because of their favorable locations and other historical factors in their favor during the important changes in the society of Neolithic and later times.

A comparable spread of a few languages, but to a lesser extent, can be witnessed in the New World although its linguistic stocks have not been charted with the care scholars have expended upon such mappings in most of the Old World. Since very few language stocks could have been represented in the Chukchee Peninsula during the Upper Paleolithic and immediately succeeding eras, the many hundreds of mutually unintelligible languages of North and South America may have stemmed from something less than a dozen to perhaps no more than five or six stocks. Presumably every language of the Americas ultimately, in one or another ancestral form, entered North America by way of Alaska, and as its descendant dialects went their different ways in the Americas, a great number of languages eventually developed. These have been grouped tentatively and have been accorded designations which are familiar working hypotheses to specialists in American linguistics. Some of the captions deserving of mention are (43) Eskimo-Aleut; (44) the Athabaskan or Nadéné languages of western North America, to which the Apache and Navajo of Arizona and New Mexico belong; (45) Uto-Aztekan, which is found from southern Idaho and Oregon to Costa Rica and which includes, among many others, the Aztec of Mexico; (46) Penutian and (47) Hokan-Siouan, which constitute aggregates of diverse languages where the hypothetical assembling has not yet been supported by sufficient documentation. Additional captions could be listed but in no instances are the evidences for the hypotheses as to stocks adequately supported by linguistic studies.

Almost all of the forty to fifty or more language groups or stocks noted above will continue to be spoken for some time to come. There seems to be little likelihood that either a blending of languages, or a surrender of all save a few, will occur in the early future.

Standard and Less-than-Standard Speech. Societies with small populations where the technological level is low as in food-gathering societies or in simple agricultural societies, and where the social systems lack inequalities or class stratifications, usually display one pattern of speech, with only minor speech variations from person to person.

On the other hand, agricultural and pastoral societies with socio-economic systems of the kind that flowered in later Neolithic and in subsequent times, with large populations, inequalities, class stratifications, and considerable specialization of labor, developed divisions such as rural versus urban, class versus class, specialized group versus specialized group, and as a result divergences in phonetics, vocabulary, grammar, and idiom appeared within the speech community. In time the speech forms employed by the members of the most privileged subgroup in such societies come to be termed good, correct, high, or grammatical and the corresponding but variant speech forms employed by members of the less fortunate subgroups are termed bad, incorrect, vulgar, slang, rustic, twangy, low, and dialect. The former become standard and preferred, the latter substandard and depreciated.

In terms of scientific linguistics, these are purely social evaluations. They are especially interesting as social phenomena, but they also have linguistic interest. Where the so-called standard is urged and spread, it has had historical consequences to language, but not because it is actually a superior sort of speech. Scientific linguistics does not accept popular value judgments of good and bad for standard and substandard speech forms. Its task is to study and formulate the linguistic and interconnected social processes that have operated in such developments. The speech forms that are most violently disapproved are as interesting and valuable examples of dynamic processes of linguistic development, as are the speech forms that are thought of as good, elegant, or beautiful.

In wealthy and literate social systems of Europe in modern times, the general acceptance of so-called grammarians' standards of correct grammar is primarily a social, not a linguistic, matter. Grammatical forms that might have died out were accorded additional decades or centuries of usage. But generally many of the speech forms that appeared among substandard speakers, and that initially were snubbed by the purveyors of good speech, have percolated into the patterns of good speech and have at length become respectable and correct.

Research Method for Unwritten Languages. A hitherto unrecorded and unknown language can usually be rapidly and fully made known to science by a scientific linguist through phonetic transcription with appended literal translation. Some thousands of words and thousands of sentences thus noted progressively reveal the grammatical forms, the vocabulary content, and the entire inventory of sound features of the language. The linguist also records transcriptions and translations of folk tales and other dictations of connected speech and makes electrical recordings, so that linguistic science may have an objective check-up on phonetic and other features of his analysis. From this material he is able to prepare an analysis of sound and structural phenomena, and a dictionary.

In a socially stratified society where markedly divergent speech forms are found within the subgroups of the community, the linguist makes notations of the speech of members of each such group. Wherever the language is the common medium of all the members of a food-gathering community or a community on a primitive agricultural level, all mentally normal persons in such societies utilize almost all the available speech forms and there are no significantly variant patterns of expression that are unfamiliar to or not employed by an individual informant.

Language Sounds: Phonetics. The oral cavity, which is nature's own elaborate equipment for sound production, is identical in all populations. It can produce thousands of distinguishable sounds, any one of which is quite as natural and potentially as easy to articulate as any other. But every language employs only a small percentage of all the possible sounds. An insufficient number of languages have been analyzed to give an exact estimate, but the average number of basic sounds, also termed sound units or *phonemes,* seems to be between twenty and forty, with some languages less and others more.

There are a number of types of sounds. One type, made by an outgoing column of air completely obstructed, for a split second, by one or more points of closure in the oral cavity, is termed a *stopped consonant:* English examples are *b, p, d, t, g, k.* A second type, which involves a continued partial obstruction, is termed a *continuant consonant,* or a *sibilant, spirant,* or *fricative:* examples are *z, s, v, f, th, sh*. A third type, termed an *affricative consonant*, involves a kind of combined articulation of the first two: examples are *dz, ts, tch*. A fourth type, which involves no obstruction to the outgoing air, is termed a *vowel*: examples are *a, e, i, o, u, aw, oy, ay*. It is noteworthy that every stock and almost every known language has some sounds of each of the types noted. This is pertinent evidence of the similarity in the linguistic potential and behavior of all peoples. Moreover, every language has far more basic sounds or phonemes than are needed to effect a massive vocabulary.

Other features of sound production, such as the use of variable lengths of sound; an accompanying tone level or change of pitch; variations in loudness or stress; and phrase or sentence melody pattern, involve technical details which cannot be summarized here. In modern times, however, all languages, no matter how primitive the technology or economy of their speakers, are on a parity in the developmental level of their phonetic features. No evolutionary highs or lows in sound production can be substantiated. No language sounds or features of sound can be evaluated as more advanced or more primitive than are any others. Sounds of so-called primitive languages which are designated as "strange" are only sounds to which one is unaccustomed. Strangeness is due simply to unfamiliarity, not to primitiveness. Moreover, differences in skin color, lip thickness, nasal width, or the like have had no influence whatsoever upon sounds. There is no evidence that African Negroids have tended to utilize certain sounds, and Chinese, Germans, or Slavs certain other sounds, as consequence of hereditary anatomical differences or different gene frequencies. Nor is there the slightest evidence that differences in climate and altitude have had any influence upon the sounds of languages of different regions. The kinds of sounds found in any area are entirely unconnected with racial or geographical factors and are caused by phonetic or linguistic factors. Anybody, in any part of the world, will learn and employ only the sounds employed in the area in which he is brought up and with sufficient practice will utter them as perfectly as anyone else.

Vocabulary. More basic than words are minimal units of distinguishable meaning, or idea-units, which number some thousands in every language. They have lately been termed *morphemes*. For example, the English word *railroads* has three such morphemes, *rail, road,* and *s* for plural number. A scientific linguist's dictionary is therefore not so much an alphabetized inventory of words as it is an inventory of morphemes together with the possible morpheme combinations such as *railroading* and *railroads.*

It is noteworthy that in every language, no matter how primitive the habitations, customs, or technology of the people who speak it, there may be found a vocabulary of morphemes and morpheme combinations large and varied enough to permit the expression of any idea known to any other people. In other words, the vocabulary of no people is either permanently handicapped or even severely limited at the moment of need to express a newly introduced concept. Every vocabulary constitutes a tool so complex and so speedily adaptable that its morpheme resources can at once be employed to denote any new and complex technological, scientific, abstractly philosophical, and poetic interests which the people may have acquired. In this sense all languages display indefinite plasticity and rapid or immediate adaptability. It cannot be shown that in the matter of adaptability of vocabulary any one language is superior or inferior to any other.

Since some languages indulge in a much larger number of patterns of morpheme combination than do others, they have much larger word-vocabularies. Eskimos, for example, employ a few thousand morphemes but hundreds of thousands of words. However, a language of five or ten thousand words works quite as well as one with greater numbers. It is the resources in basic idea-units or morphemes and not the numbers of their possible combinations in words that count.

Conditions of daily living and of social relationships in an unstratified and technologically primitive society may allow all persons to master the entire word-vocabulary. On the other hand, the conditions of a stratified and technologically advanced society allow no one the opportunity to master the word-vocabulary in its entirety. Each person masters little more than a small segment of that vocabulary and the segment so mastered includes the terms employed in his field of specialty. The size of the English dictionary is notable not because English is a superior language but because it is the vehicle of expression of a people in a social system characterized by a highly developed scientific and technological heritage and hence by a thousand or more specialized fields, each of which has rapidly developed special words. Bushman, Iroquois, or Guadalcanal Melanesian would be equally efficient vehicles for the vocabularies of specialists, and hundreds of languages, whether of Africa or Oceania, will become such vehicles if and when, in coming decades, their social systems are modernized and industrialized and their speakers rendered literate.

Grammar, or Linguistic Morphology. The structure, morphology, or grammar of a language comprises basically the patterns of arrangement of its morphemes and, as a corollary, the groupings of its morphemes into form-classes, semantic classes, and paradigmatic sets. For example, the groups of morphemes that express time of action (*shall, will, -ing, -ed*), the sex gender of the actor (Spanish *el, la, los, las*), or the number of actors (Ancient Greek singular, dual, and plural) each define a form-class, embracing all the morphemes which can be combined with those indicated. Some languages like Latin, Slavic, or Eskimo have rather complex rules governing the arrangements of their many classes of morphemes—that is, they have a complex grammar. A few languages like English and French have relatively few morphemes grouped in form-classes and have on the whole a somewhat simple grammatical structure. Although Chinese displays complexities of various kinds, as in word order, its lack of form-classes of the kind noted above warrants its being called virtually grammarless. For example, Chinese can say *dog bite man,* where each word is a morpheme and no other idea-units are added. Chinese sentences therefore have a staccato clarity, and supplementary morphemes of the kind found in many other languages the world over are absent. A language with complex grammar like Chinook in the northwest United States might express the same sentence by using many morphemes which correct grammatical usage does not allow the speaker to omit: he says *singular-feminine-subject-dog singular-masculine-object-man singular-feminine-subject-singular-masculine-object-directive-bite-instantaneous-past.* The one speaker says this simply, the other is seemingly burdened by a necessity to say much more.

Questions arise as to which language is more efficient and aesthetic and which is on a higher developmental level in its grammar or morphology—Chinese, Chinook, or English. One answer is that one language is no more nor less efficient and clear or necessarily much more aesthetically satisfying than another. Moreover, there is no historical evidence to indicate a higher developmental level for one than for another. In fact some languages employed by peoples of low economic levels, like the Eskimos or the Uto-Aztekans of Nevada, utilize an elaborate machinery of form-classes and other constructions. Chinese and English, which are used by some of the peoples of highest economic level, may be thought of as having much less grammar. Nevadan Uto-Aztekans, who are among the world's economically simplest peoples, use a grammar that is quite complex and their languages are similar to that of the Aztecs of Mexico, a group advanced in its economic structure. Scientific linguistics has therefore concluded that grammatical complexity appears to correlate little, if at all, with technological or economic levels. Whatever they may be, the ultimate causes for the development of simple or complex grammars have operated at all levels of economic development, so that simple and complex grammars have tended to develop among hunting peoples as among the wealthiest agricultural civilizations.

Language, Race, and Culture. No interconnections of cause and effect have been found between the racial characteristics of a geographical population and the speech forms employed by that population. For example, the American Indians have a tremendous number of languages, of most divergent content and structure, as well as a number of language stocks. The American languages have undergone profound changes during the past thousands of years, when the racial characteristics of the people of America have not changed to an extent great enough to account for either the linguistic or cultural diversities. Caucasoids also employ divergent languages and language stocks as do Negroids. A number of mutually unintelligible languages are found among the Australoids and Bushmen-Hottentots, and several among the Andamanese, Pygmies, Aleuts, and Eskimos. Furthermore, the population of any geographical area may take over entirely different languages. Large numbers of American

Indians, for example, speak only Spanish or English and many modern people the world over speak languages unheard by their grandparents who came from other regions. Nowhere can hereditary factors be shown to have influenced receptivity to a specific language There is therefore no direct and specific interconnection between race and language.

In discussing the relationship between language and culture it is helpful to treat phonetics, vocabulary, and grammar separately. The culture of a people has never had direct effects upon phonetics—that is, upon the kinds of sounds used. Yet there have been indirect effects. The way of life has always determined socio-economic and other relationships to adjacent peoples. It has determined their frequency of visits, intermarriages, and trading, and thus the degree of familiarity with contiguous languages. The sparser the population and the lower its technological level, the greater the familiarity with or use of adjacent languages and the greater the prevalence of bilingual and trilingual persons. Hence there is a greater degree and speed of diffusion of sound features from speech community to speech community. This is why an area such as the Pacific Northwest of America displays scores of languages of most diverse structure and vocabulary but possessed of a common inventory of vowel and consonant sounds. In other parts of the world also a fairly homogeneous inventory of sound features will be found in large regions characterized by extensive vocabulary and grammatical diversity. In short, culture and the special dynamic processes set up by one or another type of culture have had detailed effects upon features of sound although the sounds have had no effect upon the features or processes of culture. However, in more advanced socio-economic systems, where the populations have been dense and bilinguals have been relatively few, sound features do not diffuse to a comparable degree from one speech community to another.

Culture has of course had the profoundest effect upon vocabulary. It has always determined every item of vocabulary. Each morpheme, word, or other meaningful speech form connotes only that which is or has been in the culture, in the way of life and ideology of the people. For example, *house* means the kind of house constructed by the people of that culture; *dance* means the manner in which the people dance; *good* connotes the value concept created by that culture or borrowed from other cultures; *spirit* implies only the concept of a nonmaterial being or essence that is or was prevalent in the culture. Vocabulary is a tool employed by the culture not a tool which shapes the culture.

The effect of culture upon some features of grammatical structure has long been moot. Culture may tend to provide minor pressures to give formal or grammatical expression to certain groups of ideas, as for example the development of directional categories such as up-from-the-beach, down-to-the-beach, upriver, and downriver, in a number of Pacific Northwest languages. Here the daily employment by river village cultures of specific directional indications seems to have led to a necessary and stylized employment of such directional indicators. However, few such features of grammar can be so easily ascribed to a way of life, because grammatical features tend to change slowly whereas cultures change rapidly. Many features of grammar found in the more familiar languages, which in most instances are spoken by participants in wealthy socio-economic systems, are features which developed during earlier times and in other regions the cultures of which are no longer extant. The fashion by which such ancient cultures may have developed their grammatical devices cannot be found by any technique of direct observation.

The effect of features of grammatical structure upon culture is also moot. Claims have been made that a grammar possessed of a category such as that of time indicators (present, past, and future) facilitates the development of clear thinking and makes possible useful distinctions like that between the past and the present, and that the presence of a category of evidence indicators (for example, *so-they-say, I-know-from-the-evidence-of-my-own-eyes, I-know-because-he-told-me*) facilitates precision in thinking. In fact, claims have been made that the type of logic and canons of proper inference developed by speakers of Indo-European languages were influenced by grammatical features of these languages, and that a somewhat different kind of logic might have tended to evolve were another grammatical pattern employed. Such claims cannot be proved or disproved. In general it may be said that grammar, like other facets of language, seems to have had little detailed effect upon culture.

Jargons and Creolized Languages. So far only "natural" languages have been discussed—that is, languages of great complexity and morpheme resources, which have evolved over long periods of time. Although they differ notably in vocabulary, phonetics, and grammar, these languages are now and have long been on an equal developmental level. However, there are three lower levels of linguistic complexity and efficiency, which have paradoxically enough been determined by and developed only under the special conditions of most recent times. The simplest level is represented by "natural" jargons; the next simplest, by the artificially contrived desk products termed international auxiliary languages; and the third, by the rather complex idioms termed creolized languages. Culture has obviously been a strategic determinant of the sound patterns, vocabulary content, and grammatical features of speech forms such as these.

In an area of intensive commerce and employment of many languages, a small and most used portion of the speech of the natives of the area, or of those with most economic prestige, has often been resorted to by others for purposes of simple transactions and merriment. Five hundred to a thousand of the most frequent morphemes or words are used as the basis for such a jargon, with minor supplements from a few of the other languages of the region. Grammatical morphemes or niceties are ignored. Where English has been a base as in Melanesia, cultural and racist conceits characteristic of early English ventures in the area resulted in the employment of many baby-talk English morphemes or other morphemes that have connotations of a condescending sort towards natives. Similarly in several other areas a relatively grammarless jargon or pidgin arose based upon English baby talk and other English morphemes or words. On the Pacific Northwest Coast the Chinook jargon was a kind of Basic Chinook made up of several hundred morphemes and words from Chinook, with small supplementary inventories of French, English, and some local Indian languages. It too was virtually grammarless. A score of other jargons or pidgins have appeared in various parts of the world and in each instance they have served well as "natural" auxiliary or international languages for these areas.

But pidgins or jargons do not remain unchanged. In recent centuries as well as in the later Roman Empire a few of them may have constantly supplemented their morpheme content, developed form-classes, and metamorphosed into a kind of halfway stage towards a complex "natural" language termed a creolized language. However, definite evidences are lacking of such possible developments, although it is known that a creolized language appears in each instance to have developed in slave, peon, or other submerged classes. A creolized language usually appears to have developed almost spontaneously, without a preceding stage of jargon, when slave groups rapidly and directly learned a considerable part of the vocabulary and a few of the form-classes of their masters. This is how some creolized forms of French and Spanish seem to have been formed in Latin American countries. Eventually a creolized stage develops into a true "natural" language, which then takes form as a divergent dialect of the language that had been originally only partially borrowed by the poor and lowly.

The Technique of Writing. The ways of life of Paleolithic times were such that painstaking notations of things and actions were rarely made. Writing could not develop under such conditions. The people did symbolize and cartoon, but they had no incentive to represent words, morphemes, syllables, or phonemes. Early Neolithic conditions also failed to bring about a technique of morpheme or word representation. Not until later Neolithic times did any societies develop the conditions which eventuated in a technique of writing. Such conditions developed independently before 4000 B.C. in Hamitic-speaking Egypt, and before 1000 B.C. in Mayan-speaking southern Mexico or Guatemala. In Egypt and in Central America, commerce, trade, and religious organization had developed to a point where detailed notations were resorted to. There was ownership of agricultural lands and in Egypt also of domesticated animals of economic significance; a considerable development of specialized labor; specialized and full-time priesthoods; tax and tribute collections; and other unprecedented economic, social, and governmental developments. This combination of new conditions, not the appearance of a creative genius, constitutes the matrix from which techniques of writing have been developed.

In each area where writing evolved, a long inventory of cartoon representations of things and actions, the so-called ideographs, became progressively stylized into characters that numbered over 500. These in turn came to represent syllables. With later phonetic change a few Egyptian characters represented only consonant phonemes. New consonant signs were developed by the Phoenician-speaking Semitic towns, then borrowed by the Greeks, then by the Romans, and at length they became our conventional alphabet of today. An analogous development from ideographs to stylized characters occurred in Chinese-speaking eastern Asia by 2000 B.C. Whether the initial development of writing in the Far East was stimulated by Near Eastern scripts or was as independent as was the Mayan script remains to be ascertained. The clay tablet system (cuneiform) that developed in Mesopotamia about the time of the invention of Egyptian writing was perhaps entirely independent. A syllable hieroglyph script, if composed of simply drawn characters, is probably a more rapid if not in all respects a more efficient script than a phonemic or alphabet script such as that employed by Europeans from the time of classical Greece to the present.

Until the century of the universal common school and compulsory education, writing had had only slight influence upon vocabulary content or grammar as employed by the majority of the speakers of a language. It has never had a perceptible influence upon anybody's phonetics. But writing does permit vocabularies to accumulate and it salvages morphemes and words which would otherwise have passed into disuse and oblivion. Writing has also permitted the development of sciences, and of the science of grammar with the result that a few grammatical devices may have tended to be used where a nonliterate people might have dropped them more rapidly. Writing has of course had extraordinary cultural, technological, and scientific consequences by making possible the cumulative transmission of learned behavior, and facilitating communication. Its influence upon spoken language, however, has been scant and superficial until the most recent decades.

An International Auxiliary Language. Large numbers of persons who have been perturbed by intensified sentiments of nationalism and by recurrent wars have believed that a simple auxiliary language would strengthen forces for peace and good will, as well as facilitate other international relationships such as those of scientists and businessmen. In the past 75 years over 20 such auxiliary languages have been devised and some have been supported by active organizations. The best known auxiliaries are Esperanto and Basic English, each of which has numerous and enthusiastic protagonists.

Actually all the modernly contrived auxiliaries have been far more complex in sound patterns and morphology than an efficient auxiliary need be. Their sounds and morphemes are usually from no more than one or two westerly subdivisions of Indo-European. They would thus serve much better as European regional auxiliary languages than as international auxiliary languages. The essential contribution of their advocates, especially of the Esperantists, has been to persuade the peoples that an auxiliary of one or another kind is necessary as well as possible in our time. The limitations of the advocates of international auxiliary languages reside in the fact that some tend to neglect causes of war other than diversities of languages, and also in what may be characterized as their linguistic ethnocentrism and in their failure to utilize the knowledge and skills of up-to-date scientific linguists.

Sign or Gesture "Languages." A few peoples on a simple food-gathering level, such as some Australoids and Plains Indians, who had complex "natural" languages, were also able to converse to a minimal degree by the employment of small inventories of meaningful gestures. Modernized and literate peoples have worked out a number of quite different kinds of gesture or sign vocabularies that often correlate with script symbols. Both types of sign or gesture "language" merely supplement "natural" spoken languages and not too efficiently. There is neither evidence nor a likelihood that humanity has passed through a gesture-language stage.

Summary. "Primitive language" is a conventional but not at all satisfactory caption for languages of varying grammatical complexity spoken by nonliterate peoples of primitive economies. There are no differences in developmental level in phonetic or grammatical features of these or any languages, although one can observe that languages of peoples of advanced technology and considerable specialization of labor may have a larger total of morpheme combinations or specialized segments of vocabulary which supplement the vocabulary in daily use. The dynamic processes of language interconnect with culture but in different ways—phonetics and grammar only remotely, and vocabulary intimately and immediately. Each language constitutes only a tiny portion of all the possibilities available in sounds, morphemes, and grammatical features. At that, each language contains more resources in these features than are needed for efficient expression. Writing has had no effect upon sounds, a slight effect on the retention of dying grammatical forms, and a considerable effect in the supplementation of vocabulary in the case of languages which have been written for a long time. A great deal remains to be learned about the world's languages, because only a very small number have been recorded and analyzed according to the methods of modern scientific linguistics.

Although a further contraction in the number of languages spoken can be expected, with the extinction of the many languages now spoken by only hundreds of or a few thousand persons, there is little likelihood that a democratic humanity will speak fewer than many hundreds of "natural" languages for generations to come. These may be supplemented by inelegant though efficient regional auxiliary jargons, or by a single international auxiliary which will serve in international meetings, scientific journals, and various other forms of international intercommunication. There is no evidence that such a supplementary jargon would injure or tend to replace any of the surviving "natural" languages. The immediate future therefore is likely to be polyglot, the languages employed having been selected for survival by their fortunate location rather than by essential linguistic superiority.

SELECTED READINGS

Bloch, B., and G. L. Trager. *Outline of Linguistic Analysis*. Baltimore: Linguistic Soc. Amer., 1942.

Bloomfield, L. *Language*. New York: Holt, 1933.

——. *Outline Guide for the Practical Study of Foreign Languages*. Baltimore: Linguistic Soc. Amer., 1942.

Boas, F. *Handbook of American Indian Languages*. Washington: Bur. Amer. Ethnol., Bul. 40, Pt. I, 1910. Introduction.

——. *Race, Language, and Culture*. New York: Macmillan, 1940. Pp. 199-225.

Bram, J. *Language and Society*. Garden City: Doubleday, 1955.

Carroll, J. B. *The Study of Language*. Cambridge: Harvard Univ. Press, 1953.

Gleason, H. A., Jr. *An Introduction to Descriptive Linguistics*. New York: Holt, 1955.

Hall, R. A., Jr. *Introductory Linguistics*. Philadelphia: Chilton, 1964.

——. *Leave Your Language Alone!* Ithaca: Linguistica, 1950.

——. *Linguistics and Your Language*. Garden City: Doubleday, 1960.

Hockett, C. *A Course in Modern Linguistics*. New York: Macmillan, 1958.

——. *A Manual of Phonology*. Pt. I, Mem. II: International Journal of American Linguistics; Indiana Univ. Publications in Anthropology and Linguistics, Vol. 21, No. 4. Baltimore: Waverly Press, 1955.

Hoijer, H., ed. *Language in Culture*. Chicago: Univ. of Chicago Press, 1954.

Hymes, D., ed. *Language in Culture and Society*. New York: Harper and Row, 1964.

Jespersen, J. O. H. *Language: Its Nature, Development, and Origin*. New York: Holt, 1921.

Kluckhohn, C. *Mirror for Man*. New York: Whittlesey, 1949. Pp. 145–167.

Laguna, G. de. *Speech, Its Function and Development*. New Haven: Yale Univ. Press, 1927.

Mandelbaum, D. G., ed. *Selected Writings of Edward Sapir in Language, Culture, and Personality*. Berkeley and Los Angeles: Univ. of Cal. Press, 1949.

Sapir, E. *Language*. New York: Harcourt, Brace, 1921.

——. "Language," in *Encyclopedia of the Social Sciences*, IX (1933), 155–169.

——. "Language, Race, and Culture," in V. F. Calverton, ed., *The Making of Man*. New York: Modern Library, 1931. Pp. 142–156.

Saporta, S. ed. *Psycholinguistics*. New York: Holt, Rinehart and Winston, 1961.

Schlauch, M. *The Gift of Tongues*. New York: Modern Age, 1942.

Sturtevant, E. H. *An Introduction to Linguistic Science*. New Haven: Yale Univ. Press, 1947.

Thomas, W. I. *Primitive Behavior*. New York: McGraw-Hill, 1937. Pp. 49–97.

Vendryes, J. *Language, a Linguistic Introduction to History*. New York: Knopf, 1925.

Weinreich, U. *Languages in Contact: Findings and Problems*. New York: Publications of the Linguistic Circle of New York—No. 1, 1953.

Whorf, B. L. *Language, Thought and Reality*. J. B. Carroll, ed. Cambridge: Mass. Institute of Technology, 1956.

GLOSSARY

The special connotations of terms used in anthropology are listed here. To facilitate the work of students additional terms have been included in this glossary which are utilized in other textbooks but are not discussed further in this book.

ACCULTURATION. The process of the envelopment or change of culture which occurs when one socio-economic system influences another in a thoroughgoing manner.

ACHEULEAN. A Lower Paleolithic core-biface technique, present in western Europe, which is finer than Abbevillian. It is believed to have lasted to the end of the third interglacial or until a little more than fifty thousand years ago.

AFFRICATIVE. A type of consonant sound, exemplified by *ts* or *dz*.

AFRICANTHROPUS NJARANENSIS. Fossils from East Africa, possibly of the *Pithecanthropus-Sinanthropus* (*q. v.*) developmental level but the date of which is uncertain.

AGE GRADE. A social status level marked by age.

AGGLUTINATIVE LANGUAGE. A type of language whose grammatical structure is characterized by dependent morphemes (*q. v.*) or bound forms which follow one another within words according to certain rules of sequence, as for example in Turkish.

AINUS. The small remnant groups of food-gathering Caucasoid-like natives of Japan, now largely restricted to northerly Japanese islands. Ainu is a term both for a geographical population and for a linguistic stock.

ALEUTS. Residents of the Aleutian islands, who speak languages closely related to Eskimo and who have a food-gathering socio-economic system.

ALGONKIN. A linguistic stock comprising many languages of peoples dwelling largely in central-eastern Canada and the northeastern United States.

ALLOPHONE. One of the major variants of a phoneme (*q. v.*).

ALPINE. The concept of a distinguishable east-west central European ethnic subdivision or subrace of Caucasoids (*q. v.*).

AMITATE. The social relationship in which there are especially close ties with the paternal aunt (cf. Avunculate).

AMUCK, RUNNING. A culturally patterned type of abnormal mental and social behavior found in Malay-speaking countries.

AMULET. A small object, talisman, or charm which is believed to protect a person from supernatural or magical danger.

ANALYTIC LANGUAGE. A language whose grammatical structure is characterized by few or no bound forms, as in Chinese.

ANDAMAN ISLANDERS. Far Eastern pygmy people on islands south of Burma in the eastern Bay of Bengal, possessed of a food-gathering socio-economic system.

ANIMATISM. The belief in the existence of a nonmaterial supernatural essence, force, or power which resides in matter; also termed *mana*.

ANIMISM. The belief in individual spiritual beings, found among all peoples in primitive economies.

ANTHROPOID. The portion of the primate order which includes apes and humans.

ANTHROPOLOGY. The over-all term for the science of the physical, social, and cultural development and behavior of human beings since their appearance on earth. It includes several distinctive and at the same time interconnected scientific fields. These are human evolution or the science of fossil man; physical anthropology, which is concerned with the classification of living geographical populations and ethnic subdivisions and with the processes of physical growth of different peoples; archeology or prehistory; cultural anthropology, social anthropology, or ethnology; and scientific linguistics.

ANTHROPOLOGY, CULTURAL or SOCIAL (*see* Ethnology and Ethnography).

ANTHROPOLOGY, PHYSICAL (*see* Physical Anthropology).

ANTHROPOMETRY (*see* Physical Anthropology).

ANTHROPOMORPHIC. Of human form and appearance.

ANTHROPOPHAGY. Cannibalism.

APE. The type of larger anthropoid which evolved in Miocene (*q. v.*) times and is now represented by gorillas, chimpanzees, orangs, and gibbons.

APOLLONIAN. A basic culture pattern of the Southwest United States Pueblo Indians, who as described by Ruth Benedict are characterized by orderliness, ceremoniousness, formality, sobriety, and dislike for emotional instability, violence, or excess (cf. Dionysian).

ARAUCANIAN. A linguistic and cultural group of American Indians resident in Chile.

ARCTIC HYSTERIA. A type of abnormal mental behavior, probably culturally patterned, found in some Siberian societies of low technological level.

ARMENOID. The concept of a Caucasoid subrace in eastern Asia Minor and Caucasus districts.

ARTIFACT. Anything such as a tool, container, weapon, garment, or ornament, made by human hands.

ARYAN. A term used by some earlier writers as a synonym for Nordic (*q. v.*) and also employed by some earlier writers as a synonym for Indo-European (*q. v.*). Neither usage is acceptable in modern scientific writings.

ASSOCIATIONS. A term for social relationships, social patterns, or groups such as the family, lineage, community, clan, class, club, and secret society.

ATHABASKAN. A linguistic subdivision or stock possibly related to Sinitic and comprising many languages of western North America. It is a subdivision of the larger group termed Nadéné which also includes the Eyak, Haida, and Tlingit languages. Athabaskan languages are found from Alaska to Arizona and New Mexico.

ATHLETIC. A postulated constitutional type portrayed by Kretschmer (*see* Leptosome, Pyknic).

ATLANTO-MEDITERRANEAN. The concept of a western European subrace of Mediterranean Caucasoids.

AURIGNACIAN. A European Upper Paleolithic blade "industry" of Würm glaciation dating.

AUSTRALOID. A primary geographical population or race now represented by thirty-five thousand or more survivors in Australia.

AUSTRALOPITHECUS. Fossil manlike apes from Africa.

AUSTRONESIAN. A linguistic stock whose subdivisions are spoken in Madagascar, Malaya, Indonesia, Melanesia, Micronesia, and Polynesia. It is also termed Malayo-Polynesian.

AVOIDANCE. Etiquette customs characterized by complete or partial avoidance or by formalized behavior which functions to maintain a social distance between certain relatives.

AVUNCULATE. The social relationship in which there are especially close ties with the maternal uncle (cf. Amitate).

AZILIAN. A western European culture area of the Epipaleolithic (*q. v.*) age.

AZTEC. A Mexican linguistic subdivision of the Uto-Aztekan (*q. v.*) linguistic stock. The people and culture of the Valley of Mexico.

BALTIC. A linguistic subdivision of the Indo-European linguistic stock. The surviving Baltic languages are Latvian and Lithuanian (*see also* East Baltic).

BANTU. Languages of the large southern subdivision of the Niger-Congo linguistic stock of Africa.

BARBARISM. A technical term applied by some writers to peoples of Neolithic or primitive agricultural and pastoral economy; also, a term of disparagement often applied to peoples in primitive economies.

BARTER. The type of exchange of product where no form of money is employed. It may be found in any type of socio-economic system but constitutes the sole type of exchange in the economically simplest systems known.

BASQUE. A linguistic stock, also termed Iberian, comprising a number of languages of southwestern France and northern Spain adjacent to the western Pyrenees.

BERDACHE (*see* Transvestitism).

BLACKFELLOWS, AUSTRALIAN. The dark natives of Australia and the only surviving examples of the Australoid geographical population.

BLOOD TYPE OR GROUP. Persons placed in a group because of the manner of the clumping or agglutination of their red corpuscles.

BLOWGUN. A long hollow tube from which darts are expelled by blowing, used for hunting birds, monkeys, and other smaller fauna. It is found in tropical districts in both hemispheres.

BOOMERANG. A curved wooden missile, some Australian forms of which return to the thrower.

BORREBY. The concept of some anthropologists of a northwestern European Caucasoid subrace.

BOUND FORM. A linguistic form which is never spoken alone, as *de* in *demerit,* or *ed* in *asked.*

BRACHIATION. Arboreal ape locomotion involving swinging from branches; the body may be supported by the hind limbs.

BRACHYCEPHALIC. Having a cephalic index of 80 or higher; wide-headed.

BRÜNN. The concept of some anthropologists of a central European Caucasoid subrace.

BULL-ROARER. A stick whirled at the end of a string and producing a whirring noise. It was employed in ceremonials by Australians and some other peoples.

BUSHMEN. The food-gathering bands of South Africa who speak languages of the Bushman division of the Khoisan (*q. v.*) linguistic stock and who are members of the Bushman-Hottentot pygmy geographical population.

CASTE. A hereditary group the members of which are severely limited in choice of mate, occupation, social participation, residence, or habiliments. Also sometimes used less accurately to refer to a segregated minority group against which there are discriminatory practices.

CAT'S CRADLE. The game of weaving patterns with string upon the fingers, played in many parts of the world.

CAUCASOID or CAUCASIAN. The concept of a geographical population of Europe and adjacent areas, sometimes termed less fittingly the white race or whites.

CAUCASUS (*see* North Caucasus and South Caucasus).

CAVE MAN. The improbable hypothesis that Pleistocene (*q. v.*) populations, especially the Neandertals (*q. v.*), occupied caves as permanent habitations, brandished gnarled clubs, were unusually hairy and sexually uninhibited.

CEPHALIC INDEX. A mathematically expressed relationship obtained by dividing the greatest width by the greatest length of a skull, and multiplying by 100.

CHARM (*see* Amulet).

CHELLEAN. A term which was formerly applied to the Lower Paleolithic levels of culture but which is now replaced by terms such as Abbevillian and Clactonian.

CHEYENNE. A northwestern Plains Indian group.

CHIBCHA. A group of languages from Costa Rica to Colombia. Also, the culture of Chibcha-speaking Indians of Colombia.

CHIEF. A term applied by Europeans to the leader or leaders in a socioeconomic system of low technological level.

CHILKAT. A Tlingit-speaking group of southern Alaska, living in a northerly district of the Pacific Northwest Coast culture area.

CHOREOGRAPHY. The art of planning or designing dance movements and patterns and of symbolizing such dance behavior in an appropriate transcription.

CHROMOSOME. One of the particles which is composed of many genes (*q. v.*) and is visible in a nucleus prior to cell division. Each human has forty-eight chromosomes in a cell.

CHUKCHEE. A language and culture group in the Paleasiatic (*q. v.*) population of the Chukchee Peninsula of eastern Siberia.

CIVILIZATION (*see* Civilized).

CIVILIZED. A loose term, of doubtful value, applied by many writers to social systems which possess stone architecture, a technique of writing, and an economy of Late Neolithic or later developmental levels.

CLACTONIAN. An English type of stone technology of Lower Paleolithic times.

CLAN. A unilateral pseudo-kinship relationship pattern or group within a community. Clan members are such for life, practice clan exogamy, call fellow members siblings, if of the same generation, parents if of an older generation, and son or daughter if of a younger generation.

CLASS. A segment of the population whose pattern of social relationships is determined by its special ownership of the most productive resources or by its relationship to the owners of such resources.

COHUNA. An Australian fossil skull of uncertain date once believed to be late Pleistocene and pre-Australoid but now regarded as probably a member of the modern Australoid group.

COLLECTIVE RESPONSIBILITY. The lower the technological level, the larger the circle of persons relative to the size of the community with whom an individual has mutual obligations, and the larger the number who share responsibility both for that individual's welfare and for his misdeeds. In time of trouble all members of the family, extended family, clan, village, or larger community may assume responsibility for the misdeed of the offender.

COMMUNISM, PRIMITIVE. A term applied by some writers to technologically lowly socio-economic systems wherein all major productive resources are the property of the community, not of individuals, lineages, or clans. In such communities there are no inequalities in ownership of the major resources or in the distribution of major production.

COMMUNITY. A group of mutually interdependent families which live and work together in a band, encampment, village, or larger aggregate of persons. It may or may not be self-sufficient. By contrast a society is an economically self-sufficient cluster of communities which are not necessarily interdependent but which intermarry and have a common territory, language, socio-economic system, and cultural heritage.

COMPLEX (*see* Culture Complex).

CONJUGAL FAMILY. The type of family in which the relationship between husband and wife and dependent offspring tends to play a functionally primary role whereas other persons who are biologically related to this familial nucleus tend to play a secondary role in the larger family pattern (cf. Consanguine Family).

CONSANGUINE FAMILY. The type of family in which the relationship between husband and wife and offspring tends to play a functionally secondary role whereas other persons who are biologically related to this familial core tend to play a functionally primary role in the larger family pattern (cf. Conjugal Family).

CONSONANT. A sound made by a complete and/or partial closure. Examples are b, t, g, k, l, s, ts, dj.

CONTAGIOUS MAGIC. The assumption that things, actions, or forms of behavior once interconnected will consequently and at a later time be interconnected (cf. Imitative Magic).

CONTINUANT. In phonetics, a type of consonant made with partial obstruction to the outgoing column of air. Examples are v, s, m, l.

CONVERGENCE. The independent development of similar features of culture, for example, similar geometric basketry designs that are historically unconnected.

COSMOGONY. The premises regarding the origin, form, and structure of the universe.

COUVADE. A custom found in many areas, where the husband observes special taboos, restrictions, or other confining behavior for a number of days subsequent to the birth of a baby to his wife.

COWRIE SHELLS. A type of sea shell employed as money in African and Indonesian culture areas.

CREOLES. Persons who have developed a creolized language (*q. v.*) or who are hybrids of a native and an economically superior invading population, and who retain many features of the cultural heritage native to the area hybridized with features of the introduced culture.

CREOLIZED LANGUAGE. A dialect of a "natural" language, developed by a population lately enveloped by an economically superior group, taken from the basic vocabulary of the latter group and supplemented by minor portions of its grammar and other linguistic features.

CRIME. An offense which is met by community, government, or state action rather than by retaliation by the hurt individual, lineage, or clan (cf. Tort).

CROMAGNON. The western European population of tall stature, probably Caucasoid, which was also Late Upper Paleolithic.

CROSS-COUSINS. Children of siblings of opposite sexes.

CULTURAL ANTHROPOLOGY (*see* Ethnography and Ethnology).

CULTURE. The total community heritage of nonbiological, socially transmitted traits, including technological, social, ideological, religious, and artistic forms of behavior and material objects.

CULTURE AREAS. Areas within each of which lie a number of socio-economic systems and cultures more like one another than any are like the systems and cultures of adjacent areas. It is sometimes useful to divide each area into subareas.

CULTURE CENTER. The socio-economic system and culture of the most distinctive or typical communities of a culture area (*q. v.*).

CULTURE COMPLEX. Any functionally integrated and patterned cluster of culture traits within a culture or culture area, for example the horse complex of the modern Plains Indian cultures, the cattle complex of East African cultures, and the potlatch product-exchange patterns of the Pacific Northwest culture area.

CULTURE TRAITS or CULTURE ELEMENTS. The units or minimal features of socially transmitted behavior or handiwork. Each culture comprises tens of thousands of created or borrowed traits.

CUNEIFORM. The extinct hieroglyph script characterized by wedge-shaped indentations made with a reed stylus in clay, developed by Mesopotamians before 3000 B.C.

DEMENTIA PRECOX. The older name for a group of psychoses now called the schizophrenias, whose highest incidence in our society is in the 20- to 30-year-old age group. These psychoses are characterized by a splitting of the ego and the divorce of emotional and mental processes from social and physical reality.

DENTALIA. Sea shells secured at low tide and used for purposes of ornamentation and as money; on the Pacific Northwest Coast, they were collected by Vancouver Island Indians of Nootka villages and the beads were exchanged over a vast area.

DEUTERO-MALAY. The concept of a Mongoloid subrace, in a later era, which migrated from southeastern Asia into Malaysia, following an earlier migration of another Mongoloid subdivision termed proto-Malay (cf. Indonesian and Malay).

DIBBLE. A simple sharp-pointed or chisel-pointed tool, superior to and evolved from a simple root digger, sometimes equipped with a footrest, and used in the most primitive Neolithic farming communities. The plough and the hoe were probably later developments.

DIFFUSION. The spread of a feature of culture beyond the community in which it originated (cf. Stimulus Diffusion).

DIFFUSIONISTS. The term for several groups of theoreticians in anthropology who agree in the premise that the spread of features of culture is a major factor in culture history.

DINARIC. The concept of a European Caucasoid subrace, centering in the Dinaric Alps of Yugoslavia. Pronounced nasal convexity is frequent in this population.

DIONYSIAN. A basic cultural pattern of most Indians of the United States apart from those of the southwestern states. As described by Ruth Benedict the Dionysian pattern exhibits emotionally violent experiences or frenzied psychic states, the use of torture in religion in some districts, and predilection for drugs (cf. Apollonian).

DOLICHOCEPHALIC. Having a cephalic index of less than 75; narrow- or long-headed.

DOMESTICATION. The process of artificial selection in animals by which the anatomical features and central nervous system are progressively changed. The creatures breed under artificial conditions of living; complex behavior patterns determined by heredity are progressively attenuated or modified; anatomical features not successful for survival in the natural state are further developed because they have become useful or desirable for human purposes. The creatures become more plastic and teachable and after a certain degree of domestication may become incapable of surviving under natural conditions.

DRAVIDIAN. A linguistic stock of India (*see also* Veddoid).

DRYOPITHECUS. The races of erect, ground-dwelling, and omnivorous apes, the descendants of only one of which may have evolved into humans and thus survived in changed form. *Dryopithecus* first developed in the Late Miocene and spread into three Old World continents. Manlike fossil apes of *Dryopithecus* ancestry may have survived in Africa into Pleistocene times.

EAST BALTIC. The concept of a Caucasoid subrace resident in East Baltic areas.

ECOLOGY. The relations between organisms and their habitats; the continuous adaptation of human biological, social, and cultural processes and features to their changing environments.

ENDOGAMY. The restrictive customs according to which a mate can be sought, or is preferably sought, only within one's own segment of the population. There are racial, religious, class, and other endogamic rules.

EOANTHROPUS (*see* Piltdown).

EOCENE. An early division of the Tertiary, when lemurs and tarsiers had a central nervous system more complex in its structure than any other mammals. Monkeys were then only in process of evolving from tarsiers.

EOLITHIC. The "Dawn Stone Era" which preceded the Paleolithic period and characterized Late Pliocene and Early Pleistocene times until the first Pleistocene glacial age (*see* Eoliths).

EOLITHS. Extremely crude chipped flints used and supposedly made by Pliocene and Early Pleistocene prehumans during the Eolithic era.

EPICANTHIC FOLD. The fold of skin of the upper eyelid from the nose to the eyebrow. Classic Mongoloids have the most pronounced inner epicanthic folds of any populations.

EPIPALEOLITHIC, MESOLITHIC, or TRANSITIONAL. The technological and socio-economic developmental level immediately following the Old World Upper Paleolithic era and transitional to the Neolithic era.

ESKIMO. A division of the Eskimo-Aleut linguistic stock. The term is also used for an ethnic subdivision of the American Indian and Pale-asiatic peoples. The Eskimo people live mainly in arctic coastal districts of eastern Siberia, North America, and Greenland, and their economy is based upon the utilization of seal and caribou.

ETHNIC SUBDIVISION. That portion of a geographical population or major race which is distinguishable from other portions in one or more inherited anatomical features.

ETHNOCENTRISM. The ideology characterized by an unduly high evaluation of the language, and of the religious and cultural manifestations, of one's own population, and a depreciation or snobbish disapproval of such manifestations in other populations.

ETHNOGRAPHY. The scientific description of the socio-economic systems and cultural heritages of the peoples of low technological levels.

ETHNOLOGY. The scientific analysis of the socio-economic systems and cultural heritages of the peoples of low technological level, based upon ethnography, and undertaken to reveal the origins, functioning, and processes of change of their cultural features; also termed cultural anthropology and social anthropology.

EUGENICS. The study of the mechanisms of inheritance and change of human traits, with a practical perspective of selective breeding in order to improve the inherited quality of human populations. However, the scientific knowledge of problems of eugenics is still so meagre that selective breeding in humans is now impossible. A negative program of eugenics can limit the frequency of only a few genetically determined physical abnormalities or malformations.

EXOGAMY. The customs according to which a mate can be sought or is preferably sought only outside one's own segment of the population, such as close relatives, or the village, clan, or moiety.

EXTENDED FAMILY. The larger group of biological relatives which includes the individual family and a varying number of more distant kin; strong socio-economic bonds tie these individuals one to another.

EXTROVERT. A psychological type of personality and behavior pattern described by C. G. Jung. Individuals of this type direct their interests and energies outward toward people and things of the external world (cf. Introvert).

FAMILIARITY. Customs, sometimes also termed privileged familiarity, characterized by custom-sanctioned intimacies and liberties that can be taken with certain relatives such as uncles, aunts, or in-laws (cf. Avunculate, Amitate, Avoidance).

FAMILY. The universal social relationship consisting of husband, wife, and dependent offspring, and other biological relatives (cf. Conjugal Family, Consanguine Family, and Extended Family).

FELTING. The process of rolling, beating, and compressing of wool, fur. or hair, originally developed by Asian Neolithic pastoralists.

FETISH. An object to which supernatural potency is ascribed.

FINNO-UGRIAN. A linguistic stock or a subdivision of the Ural-Altaic linguistic stock. It includes languages such as Lapp, Finnish, Esthonian, Hungarian, and many others, mainly of peoples of the Soviet Union.

FOLKLORE. The orally transmitted stories, tales, and myths had by all peoples and rendered in a literary style. Folklore is often used to refer to folk tales of a less sacred or culturally less important type than myth tales or mythology. By folklore is also sometimes meant the entire body of oral literature, dance, music, sayings, and folk beliefs.

FOLK TALE. A story of the folklore.

FOLKWAYS. The modes of behavior and usages of people, sometimes termed mores, which are approved because they are the custom. They may be explicitly sanctioned by the mythology (cf. Mores).

FOSSIL. Any organic or inorganic object which has been preserved in the earth or rocks, whether because it was imperishable like chipped flints or because it was mineralized like some bones of Pleistocene animals, birds, or human populations, and which supplies information regarding zoological or cultural change.

FREE FORM. A linguistic form which can be spoken alone. A word is a minimum free form. Phrases and sentences constitute other kinds of free forms.

FREUDIAN. Referring to a premise or method first expressed in the writings of the founder of psychoanalysis, Sigmund Freud of Vienna, or to a believer in or protagonist of his ideology, methods of psychological analysis. and therapeutic procedures.

GALLEY HILL. A Late Pleistocene skeleton, found in England, once supposed to be of the same developmental level and era as the Swanscombe (*q. v.*) and the Steinheim (*q. v.*). Fluorine dating indicates a much more recent age.

GENE. A minimal and ultimate unit of heredity and the supposed determinant of specific anatomical features. Each chromosome (*q. v.*) is the carrier of many genes.

GENIUS. A concept premised upon the postulated extreme rarity of original or creative ability. The very small segment at the extreme upper end of a normal distribution curve which symbolizes the mental potentialities of a human population.

GENOTYPE. The anatomical type as determined exclusively by genes (cf. Phenotype).

GENS. A patrilineal, unilateral pseudo-kinship group within a community. An alternative and now preferred term is patrilineal clan.

GEOGRAPHICAL POPULATION (*see* Race).

GERONTOCRACY. A term applied to government by a dominant if not autocratic group of older men, ascribed with doubtful fitness to the natives of Australia.

GHOST DANCE, PLAINS. An ideology and ceremonial which spread from Wovoka, a Nevada Indian, eastwards almost to the Mississippi about 1890. It assumed the magical disappearance of the Caucasian invaders, and the return of the recently deceased Indians and of the native foods, especially the vanished buffalo.

GHOST DANCE CULTS, CALIFORNIAN. An ideology and ceremonial of the 1870's which spread beyond California. These cults assumed the magical disappearance of the Caucasian invaders, and the return of the recently deceased Indians and of the native foods.

GIGANTOPITHECUS. Fossil fragments possibly of Early Pleistocene dating from a prehuman population preceding *Pithecanthropus-Sinanthropus*.

GRAMMAR. The analysis and description of the arrangements of free and bound forms (*q. v.*). *See also* Morphology.

GRIMALDI. Cromagnon fossils, thought by some writers to have partially Negroid characteristics.

GROUP MARRIAGE. The improbable hypothesis of an early stage of the evolution of social patterns characterized by a marital and familial relationship wherein a group of males was married to a group of females without individual family units.

GUINEA-SUDAN. Once regarded as a language stock south of the Sahara, now largely a subdivision of the Niger-Congo stock (*q. v.*).

GYPSIES. Members of a European minority group partially descended from tribes which migrated westwards from northwestern India about six centuries ago. Many features of their anatomy, language, and culture survive from such a point of origin.

HAIDA. A linguistic group, probably genetically related to Nadéné, resident in the Queen Charlotte Islands off southern Alaska.

HEIDELBERG. A fossil jaw and the teeth of a Pleistocene population possibly of slightly higher developmental level than *Pithecanthropus-Sinanthropus* (*q. v.*).

HIEROGLYPH. Written characters that are highly conventionalized and a later development of picture writing. In Egypt the later and further simplified, rounded, conventionalized, and more rapidly written characters are termed hieratic.

HOE. A tilling implement with a flat blade set at approximately a right angle to the handle, and developed in the Neolithic era in both hemispheres.

HOKAN. A postulated portion of the hypothetic Hokan-Siouan linguistic stock of the Americas.

HOMONID. A member of any Pleistocene or recent species on the human line of ascent.

HOTTENTOT. The group of languages which constitutes one division of the Khoisan (*q. v.*) linguistic stock of South Africa. Also, the people who speak a Hottentot language.

HYBRID. In human heredity, any offspring of members of diverse geographical populations.

HYBRID VIGOR. The hypothesis that hybrids of healthy family lines of diverse geographical populations in a species display greater physical strength and larger dimensions of anatomical features than are exhibited in the ancestral lines that contributed to the hybrids. Hybrid vigor has not, however, been sufficiently documented for human hybrids to be regarded as proved.

IBERIAN (*see* Basque).

IDEOGRAPH. A written character or symbol for a word.

IMITATIVE MAGIC or SYMPATHETIC MAGIC. The assumption that action upon a symbol of a thing or person will cause a similar and real effect upon that thing or person (cf. Contagious Magic).

INCA. A linguistic stock, also termed Quechua, of the Andean highlands of Peru and Ecuador. Also, the economically advanced culture area of that region.

INCEST. A sexual or marital relationship prohibited because the participants are judged to be too closely related.

INCORPOREAL PROPERTY. A term for features of culture such as dances, designs, songs, magical formulae, patents, and the like, which are often privately owned in primitive economies.

INDEX. A mathematically expressed relationship between two anatomical measurements; for example, the cephalic index.

INDO-AUSTRALIAN (*see* Veddoid).

INDO-EUROPEAN. A linguistic stock of Asia, Europe, and North Africa, which comprises subdivisions such as the Celtic, Germanic, Italic, Greek, Slavic, Baltic, Armenian, Indo-Iranian, and others. The stock was formerly often termed Indo-Germanic and a few earlier writers called it Aryan.

INDONESIAN. A supposedly earlier Mongoloid migration into Indonesia, followed by Malays; also termed proto-Malay.

INFANTICIDE. The killing of infants.

INFLECTIVE LANGUAGE. A language whose grammar is characterized by many bound forms each of which have merged some distinct features, as in Latin verb suffixes.

INSTINCT. An inherited and fundamental drive or highly complex stimulus-response mechanism found in all animals with the possible exception of *Homo sapiens*. It is a dynamic base for responses and is present in all members of the species. It is not directly dependent for its existence upon environment but is determined by specific genes. Among humans, historically derived culture (*q. v.*) rather than instinct is decisive in determining the patterns of behavior.

INTANGIBLE PROPERTY (*see* Incorporeal Property).

INTELLIGENCE QUOTIENT (*I. Q.*). The mental age of a person, as measured by so-called intelligence tests, divided by his chronological age.

INTROVERT. A psychological type of personality and behavior pattern described by C. G. Jung. Individuals of this type direct their interests and energies inward rather than outward as in the case of the EXTROVERT (*q. v.*).

IRANO-AFGHAN MEDITERRANEAN. The concept of a Near East subrace of Mediterranean Caucasoids.

JARGON or PIDGIN. A means of communication spontaneously but meagrely developed, characterized by a small vocabulary and few grammatical features, usually appearing in an area of many languages and rapidly increasing intercommunication.

JEWS. Peoples who share a religio-cultural heritage termed Jewish. They are anatomically identical with populations among whom they have long resided, and therefore they are neither a race nor an ethnic subdivision. They are a segregated and discriminated-against minority group in many countries. Where local groups of Jews have lived in ghettos for centuries they have developed some minor but distinctive cultural characteristics. In central and eastern European ghettos they retained and gradually changed a western Old High German dialect which, mixed with Hebrew words, is now termed Yiddish. Most contemporary Jews in other parts of the world speak the language of the countries in which they live and participate fully in the cultures of those countries.

JOKING RELATIONSHIP. Among the Northwest Plains Indians, children of fathers who are members of the same subdivision play tricks on one another with impunity and exert moral censorship on one another, as a special form of privileged familiarity.

KEILOR. An Australian fossil fragment possibly of Solo-Wadjak and third interglacial level.

KHOISAN. The linguistic stock which comprises the Bushman and Hottentot languages of South Africa; also designated Bushman-Hottentot.

KITCHEN MIDDEN. A Mesolithic or later refuse heap or mound which contains especially large numbers of shells in addition to artifacts.

KULA RING. The ceremonialized economic interchanges described by Bronislaw Malinowski as a facet of the economic system of the Melanesians of the Trobriand Islands.

KULTURKREIS. The designation given the theory of world-wide diffusion of successive culture aggregates, advanced by German-speaking anthropologists, notably by Fritz Graebner and Wilhelm Schmidt.

KWAKIUTL. A Wakashan-speaking group of Indian villages of northern Vancouver Island.

LADOGAN. The concept of a Caucasoid subrace resident in East Baltic districts.

LANGUAGE. The complex medium of oral expression of a speech community. It is largely unintelligible to any other speech community.

LAPP. A partially Mongoloid ethnic subdivision of the Caucasoids, largely in northern Scandinavia.

LATTAH. A type of mental abnormality found in Malaya or other equatorial districts, featured by compulsive imitativeness and probably largely culturally determined.

LEMUR. The most primitive suborder of the primates, which evolved in Paleocene and Eocene times but survives in many species in Madagascar, Africa, and Indonesia.

LEPTOSOME. A postulated constitutional type portrayed by Kretschmer. Individuals approximating the type are tall, slender, narrow chested, long legged, with elongated face, long and narrow hands and feet. *See* Athletic and Pyknic.

LEVALLOISIAN. A special technique of flake chipping of Acheulean and later eras.

LEVIRATE. The custom whereby a deceased husband is replaced by his brother or other close male relative (cf. Sororate).

LINEAGE. A subdivision of a clan composed of actual not fictitious kin.

LOBOLA. The bride purchase price paid in cattle in East Africa.

"LOST WAX" METHOD. A technique invented in both hemispheres for casting metals by covering a wax model with clay and pouring molten metal into the clay mold.

MAGDALENIAN. A western European Upper Paleolithic blade "industry," other artifacts, and cave paintings.

MAGIC (*see* Contagious Magic and Imitative Magic).

MAGLEMOSIAN. A northern central European culture area of the Epipaleolithic period.

MALAY. The concept of a later and post-Indonesian Mongoloid migration into Indonesia. Also, the Indonesian language subdivision of the Austronesian linguistic stock.

MALAYO-POLYNESIAN (*see* Austronesian).

MANA. Impersonal, all-pervasive, nonindividualized supernatural power, widely if not universally believed in (*see* Animatism).

MANIC-DEPRESSIVE. The psychosis which often displays two phases or alterations of mood: acute mania, excitement, or elation, and acute depression or melancholia.

MAORI. The Polynesian people resident in New Zealand.

MARGINAL AREAS. The socio-economic systems and cultures of the communities which lie near or at the broad boundaries drawn to delimit culture areas.

MARRIAGE. A term for the social relationship of husband and wife or of plural mates; also used for the ceremony of uniting marital partners.

MATRIARCHATE. The improbable hypothesis that there were socio-economic systems characterized by preponderantly feminine property ownership and economic control, governmental management, and cultural leadership. Writers have occasionally used the term when the societies to which they referred were actually characterized by no more than parity of the sexes.

MATRILINEAL. The reckoning of group membership or descent through the mother, not the father.

MATRILOCAL. Residence by a married couple in the wife's native community.

MAYA. The language group of Yucatan and nearby areas. Also, the especially advanced Neolithic civilization of Yucatan, Guatemala, and nearby districts.

MEAN, ARITHMETIC. The most widely used of all the measures of central tendency, obtained by adding the mathematical values of a series of items and dividing by the number of items.

MEDIAN. That value which divides a series of items arranged in a frequency distribution, so that an equal number of items are on either side of it.

MEDITERRANEANS. The concept of a Caucasoid subrace around the shores of the Mediterranean, in northeastern Africa, and in southwestern Asia and beyond into India. Many Mediterraneans also are found in northwestern Europe.

MEGANTHROPUS PALEOJAVANICUS. A fossil fragment possibly of Early Pleistocene dating from a prehuman population preceding *Pithecanthropus-Sinanthropus*.

MELANESIA. The great Oceanian cluster of islands from New Guinea to Fiji inclusive. *Melanesian* means both a distinctive Oceanian geographical population which simulates Negroid features but is not genetically Negroid, and a language subdivision of Austronesian.

MENDELIANISM. The theory regarding the process of inheritance of characters, first published by Gregor Mendel in the 1860's and rediscovered about 1900.

MESOCEPHALIC. Having a cephalic index between 75 and 80; medium-headed.

MESOLITHIC (*see* Epipaleolithic).

MICROLITH. A term for exquisitely finely pressure-flaked and tiny flints of the Magdalenian, Epipaleolithic, and Neolithic eras.

MICRONESIA. The many islands north of Melanesia and northwest of Polynesia, including the Gilbert, Ellice, Marshall, Caroline, and Marianas groups. *Micronesian* means both a linguistic subdivision in the Austronesian linguistic stock, and an ethnic subdivision of the Micronesian-Polynesian geographical population.

MIOCENE. A Tertiary geological epoch during which apes were in process of development and the *Dryopithecus* apes had begun their course of evolution on the ground.

MODAL PERSONALITY, or BASIC PERSONALITY. The kind of personality most typical or most frequently found in a community. An economically advanced and stratified culture is likely to have two or more such modes or personality types.

MODE. In statistics the value at the point around which the items in a group or series tend to be most heavily concentrated; or, the most typical of a series of values.

MOIETY. In a clan society, the half of the community which may include one or more interconnected clans, as opposed to the other half which may also include one or more interconnected clans. Members of a moiety often practice moiety exogamy.

MONEY. The most portable, imperishable, neatly divisible, and socially fluid of surplus products which are exchanged, functioning as an equivalent for any other exchanged products.

MONGOL. A linguistic stock or subdivision of the Ural-Altaic linguistic stock. The term may also be used to refer to residents of modern Mongolia as well as to ancient and predatory groups whose homes were in that area.

MONOTHEISM. Belief in only one deity or in one outstandingly potent deity among some minor deities.

MORES. Modes of behavior which are approved because they are the custom and are sanctioned by the mythology (cf. Folkways).

MORPHEME. A minimal unit, composed of one or several sounds, of distinguishable meaning and function.

MORPHOLOGY. In scientific linguistics, the analysis and description of the arrangements of bound forms or parts of words, contrasted with syntax, which analyzes phrases or sentences and the interrelations of their free forms. Grammar is inclusive of both.

MOTIF. A minimal feature of plot in oral literature, of melodic pattern in music, of design in plastic or graphic art, or of symbolized expression in dance.

MOUSTERIAN. A tool technique of the Middle Paleolithic, from Europe to China, and from the later third interglacial to the middle of the fourth or Würm glacial epoch.

MUSICOLOGY. The science of the description and analysis of music, and of processes of change in music.

MYTH. A story in mythology (*q. v.*).

MYTHOLOGY. Orally transmitted literature. Sometimes such oral literature is regarded as more sacred than folklore.

NADÉNÉ. The American linguistic stock or subdivision which may be genetically related to Sinitic. It includes Eyak, Haida, Tlingit, and many Athabaskan languages.

NATION. A technical term often used for those peoples who possess a common language, territory, and cultural heritage, or who desire nationhood. Also employed by some writers as a synonym for tribe.

NEANDERTAL. The concept of European ethnic subdivisions of a Late Pleistocene developmental level immediately preceding *Homo sapiens.*

NEAR-HUMANS. Old World geographical populations from Early to Middle Pleistocene eras.

NEGRILLO. A term used by some writers for the central African Pygmy population.

NEGRITO. A term used by some writers for the Far Eastern Pygmy populations.

NEGROID. The geographical population of dark Africans of normal stature and south of the Sahara. Many writers include the Melanesians and the three geographical populations of Pygmies in a larger concept of Negroids. Most American Negro people are only partially Negroid.

NEOASIATIC. The concept of a central-eastern Asiatic ethnic subdivision also termed North Chinese Mongoloids, with less adaptation to cold than Classic Mongoloids.

NEOLITHIC. The socio-economic developmental level characterized by primitive agriculture and/or primitive pastoralism, and by a lack of bronze or ferrous metallurgy.

NEUROSIS. Mental, emotional, and motor abnormality which only temporarily or partially incapacitates and where the basic symptoms are characterized by anxiety; also termed psychoneurosis (cf. Psychosis).

NEW STONE AGE (*see* Neolithic).

NIGER-CONGO. An African linguistic stock which comprises the Bantu speaking and many Guinea-Sudan peoples.

NOMAD. A term used for peoples who change their area of residence seasonally within a larger domain which is their home country.

Nomadism in the sense of wandering without annual return is rarely found.

NORDIC. The concept of a northern European Caucasoid subrace. No satisfactory scientific formulations have been given regarding the genesis, racial ingredients, anatomical criteria, or geographic distribution of such a population (cf. Aryan).

NORTH CAUCASUS. A linguistic stock comprising several languages of the region so named.

NORTHWEST COAST, PACIFIC. A culture area as to the boundaries for which there is no precise agreement. It refers in general to the many tidewater or lower river communities from northwestern coastal California to the Yakutat in southern Alaska.

OATH. A declaration supported by an appeal to the supernatural requesting punishment in event of perjury, and employed as evidence in determination of guilt in many societies which possess primitive economies.

OEDIPUS COMPLEX. The Freudian concept of a biologically determined emotional conflict, initiated at the moment of childhood frustration at time of weaning, which is claimed to be a primary factor in later character and personality formation. Its normal course has been claimed to be characterized by repressed love for the parent of opposite sex and repressed hate for the parent of the same sex.

OLD STONE AGE (*see* Paleolithic).

OLIGOCENE. The Tertiary geological epoch in which many species of monkeys appeared. It preceded the Miocene (*q. v.*) era of the development of apes.

ORDEAL. A form of trial and procedure for securing evidence of guilt, not found in the New World. The accused drinks a poison, or immerses a body member in hot liquid, or engages in combat with his accuser.

OUTRIGGER. A pole or float braced to a canoe to lessen its chances of capsizing. This type of vessel is widely used by Oceanian islanders and also in Madagascar.

PALEASIATIC. A Mongoloid ethnic subdivision of Far Eastern Siberia, to which the American Indian and Eskimo populations are genetically related.

PALEOCENE. The first Tertiary geological epoch, during which lemurs and tarsiers appeared.

PALEOLITHIC or OLD STONE AGE. The long Pleistocene epoch characterized by cutting tools of stone that were chipped and in later epochs flaked by pressure.

PALEOJAVANICUS (*see* Meganthropus).

PALEONTOLOGY, HUMAN. The science of fossil man.

PAPUAN. In linguistics a term for a possible non-Melanesian or non-Austronesian linguistic stock or stocks of New Guinea. Also employed with confusing lack of agreement for all or some of the New Guineans.

PARALLEL COUSINS. Children of siblings of the same sex.

PARALLELISM. The independent invention of similar or identical features of culture, as New World and Old World writing, the concept of zero, bronze, and agriculture.

PARANOIA. A form of schizoid psychosis, always characterized by systematized delusions of persecution and usually accompanied by delusions of grandeur.

PARANTHROPUS. A fossil manlike ape from Africa.

PARAPITHECUS. A squirrel-sized Lower Oligocene creature, uncertainly a precursor of apes.

PASTORALISM. An economic system in which production from or with domesticated animals constitutes a major economic resource.

PATRIARCHATE. A term that is used for any society in which the feminine sex has lower status.

PATRILINEAL. The reckoning of group membership or descent through the father, not the mother.

PATRILOCAL. Residence by a married couple in the husband's native community.

PATTERN, CULTURE. The most typical, basic, or central social and correlated psychological features of a culture.

PATTERN NUMBER, MAGIC NUMBER, or MYSTIC NUMBER. The customary and stylized number of repetitions for a feature of a ceremonial, a song melody, or a dance pattern. Also, the conventional number of brothers or sisters or animals of a type, or of repetitions of an action in a story in oral literature.

PENUTIAN. A poorly substantiated but temporarily useful concept of an American Indian linguistic stock which includes many linguistic subdivisions possessing a great variety of grammatical structures.

PEPPERCORN HAIR. The extremely spiraled and tufted kind of head hair found among Bushman-Hottentot and adjacent Bantu groups in southern Africa.

PETROGLYPH. A figure, design, or symbol cut into rock.

PEYOTE. A small cactus, the upper button-like portion of which is eaten by United States Indians during religious ceremonials wherever the peyote cult has been developed.

PHENOTYPE. The physiological or living form displayed by the genetic type, and partly determined by the diet and conditions of living (cf. Genotype).

PHONEME. A minimal formal unit of sound, which usually appears in a number of major variants or allophones.

PHONETICS. The scientific description and formulation of sounds employed in language.

PHRATRY. A group of two or more clans which share in various activities.

PHYSICAL ANTHROPOLOGY OR ANTHROPOMETRY. The science of comparative human anatomical features and measurements, of the determination of causes for changes in such features and measurements, and of the genetic relationships of human populations.

PICTOGRAPH. Slightly conventionalized pictures or characters of a cartoon-like appearance, as in picture writing, which bear no fixed relation to linguistic forms, words, or morphemes, and which constitute a developmental level preceding the more conventionalized hieroglyphs that refer to words or morphemes. Rock paintings are also termed pictographs.

PIDGIN (*see* Jargon).

PILTDOWN or EOANTHROPUS. Several English fossil-like fragments once thought to be of second interglacial dating, but recently indicated to be fraudulent.

PITHECANTHROPUS-SINANTHROPUS. An Early to Middle Pleistocene developmental level of the homonid line, represented by fossils from Java and northern China.

PLAINS. Term for an American-Canadian culture area east of the Rockies and extending to the Eastern Woodlands.

PLEISTOCENE. The last 500,000 to 1,000,000 or more years of geological history, until the end of the last glacial period.

PLESIANTHROPUS. A fossil manlike ape from Africa.

PLIOCENE. The last geological subdivision of the Tertiary epoch, during which the types evolved from *Dryopithecus* to prehuman levels.

PLOUGH. The farming tool, superior to a hoe, which turns up more soil and pushes forward rather than chops backward. It was drawn by an ox or by slaves in Late Neolithic times, and enormously increased agricultural production.

PLUVIAL. Rainy; each Pleistocene glacial period of central western Europe was paralleled by a pluvial or excessively rainy climate in non-glaciated regions, though perhaps not in all.

POLYANDRY. Plural husbands, an extremely rare marital pattern, often confused with permissible sexual relations with more than one male.

POLYCHROME. Multicolored; often refers to the several colors of paints employed in rock paintings or on pottery.

POLYGAMY. Plural mates. Limited by some writers to a family pattern of one husband and plural wives; also termed polygyny.

POLYGENESIS. Independent and plural origins.

POLYGYNY. Plural wives.

POLYNESIA. The vast triangle of Oceania from Easter to Hawaii to New Zealand. Polynesian is a linguistic subdivision of Austronesian. Poly-nesian-Micronesian has been classified as a geographical population.

POLYSYNTHETIC LANGUAGE. A type of grammatical structure which ex-presses many semantically important elements, such as objects and di-rections, by means of bound forms. Examples are the Eskimo-Aleut and a number of American Indian languages.

POLYTHEISM. Belief in plural deities.

POTLATCH. A giving-away feast characteristic of the Pacific Northwest Coast.

PRE-DRAVIDIAN (*see* Veddoid).

PREFERENTIAL MATING. The rules or customs, such as levirate-sororate and cross-cousin marriage, that favor or prescribe marriages to certain individuals.

PRELOGICAL MENTALITY. The assumption of Lévy-Bruhl and others that qualitatively distinctive thinking exists among primitive peoples; that their ideas are socially not individually created, emotional not logical, premised upon mystical not concrete causality and upon identification of self and things with other beings and things.

PRESSURE FLAKING. A technique for breaking off minute flakes from chipped stones; it greatly advanced the level of cutting tools of stone during the Upper Paleolithic and Mesolithic periods.

PRIEST. The specialist and full-time functionary in magico-religious work of the economically more advanced agricultural and pastoral cultures.

PRIMATE. The mammalian order which includes lemurs, tarsiers, mon-keys, fossil and surviving apes, and *Homo sapiens*.

PRIMITIVE. A term best limited in anthropology to poor or inferior productivity of foods and artifacts, because of meagre technology, or to socio-economic systems thus handicapped.

PRIVILEGED FAMILIARITY. Customs such as the avunculate (*q. v.*) which permit or prescribe special forms of familiarity, joking, or license between individuals having a specific relationship.

PROGNATHISM. The hereditary protrusion of the upper jaw, found somewhat more frequently in Negroids.

PROMISCUITY. The improbable hypothesis of an early stage of the evolution of social patterns characterized by an absence of even temporary marital or familial unions.

PROPLIOPITHECUS. A squirrel-sized Lower Oligocene creature which appears to be a precursor of apes.

PROTO-MALAY (*see* Indonesian).

PSYCHOANALYSIS. The premises and methods initially developed by Sigmund Freud and changed and further developed by many psychiatrists who have adhered to some of Freud's basic premises.

PSYCHONEUROSIS (*see* Neurosis).

PSYCHOSIS. Mental, emotional, and motor abnormality which often permanently and completely incapacitates. Characterized by bizarre behavior, delusions, and disordered emotions (cf. Neurosis).

PYGMY. A term for Far Eastern, Congo, and Bushman-Hottentot geographical populations whose average hereditary stature is less than that of any other populations by several inches.

PYKNIC. A postulated constitutional type portrayed by Kretschmer. Individuals approximating the type are short, thick set, have a heavy trunk and short legs, rounded chest and shoulders, and short hands and feet. *See* Athletic and Leptosome.

RACE. A geographical population whose genetic characteristics are different from other geographical populations and which differs from them in one feature or in a cluster of inherited anatomical features.

RHODESIAN. Fossil fragments from South Africa, which cannot be dated but which may be of the Solo developmental level of the third interglacial period.

RITE DE PASSAGE or CRISIS RITE. A rite or ceremonial at a birth, initiation, puberty, marriage, or death, or at any time of important transformation in status or circumstance of a person or persons.

RORSCHACH. A projective technique or type of psychological test purporting to elicit responses which if correctly interpreted reveal basic features of the total personality. The test involves the use of a small series of cards with standardized ink blots into which the subject reads meanings.

SACRED NUMBER (*see* Pattern Number).

SANCTION. A reaction by most members of a community to an approved or disapproved form of social behavior. Some sanctions are spontaneous or diffuse, others are formally organized by customary or legal procedures.

SAVAGERY. (a) A derogatory term often applied to peoples with primitive economies; (b) a technical term applied by some writers to characterize the way of life of all peoples with primitive economies; (c) a technical term applied by some writers to food-gathering peoples.

SCARIFICATION. Gashes and scars deliberately made, usually in conventional patterns as permanent body decoration, most often by peoples of very dark pigmentation.

SCHIZOIDS or the SCHIZOPHRENIAS (*see* Dementia Precox).

SEMANTICS. The scientific description and analysis of the meanings attached to phonetic or any other linguistic forms.

SEMI-MONGOLOID. The concept of a hybridized geographical population of Eurasia, derived from the intermixture of Caucasoid and Mongoloid ancestors.

SEMITIC. A linguistic stock originally limited to Arabia which spread largely into northern and northeastern Africa. It is not a geographical population, race, or profile, and it is also not a religion.

SHAKER. A religion originated among Puget Sound Indians of Washington State in the 1880's. It combined Indian with Christian features and spread widely.

SHAMAN. The nonspecialist medical and magico-religious practitioner in societies with primitive economies (cf. Priest).

SHOSHONEAN. A western United States linguistic subdivision of the Uto-Aztekan linguistic stock. Shoshonean languages extended from southern Oregon and Idaho to southern Nevada and Utah.

SIB. Matrilineal or patrilineal, unilateral extended lineage or pseudo-kinship groups within a community (cf. Clan, Gens).

SIBLING. A brother or sister.

SILENT TRADE. The exchange of surplus products conducted without seeing the other trader. Objects are left at an agreed-upon spot, and the objects left in trade are later picked up. The practice is found largely in societies with the most primitive economies.

SINITIC, TIBETO-CHINESE, or SINO-TIBETAN. The linguistic stock of scores of Chinese languages and an undetermined number of additional divisions; claims have been made that these include Tibeto-Burman, Tai or Siamese. and Nadéné (*q. v.*).

SIVAPITHECUS. One of the *Dryopithecus* (*q. v.*) types from India. Its relation to the later human line is uncertain.

SLAVIC. A linguistic subdivision of the Indo-European (*q. v.*) linguistic stock, not a race, cultural heritage, soul, or temperament.

SOCIAL ANTHROPOLOGY (*see* Ethnography and Ethnology).

SOLO. Fragments, mostly skullcaps, of eleven individuals of a third interglacial population in Java and perhaps of an early Neandertaloid (*q. v.*) developmental level.

SOLUTREAN. A western European Upper Paleolithic blade "industry" of Würm glaciation dating and preceding the Magdalenian (*q. v.*).

SONANT. In phonetics, a sound like *b, d, g, z, dj, e,* made with synchronous vibration of vocal cords or voicing (cf. Surd).

SORCERY. Refers most often to evil magic.

SORORATE. The custom whereby a wife or a deceased wife is joined by or replaced by her sister or other close female relative (*cf.* Levirate).

SOUTH CAUCASUS. A linguistic stock comprising several languages of the region named.

SPEAR-THROWER. A wooden or bone piece about two feet long which permitted greater leverage and force of propulsion when hurling a dart or spear. It was used widely by Upper Paleolithic and more recent peoples and was replaced only with the spread of the bow and arrow.

SPELLS. Words recited or sung for a magical purpose, which may also be termed magical formulae or incantations.

STATE. A term used by some writers in political science for government by the owners of major productive resources. It is used by Lowie and many other writers as synonymous with autonomous village, tribe, community, or nation. Other writers use it as synonymous with any type of civil government.

STATUS. A term employed to designate rank in prestige in relation to other members of a community. Sometimes used as synonymous with class or socio-economic level.

STEATOPYGY. An especially pronounced deposition of fat on the buttocks. At one time it was supposed to be a hereditary and distinctive feature of the Bushman-Hottentot population but its derivation from distinctive genes is now doubted.

STEINHEIM. A third interglacial fossil skull found in Germany, indicating like Swanscombe a virtually modern level of development of the brain.

Stimulus Diffusion. That type of diffusion in which neither a specific culture element nor a culture complex is borrowed and adapted, but only the general idea of an element or complex. For example, the alphabet script of Semitic Ras Shamra developed only by analogy with the Phoenician script.

Stone Age (*see* Eolithic, Paleolithic, Neolithic).

Stop. In phonetics, a type of consonant made with a complete obstruction to the column of air; examples: *p, d, k̜.*

Sudanese (*see* Guinea-Sudan, Niger-Congo).

Supraorbital Ridge. The bony prominence over the eye sockets, more pronounced in Australoids than in other living populations, and well developed in most Pleistocene human fossils.

Surd. In phonetics, a sound like *p, t, k̜, s, ts,* made without synchronous vibration of vocal cords or voicing (cf. Sonant).

Survival. In social anthropology, a feature of culture retained with meagre or no functioning role, but which presumably functioned in a more significant way at an earlier time and hence points usefully, for purposes of historical perspectives, to earlier cultural forms.

Swanscombe. Well-authenticated fossil skullcap bones of the second interglacial period, found in England. A virtually modern level of brain development is indicated.

Symbiotic. Living together in more or less intimate association.

Sympathetic Magic (*see* Imitative Magic).

Syntax (*see* Morphology).

Taboo. A customary restraint or prohibition laid upon certain words, things, or actions.

Tale (*see* Folklore).

Talgai. A skull found in Australia, once supposed to be of the third interglacial period, but the claim for that age now appears to be poorly substantiated.

Tapa. The Polynesian name for a type of cloth made of beaten bark.

Tardenoisian. A French culture of the Epipaleolithic or Transitional period.

Tarsier. A Paleocene and Eocene developmental level in the primate order, which presumably gave rise to Oligocene monkeys. Several groups of tarsiers survive in Malaysia.

Taurodontism. Large pulp cavities in teeth.

Taxonomy. Classification for scientific purposes.

TEKNONYMY. The custom of naming a parent from his or her child, for example, "Father of so-and-so."

THEOLOGY. The reworked and more logical product of an earlier mythology, usually developed by a priesthood.

THRILL, RELIGIOUS. A variable stimulus-response mechanism of a special kind, believed by some writers to constitute a feature so basic to religion that it sets religion apart from other forms of behavior.

TIPI. A type of pole frame and mat- or hide-covered, cone-shaped dwelling constructed by North American Indians of the Plains culture area, and by some northeastern Asiatics.

TODA. A group resident in the Nilgiri hills of southwestern India who have been reported by several anthropologists to possess a true polyandry.

TORT. Among peoples in primitive economies a personal injury, wrong, or offense which is responded to in retaliation, revenge, or punishment not by government but only by the hurt individual or by his kinship group within the community (cf. Crime).

TOTEM. An animal associated with a clan, the flesh of which is tabooed by the clan members, who believe themselves descended from the animal and who conduct rites for it. Some writers give broader definitions, allowing for plant or other beings as clan totems, or for any zoomorphic supernatural powers as totems even if unconnected with clans.

TOTEMISM. The beliefs and practices connected with totems (*q. v.*).

TRAITS, CULTURE (*see* Culture Traits).

TRANSITIONAL (*see* Epipaleolithic).

TRANSVESTITISM. The custom whereby a member of the one sex more or less takes over the garb and manner of living of the other sex. Individuals of this kind are termed transvestites or berdaches and are not necessarily characterized by homosexual behavior.

TRAVOIS. A dog-hauled simple framework of poles employed in the Plains culture area, on which some baggage could be placed.

TRIBE. A term employed with no general agreement or precise definition, but often applied to a community or cluster of communities characterized by a common territory, language, and cultural heritage, on a technological level inferior to groups such as the Aztecs, Incas, ancient Egyptians, or Greeks.

TROBRIAND ISLANDS. A group of Melanesian islands just east of New Guinea.

TSIMSHIAN. A linguistic group resident in northwestern British Columbia.

TUNGUS-MANCHU. A linguistic stock or subdivision of the Ural-Altaic linguistic stock.

TURKIC. A linguistic stock or subdivision of the Ural-Altaic linguistic stock.

UNILINEAR EVOLUTION. The term generally employed to designate theories as to denotable stages of social, religious, linguistic, or artistic progress, where the progressive trend has been supposedly little affected by the diffusion of cultural features.

URAL-ALTAIC. The concept of a large linguistic stock which includes linguistic subdivisions termed Finno-Ugric, Turkic, Mongol, and Tungus-Manchu.

UTO-AZTEKAN. An American Indian linguistic stock whose member languages extend from southern Oregon and Idaho to Costa Rica.

VEDDAS. The small remnant group of food-gathering natives of the interior of Ceylon, who are considered the least hybridized of Veddoids (*q. v.*).

VEDDOID, INDO-AUSTRALIAN, or PRE-DRAVIDIAN. The concept of an ancient geographical population of southern Asia, now largely hybridized by large additions of Caucasoids and others.

VOWEL. A sound made without obstruction to the outgoing column of air, as in *a, aw, ow, u.*

WADJAK. Two large skulls of the third interglacial period found in Java, and considered by some writers to be of a proto-Australoid population.

WRITING. The technique which developed in human history for the first time in Egypt just before 4000 B.C., and which involves the use either of symbols for hundreds of syllables (hieroglyph characters) or of symbols for a score or more phonemes (the alphabet). A completely independent development of a technique (hieroglyph) of writing occurred in Mayan Yucatan.

ZOOMORPHIC. Of animal form and appearance.

INDEX

Index